JN115373

Building Ties between Japan and China

The Lives and Times of Tōa Dōbun Shoin Founders, Students, and Leaders

Fujita Yoshihisa

Translated by Douglas Robertson Reynolds
and Paul Sinclair

ARM

Originally published in Japanese as *Nit-Chū ni kakeru: Tōa Dōbun Shoin no gunzō* by Fujita Yoshihisa.

Toa Dobun Shoin University Memorial Center Research Series *Building Ties between Japan and China: The Lives and Times of Tōa Dōbun Shoin Founders, Students, and Leaders*; translated by Douglas Robertson Reynolds and Paul Sinclair with an introduction by Paul Sinclair.

Published by ARM Corporation
1–2, Chiyoda 3-chome Naka-ku, Nagoya 460–0012, Japan
http://www.arm-p.co.jp

Printed in Japan

ISBN 978–4–86333–208–9

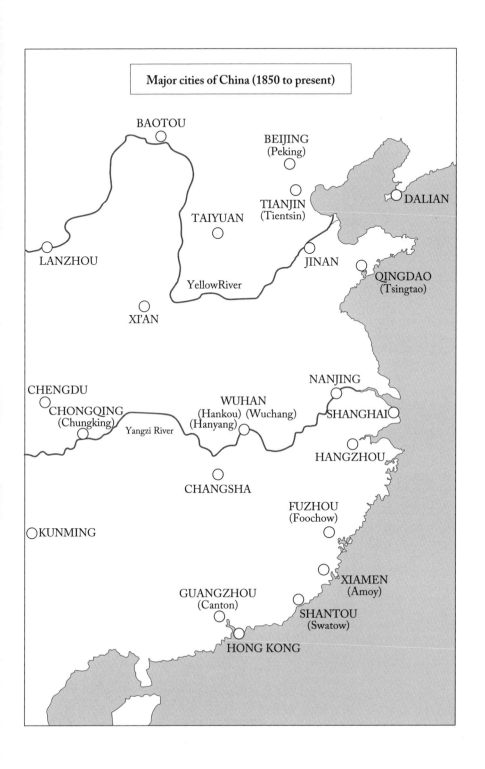

Major cities of China (1850 to present)

Introduction

As much as I have enjoyed writing the following introduction to the English translation of Fujita Yoshihisa's *Building Ties between Japan and China: The Lives and Times of Tōa Dōbun Shoin Founders, Students, and Leaders*, it should have been written by someone else. My co-translator, Douglas Robertson Reynolds, planned a lengthy introduction to the book, something he was eminently qualified to do. A senior US historian and professor emeritus of Georgia State University, Reynolds had spent 50 years exploring the transformative educational and cultural interactions between Late Meiji Japan and Late Qing China, and devoted a substantial portion of his early career to investigating the Tōa Dōbun Shoin, the topic of this book. But in March 2020, just as the book was nearing completion, Reynolds passed away after a long struggle with cancer. The passage below takes on the job Reynolds did not have time to complete. It reflects on the significance of Fujita's book, explores how the work of Fujita and Reynolds brought the Tōa Dōbun Shoin into the public consciousness in Japan, explains how the translation came about, and concludes with some observations from the introduction Reynolds had started before illness intervened.

First, *Building Ties* fills an important gap. At the time this introduction was being written, no full-length book has yet been written about the Tōa Dōbun Shoin in English, an almost inexplicable lapse given the prominent position the institution occupied in Sino-Japanese history. No book has been translated from Japanese about the Tōa Dōbun Shoin, a deficiency for which Fujita's book handily makes up. Readers will find the stories of some familiar characters like Arao Sei, Nezu Hajime, Kishida Ginkō, and Konoe Atsumaro. But Fujita's book covers lots of new ground, too. For example, Fujita's lengthy discussion of the founding of Aichi University and the Tōa Dōbun's post-war legacy will be new to many.

Second, in its sympathetic and humanistic portrayal of the founders, students, and leaders of the Tōa Dōbun Shoin, *Building Ties* breaks with 70 years of academic tradition in Japan, China, and the West.

In Japan, attitudes toward the Tōa Dōbun Shoin remain deeply ambivalent. Leftist intellectuals after the war like Ando Hikotaro despised the institution, making it difficult or impossible for bilingual Tōa Dōbun Shoin graduates to help develop Chinese language education, an area where they possessed significant expertise.[1] The tempest subsided somewhat, as Fujita notes in his book, when the Berlin Wall fell and Marxist intellectuals lost their footing in universities at the end of the Cold War. In the intervening decades, scholars of political history and international relations have been free to evaluate the institution in practical rather than moral or ideological terms. Yet the controversy lingers. To educators of the Chinese language in Japan, for example, the Tōa Dōbun Shoin potently symbolizes a lack of respect towards the modern Chinese language and modern China, a neglect reaching back to the Meiji.

In China, scholars and members of the general public still regard the school with deep suspicion. To them, detailed documentation of China's civic infrastructure, industrial capacity, and governance structures performed by Tōa Dōbun Shoin and its precursor institutions was not "research." It was deliberate intelligence-gathering designed to pave the road for Japan's eventual military incursion into China.

In the West, researchers have generally been content to nestle the institution in a larger story of Japanese imperialism. The tone was set by the GHQ/SCAP (General Headquarters of the Supreme Commanders of Allied Powers) when it shut down the parent organization of the Tōa Dōbun Shoin in 1946, labeled the institution a spy school, and subsequently refused to allow the Tōa Dōbun Shoin to be resurrected in post-WWII Japan. Post-war English-language scholarship has tended to follow this lead, seeing the institution as a kind of handmaiden of imperialism not unlike Mitsui Bussan, Yokohama Specie Bank, or the South Manchuria Railway Company.

Building Ties breaks with this tradition and tells the very human story of the Tōa Dōbun Shoin. It is a story of young men who were

---

1   Ando, Hikotaro. *Nihonjin no chūgokukan [How Japanese regard China]*. Tokyo: Keisō shobō, 1971.

recruited from Japan's countryside only to be caught up in the mayhem of social unrest, political protest, and battlefield chaos in another country. It is a story of bravery, inventiveness, perseverance, and sometimes folly. It is also a story of quiet suffering. Unlike Vietnam War veterans in the US, the Shoin graduates that returned to Japan after the war were not afforded the luxury of literature, film, and song to probe their experience in China and process the trauma war had visited on them.

Most important, *Building Ties* brings together the work of two people whose careers will be forever associated with the Tōa Dōbun Shoin. Together Fujita Yoshihisa and Douglas Robertson Reynolds changed the way the Japanese academy and Japanese general public viewed the Tōa Dōbun Shoin, making way for more nuanced (and less ideological) research on the institution's leadership, curriculum, physical facilities, and student body.

Trained as a geographer at Nagoya University, Fujita Yoshihisa initially interested himself in mountains, villages, forests, and other things that typically occupied geographers of his generation. But in 1979 Fujita took up a post at Aichi University, the Tōa Dōbun Shoin's successor institution. Once installed at Aichi, the geographer in him became fascinated with the elaborate field trips that the Shoin students had taken and the truly stunning amount of documentation they had left behind. Fujita began combing through the student graduation reports from the mandatory "Big Trips" (Dai Ryokō; Dai Chōsa Ryokō), eventually publishing his monumental five-volume series of student research trip documentation from 1994 to 2011. Fujita soon turned his attention to first-person accounts of the trips. After one of the graduates died before Fujita had a chance to talk with him, Fujita got serious. He would have kitchen-table discussions with graduates, inviting families to hear the stories. The gatherings, lectures, and symposia Fujita organized generated enormous interest in Japan and often packed conference halls and meeting rooms.

At the end of the Cold War, Fujita's writings sparked public and media interest in the extensive, detailed investigations Shoin students performed in pre-war China, and greatly increased awareness of the Tōa Dōbun Shoin itself. Influential newspaper and TV stations frequently featured Tōa Dōbun Shoin. Shoin alumni themselves began to tell their stories. That the content of this book was first serialized concurrently in several newspapers demonstrates how deeply the Tōa Dōbun Shoin has reached into the Japanese public consciousness.

Fujita became convinced that far from being a relic of a particularly difficult period in Sino-Japanese history, the Tōa Dōbun Shoin curriculum represented a distinctly modern view of China. In fact, it was a highly refined version of the *chi'iki kenkyū* (Japanese for "area studies") universities had so enthusiastically been espousing since WWII. Fujita promoted something more radical: Aspects of the Shoin program could be recreated at Aichi University. With the support of Aichi University president Makino Yoshirō (12th president, 1988–92) Fujita spearheaded an effort to consolidate graduate China research under an independent College (daigakuin). Acting as chairman of a preparatory committee, Fujita commuted back and forth to Tokyo over the course of several years to negotiate with the conservative Ministry of Education (Monbushō). The committee would eventually receive authorization to establish a PhD program called the China Research Division (Chūgoku Kenkyūka), the first independent college (daigakuin) based on a country or a region in the history of Japan's university system. The PhD program would lead to an even more ambitious experiment: In 1997, Aichi University established the Faculty of Modern Chinese Studies (Gendai Chūgoku Gakubu), a program this time directly modeled on the Tōa Dōbun Shoin. By being bold, Fujita had accomplished a lot.

Douglas Reynolds found his career similarly intertwined with the Tōa Dōbun Shoin.

From the beginning, Reynolds approached the post-war world from a distinctly Asian perspective. He began his China career early, spending 1947 to 1951, when he was age two to six in Wuhu, Anhui province. He grew up in the Philippines, only returning to the US in 1961 for college.

Columbia University, where Reynolds graduated with a PhD in 1975, would later give him a solid, old-school training on China. Because the U.S. and China lacked diplomatic relations before 1979, Columbia wisely required students of Modern Chinese History to also study Japanese language and modern Japanese history, giving students access to much of the world's best scholarship on modern China. Thus, Reynolds found himself equally comfortable with documents from Meiji Japan and Qing China, and he cultivated beautiful penmanship skills in Chinese and Japanese. He spent his entire career exploring intellectual interchange between China and Japan, leaving behind count-less articles and two important books on the topic.[2, 3] Reynolds liked both Japan and China. They were good at different things and had things to learn from each other, he liked to say.

From 1976 to 1980, Reynolds lived in Tokyo with his then-spouse, Carol Tyson Reynolds, who was a *kenkyūsei* of noted China scholar Professor Etō Shinkichi at the University of Tokyo (Tōdai). Professor Etō took Reynolds under his wing and introduced him to the rich archives of Gaikō Shiryōkan (Foreign Ministry Archives). Through this and other Japanese research materials, he stumbled upon the Tōa Dōbun Shoin. As he delved into the storied history of the institution, Reynolds recognized that its sophisticated training program was much like the Area Studies training he had experienced as a graduate student at Columbia University. It was centered on Chinese language, culture, and history with emphasis on contemporary affairs, supported by rich library holdings and a deep commitment to academic research, and included "field research" and cultural immersion requirements for its students. The only difference was that the Tōa Dōbun Shoin version of Area Studies was half a century *ahead* of the West.

Reynolds' work fundamentally changed Japanese researchers' ap-proach to the Tōa Dōbun Shoin. Not an insignificant number of Tōa Dōbun Shoin graduates returned to Japan to become academics, but the Shoin legacy was theirs to live down. For example, Ogaeri Yoshio spent three years at the Shoin in Shanghai before returning to Japan in 1929 after suffering an illness. He later became a prominent scholar of Chinese. Yet Ogaeri heaped scorn on the Tōa Dōbun Shoin and the *senmon gakkō* (specialized school) approach to Chinese, dismissing it as "unacademic." But Reynolds' work in the 1980s was saying something entirely opposite: What the Tōa Dōbun Shoin had been practicing in China was really Area Studies, a conception of international studies that had not only spread through elite universities like Columbia in the US, but had gained currency in Japan in the post-war via the Civil

2   Reynolds, Douglas R. *East Meets East: Chinese Discover the Modern World in Japan, 1854–1898: A Window on the Intellectual and Social Transformation of Modern China.* Association for Asian Studies, Incorporated, 2014.

3   Reynolds, Douglas R. *China, 1898–1912: The Xinzheng Revolution and Japan.* Brill, 2020.

Information and Educational Section in the GHQ. That Reynolds was asked to review the eightieth anniversary Tōa Dōbun Shoin history volume in 1986[4] suggests that the Tōa Dōbun Shoin supporters in the university system deeply appreciated the normalizing effect Reynolds' research had on the public perception of the Tōa Dōbun Shoin.

The story of how *Building Ties* got translated actually stretches back 25 years. My thesis supervisor at the University of Toronto passed along Reynold's 1986 article, "Chinese Area Studies in Prewar China: Japan's Tōa Dōbun Shoin in Shanghai, 1900–1945."[5] The essay was the *Journal of Asian Studies* at its elegant best: richly detailed but fascinating to curious, non-specialist readers too. I was disappointed to find Reynolds had not chosen to publish a book on Tōa Dōbun Shoin as the *JAS* article had hinted.

Rather than the complex backdrop of political history, it was what Reynolds wrote about the Tōa Dōbun Shoin learning environment that intrigued me. The experience of the young Tōa Dōbun Shoin recruits Reynolds' article so vividly described reflected my personal experience. When I got off the plane in Beijing in August 1994 I was not unlike the Tōa Dōbun Shoin recruits: I was from the countryside and about to embark on a big adventure that would change the course of my life. I watched fascinated as old China hands jabbered in Chinese, laughing and talking effortlessly with the locals, or so it seemed. Thus, I aspired not to crack China's ancient cultural secrets through quiet scholarly pursuit but rather to immerse myself in a vibrant Chinese-speaking workplace, just as the Tōa Dōbun Shoin students had done a century before.

In 1997, I was on an exchange program at Nagoya University when I was astonished to discover that in April of that year Aichi University

4   Reynolds, Douglas R. Review of *Tōa Dōbun Shoin daigakushi: Sōritsu hachijusshūnen kinen shi* [Tōa Dōbun Shoin university history: Commemorative publication on its founding], by Koyūkai Daigakushi I'inkai [Tōa Dōbun Shoin alumni association publication committee], *Ajia kenkyū* [Asia Research] 33, 2 (1986).

5   Reynolds, Douglas R. "Chinese Area Studies in Prewar China: Japan's Tōa Dōbun Shoin in Shanghai, 1900–1945," *The Journal of Asian Studies*, 45, no. 5 (November 1986), 945–970, details the pioneering Area Studies program of Tōa Dōbun Shoin. See also Reynolds, "Training Young China Hands: Tōa Dōbun Shoin and Its Precursors, 1886–1945," in *The Japanese Informal Empire in China, 1895–1937*, eds. Peter Duus, Ramon H. Myers, and Mark R. Peattie (Princeton, N.J.: Princeton University Press, 1989), 210–271.

had just opened a Chinese studies faculty entirely based on the Tōa Dōbun Shoin curriculum. Everything about the new faculty interested me. The lavish promotional pamphlets contained a big spread of the Bund, Shanghai's vibrant center, not photos of water buffalo in the countryside working tiny plots of land. It further intrigued me that while the Japanese media made much of the new "Aichi model" and the resurrection of a century-old approach to China, mention of the Tōa Dōbun Shoin was not prominently featured in the promotional materials. I went out to Aichi University's Miyoshi campus, talked to the teachers and administrators in my broken Japanese, and gathered all the information I could about the new curriculum. Over the years, I began to collect documents written about the Tōa Dōbun Shoin. I interviewed a Tōa Dōbun Shoin graduate, and attended several functions where the graduates were present, at one point hearing a group of them enthusiastically singing their school anthem, all of them out of tune. At some point around 2013, I was kindly introduced to Fujita Yoshihisa by one of my mentoring teachers in Japan.

Tucked in the back corner of the Aichi University's Toyohashi campus and housed in pre-war army barracks, the Tōa Dōbun Shoin memorial center and display rooms offer a trip back in time. One summer day in about 2016, I sat with Fujita Yoshihisa in the research room at the center discussing the Tōa Dōbun Shoin legacy and his role in resurrecting the Shoin tradition at Aichi University. He held up the Japanese version of this book. "Perhaps you could translate this," he said with a smile. I thought about it for a couple days and mailed him back. *Yep, I was doing it.* I translated one chapter, wrote a rationale outlining why Fujita's book needed to be translated into English, and started approaching publishers. Struggling to get any response from publishers and not sure which ones to target with this unique Sino-Japanese topic, I reached out to the most logical person: Douglas Reynolds.

Reynolds' involvement in the project began slowly. He began looking over some of what I had written. But before long, we began collaborating and worked out a system. I would translate a chapter, tracking down difficult readings of persons' names and finding the standardized translations of historical events and concepts readily available on the internet. Reynolds would step in, straighten up the terminology, judiciously add glosses in places that merited them, and magically turn the paragraphs into readable prose.[6] No matter how often I reworked them, my paragraphs remained clunky, so these transformations amazed me. Once each chapter was done, Reynolds would patiently answer my questions and we would chat by email, and occasionally by phone, about what we had read. Was Arao Sei adopted in the modern sense of the word? Was Nezu Hajime an alcoholic? What was Chinese scholars' assessment of the research that got done at the Tōa Dōbun Shoin? Intrigued with his Ivy League education about China and Japan, I also peppered Reynolds with questions about his career.

While I have done my best to work the bugs out of the English manuscript in the final editing process, I will have missed things Reynolds would have caught. For these defects, I will take the blame. In the end, Reynolds not only rescued the project, he made his expertise and insights freely available to me, ultimately giving the translation the quality the book deserves. For this last chapter of his life, I was his student. For that, I will always be grateful to him.

Reynolds had begun what was going to be a long introduction to the book. These initial paragraphs written before sickness stalled work are going to have to serve as Reynolds' last words on the topic.

Fujita's book, *Building Ties between Japan and China: The Lives and Times of Tōa Dōbun Shoin Founders, Students, and Leaders*, is wonderful and long overdue. It breaks new ground in our understandings of both modern Japan and modern China.

Readers are fortunate that it is authored by veteran of Tōa Dōbun Shoin studies, geography professor Fujita Yoshihisa. Published in 2012, this book could only have been written by Professor Fujita, and only in the new century. Prejudicial perspectives of the late-twentieth century often dismissed Tōa Dōbun Shoin mindlessly as a "spy school." Aichi University itself, with faculty and students repatriated from overseas schools in Taiwan, Korea, China, and Manchuria, had internationalist outlooks at odds with Japan's Cold War conservative mainstream after the war. By 1972, however, normalization of diplomatic relations between Japan and China enabled Aichi University to begin cultivating ties with Nankai University in Tianjin and with Shanghai's Jiaotong

---

6   Reynolds adds occasional observations in footnotes beginning with "Trans. note." Glosses in square brackets in text are his.

University, moving toward academic exchanges and joint research projects. Since the 1990s, new research led by author Fujita has brought about fresh understandings that showcase the uniqueness of Tōa Dōbun Shoin.

Paul Sinclair
November 2023

Table of Contents

Chapter 1. Prologue

Japanese supporters of China's 1911 revolution

The day October 10, 2011 was exactly one hundred years after the outbreak of China's 1911 Xinhai Revolution. On that anniversary, China, Taiwan, and even Japan sponsored lectures, symposia, and exhibitions to reassess the achievements of Sun Yatsen (Sun Zhongshan, 1866–1925), leader of the 1911 Revolution.

Few people know that at the time of the 1911 Revolution Japanese students were present in the region extending from Wuchang (present day Wuhan) in Hubei province to Chengdu in Sichuan province. Drawn into the turmoil, they recorded all these events. One of these students, Wada Shigejirō, vividly described the mayhem he observed after his arrival at Chengdu: "The rumble of cannon and gunfire is all around us. Even this morning, countless dead and wounded soldiers are being transported into the city...." The person depicting this scene was none other than a student of Tōa Dōbun Shoin in Shanghai.

Tōa Dōbun Shoin (East Asia Common Culture Academy) was established in 1901 in Shanghai in the image of Nisshin Bōeki Kenkyūjo (Japan-China Trade Research Institute), a practical school of business established in Shanghai in 1890 [the subject of Chapter 2]. Tōa Dōbun Shoin's parent organization was the non-governmental Tōa Dōbunkai (East Asia Common Culture Association) in Tokyo, headed by Prince Konoe Atsumaro [subject of Chapter 3]. Its first headmaster was Nezu Hajime [subject of Chapter 4]. Tōa Dōbun Shoin was a business school designed to train students for trade with China. Konoe and Nezu together developed a unique recruiting template whereby two outstanding students were selected from each of Japan's prefectures and metropolises. Full expenses for students, including tuition and transportation to China, were then covered by that student's home government.

Tōa Dōbun Shoin campus in the Xujiahui district of Shanghai in around 1917

It was no coincidence that the school was situated in Shanghai [subject of Chapter 5], Asia's largest and most international city at the time. Konoe Atsumaro had spent several years as a foreign student in Europe, and he wanted to inculcate in his young students the international perspective he had absorbed and train new talent for nation-building. Nezu Hajime, for his part, sought to instill in his students a spiritual ethos of *rinrigaku* (moral philosophy) grounded in Chinese classical learning, by which method students might concurrently acquire a thorough mastery of the Chinese language. Simultaneously, Nezu pushed to give students a thorough knowledge of China as well as of Manchuria and Southeast Asia, through on-site field investigations. As a result of these investigations, students such as Wada Shigejirō left behind real-life records and reports, which amassed in large quantities [the subject of Chapter 6].

Shoin graduates and others affiliated with the school were active in a variety of endeavors. Among those graduates were the two Yamada brothers, Yoshimasa and Junsaburō, important supporters of Sun Yatsen, leader of the 1911 Revolution. Sun and the Yamada brothers devoted themselves to the same goals: establishing a China independent of western Powers and strengthening cooperative ties between Japan and China. Tōa Dōbun Shoin itself endeavored to build up ties with China by invigorating trade between the two, while struggling to raise China's status vis a vis western Powers by strengthening China's economy. Indeed, considering like-minded Japanese patriots (*shishi*) such as Miyazaki Tōten,[1] Tōyama Mitsuru,[2] Inukai Tsuyoshi,[3] and Umeya

---

1   Miyazaki Tōten (1870–1922). Originally named Torazō, Miyazaki was the eighth son of a wealthy farmer in Arao village, Kumamoto prefecture. Influenced by his elder brother Tamizō, Miyazaki came to know Sun Yatsen and went on to become a devoted supporter of Sun's revolutionary cause. For purposes of the revolution, Miyazaki acted as an intermediary between Chinese warlords.
2   Tōyama Mitsuru (1855–1944). Born in the castle town of Fukuoka, Tōyama fell early under the influence of Saigō Takamori. Later, he stood out among Japan's right-wing ideologues, espousing statism (*kokkashugi*) and Pan-Asianism (*Ajia shugi*). He was representative of the Fukuoka Gen'yōsha (Black Ocean Society), and beginning with Sun Yatsen, supported Asian revolutionaries.
3   Inukai Tsuyoshi (1855–1932). Born in the domain of Okayama, Inukai was involved in party politics spanning the Meiji, Taishō, and Shōwa periods. He advocated commoner voting rights as well as the people's rights movement, promoted Pan-Asianist, and supported Sun Yatsen.

Shōkichi[4] who all supported Sun's cause, Japanese played an important auxiliary role in China's 1911 Revolution.

Tōa Dōbun Shoin promoted the education of a number of Chinese students, and produced many talented Japanese who helped to build ties between Japan and China. However, during the Sino-Japanese War [1937–45], students participated in Japanese aggression against China by serving as military interpreters and as student soldiers, unfortunately marring this record of bridge builders. This book shines a light on Tōa Dōbun Shoin, embracing not the "myth" but the "realities" of this illustrious institution. If this rethinking can foster better ties between Japan and China, I would be delighted.

Lead-up to revolution and the death of Yamada Yoshimasa

The year 1911 is known in the Chinese calendar as "*xinhai*," so China's 1911 Revolution is known as the "Xinhai Revolution" (*Xinhai geming*) among Chinese and Japanese. For about 250 years, since 1644, the Qing dynasty[5] under Manchu conquerors had ruled the Han people of China. On October 10 in the year of *xinhai*, ["Double 10" (*shuang shi*) in Chinese—the tenth day of the tenth month], an armed uprising to overthrow the alien Qing dynasty occurred at Wuchang in Hubei province. For that reason, Double 10 is celebrated as the date of the outbreak of the 1911 Revolution.

By the mid-nineteenth century, western Powers encroaching on China's sovereignty were weakening the Qing dynasty and turning China into a semi-colony. China lost the Opium War[6] to Britain start-

---

4   Umeya Shōkichi (1869–1934). Born in Nagasaki prefecture, Umeya started a photography shop in Hong Kong where he met Sun Yatsen. He helped finance Sun's revolutionary activities through his trading company and a moving picture company.

5   Qing dynasty (1644–1912). In 1616, the leader Nurhaci united the Jurchen people in Northeast China and declared independence of the Ming dynasty. As civil war weakened the Ming, this group (now calling itself Manchu) expanded south and consolidated power over China. The Manchus, although having their own script and independent culture, assimilated much of Han culture. By the latter half of the nineteenth century, western Powers expanded into China and reduced it to something of a semi-colony. The Qing dynasty collapsed in 1912, following China's 1911 Xinhai Revolution.

6   Opium War (1839–42). This war between China and Great Britain was triggered by a ban on British opium trade. England, struggling with a large trade deficit, had been exporting increasing quantities of opium to China. The Qing court dispatched

ing in 1839, was devastated between 1850 and 1962 by the Taiping Rebellion, and then in 1894–95 defeated by Asia's newly-risen power, Japan. As outside Powers strengthened their grip on China, nationalistic emotions gave rise to the Boxers,[7] a religiously-inspired martial-arts folk movement united under the slogan "support the Qing, annihilate the foreigners."

Taking advantage of these anti-foreign sentiments, the Empress Dowager Cixi (1835–1908) declared war against foreign Powers. This provided the Powers [including Japan] the pretext to invade China. The Empress Dowager likewise used these developments to check reform groups inside China. Adding to instability, the Empress Dowager in her later years had not made provisions for an heir, so the dynasty suddenly lost its core leadership upon her death.

During these years, anti-Qing political thought and activities of revolutionary groups gradually gained strength. A representative of one of these groups, Sun Yatsen (Son Bun in Japanese), an aspiring medical doctor, had gone to Hawai'i for his early education. There he awakened to the need to rescue China from its growing difficulties. The first anti-Qing uprising led by Sun occurred in 1900 in his home province of Guangdong at Huizhou,[8] and it failed. One of those who died in the Huizhou uprising was Yamada Yoshimasa, a student at Nankin Dōbun Shoin in Nanjing, an immediate precursor to Tōa Dōbun Shoin in Shanghai.

Lin Zexu as special envoy to halt the trade. After Lin declared a ban on British opium (and destroyed British opium stocks), Great Britain declared war on China. England, after winning the war, acquired Hong Kong and also special rights in five so-called treaty ports along China's coast, including in Canton (Guangzhou) and Shanghai.

7   Boxer Rebellion (1900). The Yihetuan or "Boxers" began in Shandong province as an anti-foreign movement opposed to western encroachment and Christianity. As the movement spread to Beijing, the Empress Dowager Cixi—the dominant political figure of the late Qing dynasty—threw her support behind the Boxers and declared war on the Powers. China lost the war, forcing the dynasty to carry out reforms that weakened it politically. The 1911 Revolution brought about the dynasty's final collapse.

8   Huizhou Uprising (1900). The first armed uprising to overthrow the Qing dynasty planned by Sun Yatsen. It failed partly because weapons from Japan were not delivered. Yamada Yoshimasa, who died in the action, was later praised as a martyr by Sun Yatsen.

Shoin students being protected by the revolutionary army. This flag is again seen in the possession
of the Shoin travel group in another photograph
below.

Despite the failure at Huizhou, anti-Qing uprisings spread to other
parts of China. In 1905, the long-time imperial examination system[9]
for service in China's imperial bureaucracy was abolished. Having lost
this pathway to success, young Chinese intellectuals and students who
had returned from abroad joined various armies, gradually enhancing revolutionary movements while fueling nationalism inspired by
slogans such as "Down with the Qing" and "Annihilate the Manchus,
Revive the Han." Amidst all this, in order to ensure payment of
reparations owed to foreign countries, the Qing government national-
ized several provincial railway lines [starting in May 1911; it then
sold those railway rights to foreigners]. In Sichuan province, Chinese
investors and others rose up in opposition to nationalization, and organized the Sichuan Railway Protection League (Baolu Tongzhihui).
In early September, in the capital of Chengdu, dozens of petitioners
were shot by local government troops, after which citizens in the tens
of thousands surrounded the capital. To suppress these protesters, the
Qing court ordered Duanfang,[10] Superintendant of the newly national-

---

9   Imperial Examination System. Originating in the Sui dynasty (581–618), this sys-
     tem tested the knowledge of candidates for high office in China's imperial bureau-
     cracy. Its many problems as well as its obstructive effect on China's modernization
     led to its abolition in 1905.
10   Duanfang (1861–1911). A Manchu, Duanfang was active in government service
     from 1882. During the Boxer Rebellion he was praised for his actions. He also
     served with distinction as Acting Governor General and Governor General of a

ized Sichuan-Hankou Railway, to reinforce Sichuan with troops from Hubei's New Army—the new modernized army of the Qing.

The situation was volatile. Qing troop strength in the Hankou area had just been reduced. Revolutionaries in Wuchang, one of the three cities which make up today's Wuhan, succeeded in seizing power. The other two cities of Hankou and Hanyang would not fall so easily, so that fighting continued into November. Ironically, Li Yuanhong,[11] commander of Qing forces who had been captured by the revolutionaries, was later put in charge of Wuchang's revolutionary army. More astonishingly, Li Yuanhong served twice as president of the Republic after 1911. Such is political power in times of turmoil.

After the post of president had been granted to Yuan Shikai[12] in 1912, Sun Yatsen carried out a Second and then a Third Revolution to gain this post for himself.

Shoin students caught in the middle

The chaos of the 1911 Revolution has been the subject of considerable research. The basic source materials for that research have been government records preserved in the documentary holdings of the Chinese bureaucracy. Few of these official records capture the heated excitement of the moment like the vivid unofficial reports—almost like can-

---

number of provinces. After touring Europe, the United States, and Japan in 1905, he advocated for China's adoption of a constitutional monarchy system modeled on Japan.

11 Li Yuanhong (1864–1928). A naval officer in the late Qing and early Republican eras, Li had studied in Japan. Zhang Zhidong, Governor General of Hubei and Hunan provinces, had appointed Li head of his New Army based at Wuchang, where Li was captured by revolutionary forces in 1911. The Hubei Revolutionary Army subsequently appointed Li their commanding officer. Later, Li twice served as President of the Republic, though with limited success. In 1920, on the occasion of the twentieth anniversary of Tōa Dōbun Shoin, Li wrote the congratulatory calligraphy on a scroll, "Smooth sailing" (yidao tongfeng).

12 Yuan Shikai (1859–1916). A military leader of the late Qing and early Republican periods, Yuan was a leading government official. After the Sino-Japanese War of 1894–95, Yuan promoted China's military modernization, served as Governor General of Zhili and Beiyang Dachen (High Commissioner for Military and Foreign Affairs in North China), and enjoyed the trust of Empress Dowager Cixi. During the 1911 Revolution, he returned to power, serving first as provisional president of the new Republic and later as President. In 1915, he attempted to establish himself as emperor. Failing to obtain support, he died in 1916.

did photographs—by Shoin students who observed events firsthand.

We begin by introducing the 1911 Revolution from its outbreak in October, continuing through November. The epicenter encompassed an area that spanned Wuhan in Hubei westward to Chengdu in Sichuan, roughly following the course of the Yangzi River. At Wuhan, where the Hanshui River flows into the Yangzi, revolutionary battles swirled like whirlpools. Tōa Dōbun Shoin students were present to capture the moment.

Six members of the the Sichuan group. Wada Shigejirō is in the back, second from right.

The Big Trip is described in detail in Chapter 6. Here we simply note that the Big Trip involved field-research travel (*chōsa ryokō*) of three to six months conducted mostly on foot. Organized into *ban* or small groups, Students in the final year of their programs were assigned a travel itinerary along with selected topics to be investigated. Students in 1911 had been organized into twelve *ban*, each responsible for writing a Field Research Report (*chōsa hōkokusho*) that served as a student's graduation thesis. Two groups (*ban*) of students on their "Big Trips" (*dai ryokō*) happened to be on the scene of the unfolding revolution.

The Sichuan Group of six students left Shanghai on June 25, and then travelled up the Yangzi River. Passing the mountainous region at the border of Hubei and Sichuan provinces, they reached Chongqing on September 13. They remained in the region until November 6, when the area suddenly erupted in chaos. Wada Shigejirō who had gone alone to Chengdu was left behind, while the remaining group members, avoiding the war zone of Wuhan, arrived back in Shanghai on November 21. Theirs had been a 150-day adventure.

First word that something had gone awry reached the group after September 17, with information that one chapter of the Sichuan Railway Protection League opposed to nationalization of the railways had rioted in Chengdu. The team may at first have suspected that this story was just one more Chinese rumor of the kind that often circulated.

However, once in Chongqing, they saw the reality with their own eyes. One student recorded the tense atmosphere of the city, observing, "On the streets we saw citizens carrying guns and knives, and we realized we were witnessing dangers related to the Chengdu riots." The next day, when they set out to do research, the report continued: "There was a frenzied atmosphere on the streets. No matter what we did, we were mistaken as suspicious characters. We got nothing done." Clearly, the atmosphere was not conducive to research.

Meanwhile, a telegram came from a fellow Japanese in Chengdu saying to stay away from the city because of riots by the Sichuan Railway Protection League. Orders also came from the Japanese consul forbidding travel to Chengdu. These communications reveal the concern of Japanese in Chengdu toward the riots that had brought disorder to their city.

Geography of the Xinhai Revolution

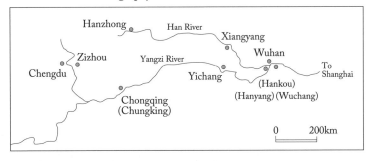

In cases like this, most Shoin Big Trip groups would ignore the warnings and go their merry way. But this time, the Sichuan Group sent Wada by himself to the group destination of Chengdu, and everyone else decided to head home. A telegram came, however, reporting that Yichang, on the Yangzi River along their route home, had fallen to the revolutionary army. "Our team can go neither forward nor backward. We are totally stuck in the middle," one journal stated. "Chongqing is getting more dangerous by the minute," vented another stuck in Chongqing.

Japanese in Chongqing gathered at the Japanese Residents Association. Fearful of [anti-foreign] activities by unruly revolutionary

9

armies, they made plans to protect their assets, secure food, and establish methods of evacuation. The situation was so tense that it led to the decision to evacuate Chongqing by boat, one journal reports.

A Shoin student … and some miraculous escapes

The Shoin students at Chongqing headed as a group for the docks. On their way, they passed Superintendant of Railways Duanfang's military procession, which was headed to Chengdu to suppress the rioters. One student saw the procession as a tragic omen: "A summer insect is flying straight into the flames." The journal added, with respect to Duanfang's demeanor: "One always has a moment of resignation on the way to one's place of death. Now, watching [Duanfang's] grand procession with bamboo screen raised, him calmly smoking, he seemed very brave. Seeing that level of resignation, one thinks about the kind of character he had." From this description, we get a sense of Duanfang's state of mind.

Wada Shigejirō, the member who travelled to Chengdu, fled from Chengdu and reached Zizhou on November 24, 1911. Duanfang, leading his army of more than a thousand men from Chongqing, had also arrived there. Part of his army had been sent on to Chengdu, but Duanfang himself had decided to remain at Zizhou. Wada's journal wonders about the reasons for his hesitation to proceed to Chengdu.

Three days later on November 27, Duanfang was stabbed to death by one of his own New Army soldiers opposed to the rioting. The soldier appears to have been after money used for military expenses, but Wada speculates that it was brought on by Duanfang's hesitation. Whatever the reasons, it was a "shameful act," Wada asserts. The death of Duanfang immediately propelled the Sichuan railway protection movement closer to a revolutionary movement.

Japanese citizens in Chengdu at the time of the Xinhai Revolution. The Japanese flag is visible.

In the aftermath, Wada Shigejirō hurried back to Chongqing as intervening counties and cities fell to revolutionaries one after the other. At one point, he was captured by insurgents toting muskets and curved swords. Wada protested that he was simply a Japanese traveler accompanied by a Chinese porter ("coolie"). He somehow managed to get them both released. Immediately after this incident, the two were chased down and captured by more than one hundred insurgents—who were also brandishing muskets and curved swords. One of the insurgents swung his sword downward at Wada, aiming for his neck. But the sword only grazed his neck then buried itself in the dirt. Wada showed the insurgents his Japanese belongings, and insisted he was Japanese. Once again, his life was spared.

Next, Wada was captured in Yongchuan County on suspicion of belonging to Duanfang's army. A young man stepped out of the crowd, saying that he had been taught by a Japanese teacher whom he respected, and for this reason Wada should be spared. This was yet another case of a miraculous escape from death. Wada struggled to understand if the Chinese who kept capturing him were part of the revolutionary party, part of the Sichuan Railway Protection League, or simply bandits. He would recall later that he was fortunate in not having had any valuables on his person.

The young man who had saved Wada in Yongchuan County wrote a letter of introduction for Wada addressed to Liu Tongling of that county. After its delivery, Wada was issued a passport under authority of the Xinzheng Reforms of 1901–12. It is dated "Issued in the Year of the Yellow Emperor, year 4609 month 10 day 8," while its official chop reads, "Stamped by the Military Commander of Yongchuan County, Military Government of the Republic of China." From the date and name of the authority on this passport, Wada finally had a sense of what was going on around him.

From Wada's various records, we are able to discern the gradual transition from a state of anarchy to a state of order based on the power of Duanfang and others.

An escort for Shoin students by the revolutionary army

Another Big Trip group—the "Hanzhong Group"—was caught up in the 1911 Revolution. This group of six had left Shanghai on June

29, 1911 and headed for Hanzhong [in Shaanxi province] by way of Beijing, Xi'an, and the Qinling Mountains, from where they headed south. They returned to Shanghai following the Hanshui River down to Hankou, and completed their travels after 136 days. Overland travel was most common, and involved encounters with bandits and the traverse of war zones. This Big Trip was literally an "adventure."

The first word of disaster came to the group on October 17 from the magistrate of Guanghua County, who told them of "a violent uprising at Wuchang." The magistrate's face showed real uneasiness. Then, passing through Shayang County, students saw columns of soldiers with swords drawn. Spying a flotilla of four or five boats flying white revolutionary army flags, they knew that Shayang had been occupied by revolutionary troops.

Downstream at Xiangyang, gunships meant to control river pirates had been sent down to Hankou to help quell the Wuchang uprising. The students anticipated that a wave of bandits would move into the vacuum.

Sure enough, the boat they were on was attacked by a gang of bandits brandishing curved swords and kitchen cleavers. All of the students' belongings were taken. As this was going on, out of the corner of their eyes they saw army units wielding spears on both banks of the river, flying the white flag [of revolutionary army forces]. Not long after, they were ordered into a small boat by two men and taken to the head bandit for a meeting. The head bandit's name was Liu, and student accounts report that his eyes had a strange shine to them.

Bandit Liu suddenly pulled from his breast pocket the business card of

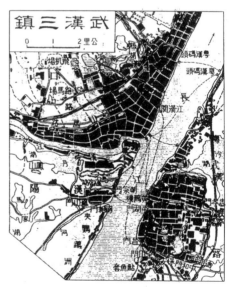

The Tri-cities of Wuhan. Northern portion on left bank is Hankou; southern portion is Hanyang. Right bank is Wuchang.

Nezu Hajime, headmaster of Tōa Dōbun Shoin. He told the students, "The local revolutionary army held a council according to which the theft of your belongings was totally unwarranted. I sincerely apologize.... As students of Tōa Dōbun Shoin, you should be treated with respect. I am returning all the items taken from you by the bandits." So saying, he returned their clothing and blankets. As if this were not enough, the group was taken to a back cave where all their notes and personal effects were returned to them. From this story, we can see that the school and its headmaster were held in high regard even by "bandits" at the time.

En route home, the Shoin group called upon the main regiment of the revolutionary army. Two to three hundred bloodthirsty soldiers, knives drawn, surrounded them while they met face to face with the two leading generals Jin Yitang and Zou Zongmeng. Jin was old gentry from a distinguished local family, while Zou was the fortieth generation of a wealthy family. "Japanese and Han Chinese are brothers (*tongbao*)," they said, and promised to escort the group to safety. This account reminds us that the revolutionary army leadership often came from noted and privileged families, cooperating to form a new political structure.

As promised, the Shoin group of six was taken to Hankou by a flotilla of fifteen boats carrying more than five hundred men. On board was a vertical flag announcing the flotilla's charge, "Under orders to escort students from Great Japan (Da Riben)." Another flag read, "Revive the Han, Annihilate the Manchus." Both were seen by thousands of people. At Wuchang, the students

Six members of the Hanzhong Group. The vertical flag (*nobori*) can be seen flying on the boat of the revolutionary army. The characters read "Dai Nippon Daigaku" (Greater Japan University).

reported dancing with abandon naked (*hadaka*) with the army generals, and exchanging poems at poetry parties. Here is unassailable evidence that this group formed strong bonds with the officers.

Later, the group found itself in life-and-death situations as battles raged in the tri-cities of Wuhan. The students were present as well for the solemn ceremony at which Li Yuanhong handed his sword of the Qing high command over to the revolutionary Huang Xing.[13]

These accounts of Shoin students depict actual conditions over a wide area during the 1911 Revolution. They are valuable records, found nowhere else.

---

13   Huang Xing (1874–1916). A revolutionary of the late Qing and early Republican periods, Huang formed the Tongmenhui (United League) in Tokyo in 1905 together with Sun Yatsen. As Sun's right-hand man, he assumed responsibility for military operations. During the 1911 Revolution, Huang directed matters at Wuchang, and was named Commander-in-Chief of the Revolutionary Army. Over the years, Huang had to flee to Japan more than once.

Chapter 2. Arao Sei Reconsidered

A Hong Kong TV program

The previous chapter told about the valuable records left behind by Tōa Dōbun Shoin students reporting their first-hand experiences of China's 1911 Revolution. A later chapter details the China research carried out by Shoin students. But for the origins of this research element of the school, we must first look to Arao Sei.

In Japanese biographical dictionaries, the name Arao Sei has come to be associated with the phrases *"Chūgoku mondai no shishi"* (a patriot connected to the China question) or *"Tairiku rōnin"* (a continental adventurer). The term *Tairiku rōnin* is a concept not readily defined. The term refers generally to "Japanese wanderers—mainly discontented former samurai and ultra-nationalists—who engaged in various activities on the China mainland during the Meiji [1868–1912], Taishō [1912–1926], and early Shōwa [1926–1989] periods." In post-World War II biographical dictionaries, Arao Sei continues to be called a *Tairiku rōnin*.

Arao Sei

In 2010, a Hong Kong television station producing a history of Japan-China relations visited our Tōa Dōbun Shoin Memorial Center at Aichi University seeking materials on Arao Sei. Happy to support the endeavor, the Center [represented by Fujita himself] explained Arao Sei's role in Japan-China relations as follows.

Arao took a broad view of Asia's problems. He sought a path toward the coexistence of Japan and Asia, a position that served later as a starting point for the notion of "Asianism" (*Ajia shugi*). Following the Sino-Japanese War of 1894–95, Arao invoked the concept of the Kingly Way (*Ōdō shisō*; a traditional Chinese concept) to argue that Japan must *not* demand Chinese territory and monetary reparations after the war. Such thinking merits our remembering, I told the TV station. I observed further that Arao's reputation had been elevated in Japan by republication in 1997 by Murakami Takeru (son of Murakami

Tokutarō,[1] a Shoin graduate) of an expanded version of the late-Meiji work by Inoue Masaji, *Kyojin Arao Sei* [Arao Sei: A Giant]. I mentioned that I looked forward to seeing the final broadcast.

An internet search later revealed a documentary-style program in the station's archives with the title, "Secret Records of Japanese Spy Activities in China." To our astonishment, the very first entry was Arao Sei. We stood in mute amazement, feeling we had been deceived.

The seeds of this documentary's interpretation seem to trace back to a book entitled *Jindai Zhongguo waidie yu neijian shiliao huibian* [Archival Materials on Foreign Spies and Domestic Traitors in Modern China], compiled before 1949 during the Republic period. According to this work, most Japanese who visited China during the late Qing were "spies." All my talk about remembering the legacy of Arao Sei did nothing to change this deeply entrenched notion.

In general, when assessing historical figures, the larger their footprint the more diverse their assessments. Needless to say, assessments will differ according to the times and to a person's place. Arao Sei was no different. Arao Sei shaped the founding and development of Tōa Dōbun Shoin and contributed to its special character. I want to consider his thinking—which was both farsighted and practical—in the context of modern Japan-China relations.

The guiding role of Kishida Ginkō

First, we need to look at Arao Sei's life beginnings.

Arao was born in 1859, the eldest son of Arao Yoshinari, a samurai retainer in the feudal domain of Owari (the western part of Aichi prefecture today). During the great transition from the late Tokugawa to early Meiji, the family moved to Tokyo where they ran a household

---

1   Murakami Tokutarō graduated from Tōa Dōbun Shoin as part of its 18th entering class (1918). In 1935, Ōuchi Chōzō, sixth headmaster of Tōa Dōbun Shoin, established on campus the expansive Shinto shrine Seia Jinja 靖亜神社 [Trans. note: The resemblance in name to the Yasukuni Jinja 靖国神社 in Tokyo, established by the Meiji Emperor in 1869 for repose of the souls of war dead], to honor the *san seijin* 三聖人 (three saintly founders) Arao Sei, Nezu Hajime, and Konoe Atsumaro. After the war, Murakami Tokutarō established his Tōkō Shoin 東光書院 in Musashiranzan in Saitama prefecture, at which time he also rebuilt the Seia Jinja. Each year, on the date of its resurrection, a ceremony is held at Seia Jinja to revere the *san seijin*.

goods shop. New laws permitting samurai to engage in commercial activities had not yet been enacted, however, and the family struggled. A police inspector, Sugai Masami (later governor of Tochigi prefecture) of the Kōjimachi Police Station, lived nearby. Noticing the family's struggles, he took young Sei into his household as a student and raised him. In 1878, the eleventh year of Meiji, Arao Sei entered the Army Kyōdōdan for non-commissioned officers to continue his studies. There, he poured himself into language study and achieved the rank of sergeant. He proceeded on to Shikan Gakkō [Japan's leading military academy] where, at age 24, he was promoted to the rank of second lieutenant in the Army Infantry. In 1883 he was assigned to the Kumamoto Garrison. He gradually gained a name for himself in Kumamoto City for his exceptional abilities and positive attitude.

In Kumamoto, Arao met Obata Masabumi, a man returned from Qing China after having been dispatched there as a student. Arao, who had already studied classical Chinese (Kangaku), learned about Chinese affairs now directly from Obata and studied modern Chinese language with him. He set his mind on going to Qing China. Subsequently, Arao was transferred to the China Division (Shina Bu) of the Army General Staff (Sanbō Honbu) and, in 1886, finally got his chance to go to China. Unable to separate from the army as he had wished, he landed at Shanghai still with the military. Once there, Arao took to China like a fish to water.

Kishida Ginkō in his later years

Shanghai at that time was a genuinely international city. Back in the thirteenth century, fishing villages spread out along the sand bars at the broad mouth of the Yangzi River. Thus, in the context of China's long history of cities, Shanghai's establishment was very new. In 1842, under the Treaty of Nanjing that settled the Opium War, Shanghai was opened as a "treaty port," and western Powers one after the other established protected Settlement areas (zujie) there. Stretched out along the left bank of the Huangpu River, tall buildings were erected by different Powers, buildings that served as the city's financial center.

Toward the end of the Tokugawa shogunate in 1862, Takasugi Shinsaku[2] from the domain of Chōshū had visited Shanghai, astonished at what he saw. Seeing the way that white people lorded it over the local Chinese population, he had a dreadful thought: "Is this Japan of the future?" Under such circumstances, if Arao had landed in Shanghai on his own, he would not have accomplished much. Thus, it helped that someone was present to instruct Arao on the realities behind appearances. That person was Kishida Ginkō.

Kishida Ginkō (1833–1905) was the father of noted artist Kishida Ryūsei. Born in Mimasaka in present day Okayama prefecture, Ginkō went to Edo [today's Tokyo] to study at the end of the Tokugawa shogunate. Having developed an eye ailment, he sought out the American doctor James Hepburn[3] who lived in nearby Yokohama. This experience opened up a new world to him. Hepburn recognized a special talent in Kishida and invited him to assist in compiling Japan's very first Japanese-English dictionary, *Waei gorin shūsei* (A Japanese and English Dictionary). In 1866, Kishida accompanied Hepburn to Shanghai for eight months to print the dictionary, which was published in 1867. Back in Japan for the next ten years, Kishida pioneered the founding of several newspapers and became a leading journalist. All the while, his interest in China grew, as he compiled and authored various materials on China's history and geography. This interest brought him back to Shanghai in 1878, where he opened a branch of his Tokyo store Rakuzendō 楽善堂 that sold Hepburn's eye medicine, books, and other goods. Sales of the eye medicine in China were prolific, earning him a

---

2   Takasugi Shinsaku (1839–1867). A samurai of the Chōshū domain, Takasugi studied under Yoshida Shōin (1830–1859) at his famous private school. Carrying on Yoshida's dream to topple the Tokugawa shogunate, Takasugi was a central figure during the period leading up to the Meiji Restoration of 1868. In 1863, he organized the Chōshū Kiheitai militia which included non-samurai volunteers. With these, he helped to defend the port of Shimonoseki after its bombardment by British and American warships, and was entrusted at age 25 to negotiate a peace. His promising life was cut short at age 28 by tuberculosis.

3   James Hepburn (1815–1911). Hepburn, an American medical doctor, came to Japan as a medical missionary in 1859. He was based in Yokohama. After curing Kishida Ginkō of his eye ailment, Hepburn invited Kishida to collaborate on his Japanese-English dictionary project, later bringing Kishida to Shanghai to print the dictionary on advanced Shanghai presses. In Yokohama, Hepburn and his wife Clara founded the Hepburn School, while successive editions of his dictionary popularized the Hepburn romanization system, today's standard.

small fortune. Kishida thus became Japan's first real international entrepreneur.

In 1886, noting Arao's passion and ambition as he settled into Shanghai, Kishida moved ahead with plans to open a branch store in Hankou to sell medicine and books. Unlike Shanghai, which was dominated by western Powers, Hankou was located in the geographical heartland of Qing China where the Yangzi and Han Rivers converged. It was also pivotally at the center of a network of roads. If one wanted to understand China, this was the place to be.

Hankou Rakuzendō: A gathering place for young Japanese

Arao Sei opened the Rakuzendō branch at Hankou (one of the tri-cities of Wuhan) in 1886, as a general store that sold both medicine and books. Not everything is known about Arao and his branch Rakuzendō. What is certain is that a major purpose was to gain knowledge of the sprawling geography of Qing China. Until then, Japan's intellectuals knew little more about China than as an exquisite world depicted in Chinese classical poetry and literature. Now, a curiosity had developed to learn about the real China.

It is hard to think of the Arao group's research activities at Hankou as "spy" activities. In 1894–95 when the Donghak Peasant Rebellion[4] occurred in Korea, Arao [as a Japanese] held views that opposed Qing intervention in Korea. In Arao's Hankou period, Japan and China were not at odds. The group's many research reports were edited quite quickly into a large compendium under the sure hand of Nezu Hajime [founding headmaster of Tōa Dōbun Shoin], and then published. None of the information gathered was clandestine or covert.

Gathering information on Qing China was not something Arao could do by himself. He thus invited young men from Japan already in Shanghai or Tianjin to join him in Hankou. Among these Japanese

---

4 Donghak (or Tonghak) Peasant Rebellion of 1894. Often simply called the Donghak (Tonghak) Rebellion, this 1894 uprising was fueled partly by disruptions resulting from the inability of the Min government to halt the influx of foreign capital [including Japanese capital]. The Min government requested military support from the Qing government, prompting Japan to dispatch Japanese troops to protect its citizens. Clashes occurred between Chinese and Japanese troops, triggering the outbreak of the Sino-Japanese War in 1894–95.

were Munakata Kotarō,[5] Yamauchi Iwao, Ibuka Hikosaburō, Takahashi Ken, Ura Kei'ichi,[6] Yamazaki Kōzaburō, Fujishima Takehiko,[7] Ishikawa Goichi, Kitamikado Matsujirō, Kawara Kakujirō, and Nakanishi Masaki—all men in their twenties.

Arao gave his recruits a basic knowledge about China in the manner of a private academy (*shijuku*), which provided a kind of institutional framework for the Hankou Rakuzendō. Using the character "*dō*" (堂) from Rakuzendō, all members were called "*dō'in*" and placed under a team leader "*dōchō.*" Those sent out to do field research were called "external members" (*gai'in*), and those who managed the everyday affairs of the store were called "internal members" (*nai'in*). Arao instructed everyone to treat Chinese with consideration and to assume the guise of merchants. Among the *nai'in* were editorial managers or *hensankakari*, responsible not only for organizing incoming reports but also for gathering information from various local newspapers.

Arao Sei (middle) and recruits for Hankou's Rakuzendō

5 Munakata Kotarō (1864–1923). Born in Higo domain (Kumamoto), Munakata went to China where he met Arao Sei. At Arao's Hankou Rakuzendō, he gathered a massive amount of information about Qing China. During the Sino-Japanese War, intelligence collected by him about the Qing Navy contributed to Japan's naval victory.

6 Ura Kei'ichi (1860–1889). Born in Hizen (Nagasaki), Ura was a member of Arao's Hankou Rakuzendō. Together with Fujishima Takehiko, he headed for Ili in distant Xinjiang. After reaching Lanzhou, he was never heard from again.

7 Fujishima Takehiko (1869–1894). Born in Kagoshima, he too became a member of Arao's Hankou Rakuzendō. He travelled to Lanzhou with Ura Kei'ichi, en route to Ili. He returned to Japan, then crossed back to China while tensions were rising. Captured by Qing authorities, he was executed in 1894.

Significantly, among the topics assigned to *gai'in* for research was the "People Section" (*jinbutsu no bu*). Following Japanese typologies, Chinese were designated as *kunshi* (official), *gōketsu* (great man or hero), *gōzoku* (powerful family or clan), *chōja* (rich person), *kyōkaku* (chivalrous person), and *fūsha* (very wealthy person). Ranking Chinese in this manner clarifies one purpose of their research [that is, social ranking—mistakenly thought to mimic Japan]. They also investigated Chinese secret societies such as Gelaohui [Elder Brother Society],[8] Jiulonghui [Nine Dragon Society], Bailianhui [White Lotus Society], and horse bandits.[9] What they did would be called field work today. They predictably gathered information on essential topics of historical geography (*chishi* 地誌) such as soil conditions, transportation, food supply, factories, military systems, population, and local customs. These investigations served as the model for *chōsa ryokō* (research trips) of later students at Tōa Dōbun Shoin.

Under instructions from Arao, *gai'in* scattered in every direction. Given the nature of their assignments, some *gai'in* unsurprisingly took on the character of *Tairiku rōnin* [continental adventurers]. Some even made names for themselves. It must be remembered that *gai'in* traveled in unfamiliar territory, and troubles were never far off. Not a few died or were unable to make it back to Hankou. While Arao was able to gather a good many reports this way, he felt torn by the limits of this Hankou approach.

Training experts for the Japan-China trade

Arao Sei returned to Japan in 1889, his experience with Rakuzendō in Hankou at the front of his mind. Instead of a private academy (*shijuku*), he now saw the necessity of establishing a school in Shanghai that

---

8 Gelaohui (Elder Brother Society). Gelaohui was a secret society in Qing China. In the early eighteenth century, it spread from Sichuan province down to the lower reaches of the Yangzi River. From its peasant base, it began to attract regional leaders. The group mounted anti-Qing and anti-French movements and played a role in China's 1911 Revolution.

9 Horse bandits (Ch. *mazei*; J. *bazoku* 馬賊). Originally, *mazei* were local self-defence forces in Northeast China (Manchuria) during the early Qing dynasty. As the dynasty weakened, however, they became bandit units that attacked towns and villages. The later leaders Ma Zhanshan and Jiang Zuolin both came out of horse bandit groups.

would methodically teach practical skills. Setting out to make this a reality, he ended up by establishing Nisshin Bōeki Kenkyūjo 日清貿易研究所 (Japan-China Trade Research Institute). As its name suggests, its purpose was to train experts for trade between Japan and Qing China. His concept for this "business school" (*bijinesu sukūru*) flowed directly into the later Tōa Dōbun Shoin.

Back in Japan, Arao first met with Prime Minister Kuroda Kiyotaka,[10] Minister of Finance Matsukata Masayoshi,[11] and other political leaders of the time. Having received their blessing along with letters of introduction to the heads of Japanese prefectures and metropolises, Arao travelled throughout the country passionately advocating the need to produce experts for Japan-China trade.

Prefectural heads welcomed Arao's ideas, which were backed by his three years of real experience in Qing China. In pursuit of his designs, Arao organized Ajia Kyōkai [Asia Association], proposing a grand plan to set up an affiliated Asia Trade Research Institute (Ajia Bōeki Kenkyūjo) that would recruit students from various Asian countries and also organize branch associations in different countries of Asia. Arao explained the rationale for his ideas as follows.

For Japanese to achieve superior skills in trade and industry (*shō-kōgyō*), they must also develop practical skills in commerce and trade (*tsūshō bōeki*). Although Europe and America at the moment enjoyed the advantage of a head start, Arao insisted that "Our country is similar to our neighbor Shina koku (China) in its customs, in its people's character, and in a hundred other ways." [Trans. note: That Arao uses Shina koku 支那国 here to mean "China," as distinguished

---

10   Kuroda Kiyotaka (1840–1900). Born into a samurai family in the large domain of Satsuma, he led troops against the final resistance of the Tokugawa in Hokkaidō. After defeating the forces of Enomoto Takeaki (1836–1908), Dutch-trained Tokugawa loyalist and naval commander, Kuroda persuaded Enomoto to join the new Meiji government. Kuroda himself was placed in charge of the colonization of Hokkaidō, and in 1877 he gained recognition for suppressing the Satsuma Rebellion. After serving as Speaker of the Privy Council, he served as Prime Minister in 1888–89.

11   Matsukata Masayoshi (1835–1924). Born into a samurai family in the Satsuma domain, he became involved early in local government finance and interested in fiscal monetary policy. In 1873, he carried out a major land tax reform, and after the Satsuma Rebellion, as Minister of Finance he carried out a policy of raising taxes that came to be known as the Matsukata Deflation. Prime Minister twice, he formed two cabinets and introduced the gold standard.

from Shinkoku 清国 meaning "Qing-dynasty China."] We must absolutely promote Nisshin Bōeki 日清貿易 (trade between Japan and Qing China), he asserted, but Japan lacks the talent to pursue this end, and must immediately train such talent. Arao went on to identify the practical points most needing attention, based on his own experience. He emphasized that what was needed was not simply to study trade (*shōgyō*) as a classroom topic, but to plan a school (*gakkō*) that trained students in Chinese ethical values (*gi-toku*) and provided practical skills that made possible business dealings with Qing China. What resulted was Japan's very first school to train people for international business. Indeed, the concept for the institution foreshadowed the course of Japan's [post-Tokugawa] development.

The following year [in 1890], two hundred Japanese students arrived in Shanghai, including publicly-funded students. With that, Nisshin Bōeki Kenkyūjo was launched. Designed to achieve the school's mission, the curriculum included Chinese language, English language, commercial geography, Chinese commercial history, bookkeeping, accounting, commercial customs, trade theory, economics, law, Japanese and Chinese literature, and physical education.

Unfortunately, management of the school did not go well from the outset, partly due to financial difficulties. The Japanese government was unable to fund the school because of political divisions, and Arao was unable to extricate himself from a funding shortfall not unlike that of his Hankou Rakuzendō days. Making things worse, diseases endemic to the wetlands around Shanghai felled many students. Student unrest followed, and dozens of students quit the school.

Graduates of the Nisshin Bōeki Kenkyūjo in 1893

Faced with the need to revamp the school's management, Arao called upon Nezu Hajime, a supporter of his plans, to come take charge and get the school back on track. In this way, after three years [in 1893], slightly under ninety students graduated and went out into the world. Soon after [in 1894], however, the Sino-Japanese War broke out and Arao's school was dissolved for lack of ongoing support.

Compilation of *Shinkoku tsūshō sōran*

During Arao's Rakuzendō days in Hankou, he had gathered enormous quantities of information while running his branch store. This included a prodigious number of reports compiled by young *gai'in* (outbound team members) who had travelled around the interior of Qing China largely on foot. What had happened to all the Rakuzendō records?

As mentioned above, Nezu Hajime had taken over management of Arao's Nisshin Bōeki Kenkyūjo, serving as Acting Institute Director from 1891. Over a five-month period, Nezu sorted through the vast amounts of materials on Qing China, and in 1892 *Shinkoku tsūshō sōran: Nisshin bōeki hikkei* [Commercial Handbook of Qing China: Essentials of Japan-China Trade] was published by Nisshin Bōeki Kenkyūjo in three volumes of two thousand-pages.

Back in 1878, Nezu and Arao had been students together at the Army Rikugun Kyōdōdan, predecessor to the Army Rikugun Shikan Gakkō [Japan's Military Academy], where they had become bosom buddies. A top student, Nezu was a man of passion and something of a rebel and eccentric. One way of understanding Nezu as a thinker is to recollect the ascetic manner in which he compiled this work. In 1891 [at Nisshin Bōeki Kenkyūjo], Nezu for nearly half a year secluded himself in his room, eating just two meals a day, while he compiled and wrote up Arao's materials. He barely slept, literally. Nezu later recalled that his body remained so motionless that mice grew bold and ran up and down his knees and shoulders for fun. Nezu would go on to become the founding headmaster of Tōa Dōbun Shoin and pillar of "the Shoin spirit" (*Shoin no seishin*).

Born of an Arao-Nezu nexus, *Shinkoku tsūshō sōran* details the essentials of Qing China commerce. Volume One, for example, tackles the topics of commercial geography, general systems, shipment of goods, finance, transport, occupations, and miscellaneous notes; and Volume

25

Two introduces goods that can be traded such as handicrafts and products of land and sea. The topic commercial geography (*shōgyō chiri*), by way of example, brings together Qing China's physical location, land area, population size, ethnic makeup, topography, mountain ranges, rivers, coastlines, and islands; next, it describes the geography of each of China's eighteen provinces; finally, it provides essential information about each of China's fifteen ports as well as Hong Kong. Following up with

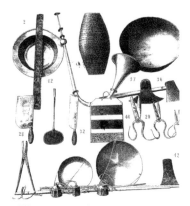

Illustrations of copper goods in the *Shinkoku tsūshō sōran*

topics such as climate, customs, education, and religions, this work can be called the first basic Qing China historical gazetteer (*chishi*) in Japanese hands.

The section on general systems (*shosei* 庶制) has twelve chapters including government organization and finance, taxation, and postal service. The section on miscellaneous notes (*zakki* 雑記) is of special interest for the information it offers on various commercial organizations, protocols for official visits and banquets, practices related to housing rentals, visas, matters related to travel, and points of importance related to business dealings. Volume Two introduces actual products illustrated by exquisite copper engravings. In addition to this content, the volumes record the history of China, and the history of agriculture and commerce and industry. *Shinkoku tsūshō sōran* is at once a work of history, a work of geography, and an encyclopedia that leaves no aspect of China untouched. The first work to introduce the real China to Japan, it became a best seller and propelled Nisshin Bōeki Kenkyūjo to fame.

Ancient Greek thinkers and philosophers, and onward up to Kant and Lenin, grounded the structure of their thinking and philosophies on a knowledge of world geography. One can say that Arao and Nezu likewise constructed their own thinking on *chishi* 地誌 or historical gazetteer-like foundations.

Lamentably, Arao Sei's work was not to continue. From Kyoto [where he sat out the war of 1894–95], he wrote two short [pro-peace] opinion pieces, "Tai-Shin iken" [An Opinion on Qing China] and "Tai-

Shin benmō" [In Defense of Qing China]. After the war ended, he went to Taipei [in Taiwan, now a possession of Japan], where he hoped to make a reality of his vision for an Asia network. In 1896, however, he died in Taiwan of cholera at the young age of 38.

Chapter 3. The Foresight of Konoe Atsumaro

Alarm at western powers' Asia strategies

As described previously, from the latter half of the 1880s through the first half of the 1890s, Arao Sei transmitted information about Qing China (Shinkoku) to Japan using the format of traditional historical gazetteers (*chishi* 地誌). To promote trade between Japan and China, he established Nisshin Bōeki Kenkyūjo in Shanghai to train Japanese experts in trade. This was his first step toward a network of links between Japan and China. His plans to develop a broad network of links between Japan and Asia came to an end with his death in 1896 at the young age of 38. Stepping in to fill this void was Konoe Atsumaro.

Photo of Konoe Atsumaro held at the Tōa Dōbun Shoin Memorial Center at Aichi University

Konoe Atsumaro (1863–1904) was born in Kyoto in 1863 [into a family of high nobility]. His father Tadafusa had died young, so Atsumaro was raised by his grandfather Tadahiro whom Atsumaro later succeeded as family head. By 1884, through self-study he had learned English along with Japanese and Chinese literature, and that year was elevated to the grand rank of Prince. From 1885 to 1890, he went to Austria and later studied in Germany at Bonn University and Leipzig University. There he directly experienced what it was like in advanced European nations and learned about global strategy. Back in Japan, he became a member of the House of Peers, serving as its president from 1896 to 1903. Konoe emerged as an enlightened leader promoting the modernization of Japan.

As is well known, the Konoe family was the leading family of the *go sekke* [the Five Regent Households]. When Atsumaro became president of the Gakushūin Peer's School in 1895, he attempted to use education to elevate the social status of Japan's aristocratic families. At the same time, he was a strong critic of clan politics (*hanbatsu seiji*) and of self-serving political parties, which dominated the politics of the day.

His posture is evident throughout his *Konoe Atsumaro Diaries* [*Konoe Atsumaro nikki*].[1] Once his position became known, many individuals and their organizations sought him out. The warm welcome he extended these groups raised the public's estimation of Atsumaro.

Atsumaro's view that western incursions into China and Southeast Asia should be stopped was a view shared by Kuga Katsunan,[2] Nakae Chōmin, Shirai Shintarō, Ōi Kentarō, Shiga Shigetaka,[3] and Miyake Setsurei.[4] In 1891, these individual and others organized the Tōhō Kyōkai 東邦協会 [Society of Eastern Nations], with the purpose of supporting research on the region and the activities of Japanese therein. Atsumaro served as its vice-chairman.

---

1   *Konoe Atsumaro Diaries*. Konoe kept a detailed diary of essential events in his busy life. In 1968, the entries from February 1895 to March 1903 were released to the public in five published volumes. These vividly describe meetings with a wide range of important people both Japanese and foreign and record gatherings and events. Its pages bring modern Japanese history alive. Included in the publication are personal letters, which provide documentary support for content in Konoe's diary entries.

2   Kuga Katsunan (1857–1907). Born in Tsugaru (Hirosaki) domain in today's Aomori prefecture, Kuga began his studies at the respected local Tōō Gijuku before moving to Tokyo. In time, he served as editor-in-chief of the influential newspaper *Nippon* [Japan] and helped found the magazine *Nihonjin* [Japanese People], through which he promoted idealistic Japanese nationalism. He stands out for the breadth of his political commentaries. After the Sino-Japanese War he began to espouse liberalism.

3   Shiga Shigetaka (1863–1927). Born in Mikawa no kuni (today's Okazaki, Aichi prefecture), Shiga graduated from the Sapporo School of Agriculture in 1884. In 1886, he travelled for ten months around the Pacific Ocean, visiting Australia and New Zealand. His *Nanyō jiji* [South Sea affairs], published in 1887, brought him fame. Editor-in-chief of the magazine *Nihonjin* [Japanese People], Shiga served as head of the Bureau of Forestry in the Ministry of Agriculture and Commerce and involved himself in politics. In 1894, he published *Nihon fūkei ron* [On Japan's Scenic Landscape], which increased his reputation as an enlightened geographer. [Trans. note: Geography was a topic of passionate interest among Japanese during the Meiji period.]

4   Miyake Setsurei (1860–1945). Born in the populous Kaga (Kanazawa) domain, Miyake graduated from the University of Tokyo's Department of Philosophy in 1883 and became a leading philosopher, prolific writer, and proponent of a distinctive Japanese culture and identity. He helped found the Seikyōsha (Society for Political Education) in 1888 along with its magazine, *Nihonjin* [Japanese People]. His essays appeared widely in such publications as the newspaper *Nippon* [Japan], *Kokumin no Tomo* [Friends of the Japanese People], and in *Nihon oyobi Nihonjin* [Japan and The Japanese People], the new name of *Nihonjin* from 1907.

Although deficient in concrete activities, this society had about one thousand members and published a number of local research reports and society news. After Japan's victory in the Sino-Japanese War, however, public attention turned almost wholly to China. Tōhō Kyōkai membership plunged, and the organization lost momentum.

Thereafter, organizations advocating new relationships between Japan and Qing China appeared one after the other, including Dōbunkai founded by Atsumaro. Tōakai was another representative of this genre of organization.

The *Konoe Atsumaro Diaries* reveal the international sensibilities of Konoe at the time—his concern with strengthening postwar cooperation between Japan and Qing China and also with sounding the alarm about Russian incursions into Chinese territory. The diaries also make known Atsumaro's response to the Asia strategies of western Powers as witnessed in Europe, and his sense of himself as a leader of Japan.

Tōakai and Dōbunkai merge

Tōakai 東亜会 [East Asia Association] was launched in 1897 [in the aftermath of the Sino-Japanese War]. Tōakai was distinctive in the diversity of its membership and their relative youth. Membership included the likes of Miyake Setsurei, Shiga Shigetaka, and Kuga Katsunan, publishers of the magazine *Nihonjin* 日本人 [Japanese People]; persons associated with Genronha 言論派 [Freedom of Speech Group] and Seikyōsha 政教社 [Society for Political Education] which held that Japan must directly defend its culture from the menace of westernization; *Tairiku rōnin* continental-adventurer types such as Uchida Ryōhei,[5] Hirayama Shū,[6] and Miyazaki Tōten; and Inukai Tsuyoshi and the stu-

---

5 Uchida Ryōhei (1874–1937). Born in Fukuoka, Uchida was an active ultranationalist who joined the Gen'yōsha (Black Ocean Society) early in life, and in 1894 at the time of the Donghak Peasant Uprising, he traveled to Korea. Besides assisting Sun Yatsen and his early Gemingdang [Revolutionary Party], Uchida supported leaders of various independence movements in Southeast Asia. He helped to develop the movement known as "Japanism" (*Nihon shugi ron*).

6 Hirayama Shū (1870–1940). Born in Fukuoka, he had met Sun Yatsen in China. Together with Miyazaki Tōten, Hirayama supported Sun's revolutionary activities in China and assisted Sun during his periods of refuge in Japan, including after his failed Huizhou uprising.

dent Inoue Masaji. Its stated purpose was to debate problems related to Qing China, and to publish its findings.

The year after Tōakai's founding witnessed the Hundred Days Reform in China, which carried out radical reforms under the Guangxu Emperor (1871–1908). Those reforms were reversed by conservatives supported by the Empress Dowager Cixi, bringing the movement to defeat. The two leading reformers Kang Youwei[7] and Liang Qichao[8] were forced to flee for their lives to Japan. Once there, Tōakai made the bold decision to admit both as members, even amidst financial difficulties.

Dōbunkai 同文会 [Common Culture Association], meanwhile, had been set up in 1898. According to the Konoe diaries, in June 1898 Konoe charged Nakanishi Masaki,[9] Ōuchi Chōzō,[10] Shiraiwa Ryūhei, and Ide Saburō[11] to draft a charter for the organization. Konoe had

---

7 Kang Youwei (1858–1927). Kang was born in Guangdong province. After studying the Chinese classics, he turned his attention to western thought. When China lost the Sino-Japanese War, he began to promote reform. Through his writings, he directly influenced the Guangxu Emperor's thinking about reform. [These were largely Meiji-style reforms with which Kang had become familiar.] After suppression of the 1898 Reforms, Kang took asylum in Japan. He shared a close bond with the younger Liang Qichao, also from Guangdong.

8 Liang Qichao (1873–1929). Liang was born in Guangdong province. When he met Kang Youwei, their ideas resonated, and the two enjoyed a close working relationship. After 1898, Liang too fled to Japan, his base for the next dozen years where he wrote prolifically and brilliantly, absorbing [and sometimes plagiarizing] modern Japanese writings. Although an advocate of freedom of speech, Liang was cautious about more extremist revolutionary doctrines.

9 Nakanishi Masaki (1858–1923). Born in Mino (Gifu), Nakanishi was sent by the Ministry of Foreign Affairs to Beijing at the age of 28 for language study. Nakanishi travelled widely around China and became a member of Arao Sei's Hankou Rakuzendō. Subsequently, he assisted Arao in the establishment of his Nis-Shin Bōeki Kenkyūjo in Shanghai.

10 Ōuchi Chōzō (1874–1944). Born in Fukuoka prefecture, Ōuchi studied at Columbia University after which he joined the faculty of Waseda University in Tokyo. Attaching himself to Konoe Atsumaro, after Konoe's death in 1904 Ōuchi entered politics to carry on Konoe's vision. Later, as president of Tōa Dōbun Shoin University, he strove to preserve and nurture its liberal values.

11 Ide Saburō (1862–1931). Born in Higo (Kumamoto), Ide went to Shanghai to study Chinese. Learning of Arao's Hankou Rakuzendō in 1886, he joined as a member. In 1898, Konoe enlisted Ide to help draft the charter for his Dōbunkai. Ide served both as a director of the organization in Tokyo and as president of its Shanghai chapter. In Shanghai, he contributed reports on Shanghai affairs to *Tōajiron* [East Asia Review] and founded the Chinese-language newspaper *Shanghai ribao* [Shanghai Daily].

already published several thought pieces on Asia. The idea of "Asianism" (*Ajia shugi*) comes across in his writings, as expressed in Konoe's bold declaration "The East is the East of Easterners" (*Tōyō wa Tōyōjin no Tōyō nari*). From this stance derived Konoe's notion to "Protect China" (*Shina hozen ron*). Dōbunkai was conceived as a first step in the realization of his Protect China ideal.

Tōa Dōbunkai first set up in Tokyo-Akasaka Tameike

The purposes of Dōbunkai were several: to conduct investigations and research on Qing issues and to support business and industry; to establish in Shanghai a Dōbun Kaikan [Common Culture Hall] and a Dōbun Gakudō [Common Culture School]; and to actively engage in cultural and educational exchanges between Japan and Qing China. Besides magazines in Tokyo and Shanghai, it published Chinese-language newspapers in various cities. Overall, it endeavored to develop trade and industry in both countries while avoiding political entanglements.

For its membership, Atsumaro extended invitations to members of the House of Peers such as Nagaoka Moriyoshi,[12] Tani Kanjō,[13]

---

12   Nagaoka Moriyoshi (1842–1906). Born in Higo (Kumamoto), Nagaoka studied in the United States and Europe in his early thirties, from 1872 to 1879, [thus sharing overseas perspectives with Konoe]. In 1880 he was appointed Japanese Minister to Holland and also served as Minister to Belgium. Awarded the title of viscount, he was a member of the House of Peers during the period he helped to found Dōbunkai.

13   Tani Kanjō (1837–1911). Born in Tosa domain (Kōchi prefecture, Shikoku). In his youth, he was an ardent admirer of Sakamoto Ryōma (1836–1837), a fellow samu-

and Kiyoura Keigo[14] as well as to Kashiwabara Buntarō, Ioki Ryōzō, Nakano Jirō, Tanabe Yasunosuke, Takahashi Ken, and Kishida Ginkō. Members of Arao Sei's circle and young graduates of Nisshin Bōeki Kenkyūjo were likewise brought in.

However, Dōbunkai also struggled with finances. Its plans, ambitious and sweeping, found few donors. Dōbunkai decided therefore to look to the government, knowing the availability of possible funding from the Ministry of Foreign Affairs. Tōakai, as mentioned, was in similar financial straits. The Foreign Ministry responded that it could provide financial assistance only on condition that the two organizations merge to achieve savings.

The two associations, though different in approach, shared the same general interests. Some members even belonged to both associations, so that their merger should have been easy. Atsumaro, however, was resolutely opposed to granting membership to Kang Youwei and Liang Qichao because he wanted to avoid any perception of the new association being anti-Qing. Ultimately, Tōhō Kyōkai had to step in to mediate.

The merged association, Tōa Dōbunkai [East Asia Common Culture Association], combined the names of the two and was born on November 2, 1898. Consisting of members with a variety of experiences in Japan-Qing relations, it was the largest people's organization (*minkan soshiki*) dealing with Japan-Qing questions. Konoe Atsumaro assumed the role of president and assigned capable members to serve as directors and advisors.

---

rai who dedicated himself to overthrowing the Tokugawa shogunate. Tani, a general in the new imperial army, in 1877 defended Kumamoto Castle against the fifty-two day siege of Satsuma Rebellion forces. Named president of the Gakushūin Peers School in 1884, he was ennobled with the rank of viscount in 1890 and entered the House of Peers. He opposed the policies of Europeanization of Itō Hirobumi (1841–1909), opposed territorial expansion after the Sino-Japanese War of 1894–95, and was a rare anti-imperialist opposed to the Russo-Japanese War of 1904–05.

14   Kiyoura Keigo (1850–1942). Born in Higo (Kumamoto), Kiyoura won favor with Yamagata Aritomo (1838–1922), Marshall of the Japanese Army, who appointed him head of the Police Bureau of the Home Ministry in 1884. Becoming active in politics, Kiyoura served as Prime Minister in 1924 after Yamagata's death. For his service to imperial Japan, he was successively elevated to the peerage ranks of baron (1902), viscount (1907), and count (1928).

Meeting Liu Kunyi and Zhang Zhidong

Thus, Tōakai and Dōbunkai merged, reborn as Tōa Dōbunkai with Konoe Atsumaro as head. The new association committed itself to the following principles: "1) The protection of 'China' [*Shina no hozen*]; 2) assistance with reforms in 'Shina' and Chōsen (Korea); 3) research on the affairs of 'Shina' and Chōsen, and 4) arousal of public opinion."

The new association's prospectus opened with the statement, "Japan and China have interacted with each other for so long that their cultures intertwine and their customs are similar. In terms of affection they have the closeness of older and younger brother, and in terms of interaction they are like lips to teeth." The founding of Tōa Dōbunkai, it explained, manifests the desire for the governments of Japan and China to redouble their formal and ritual ties and for intellectuals and leaders to seek mutual enrichment and strengthening (*fukyō* 富強). It was Atsumaro's conviction that through the protection of China (Shinkoku) and through Japan-Qing cooperation (Nisshin *teikei*) that western Powers could be checked.

The inaugural issue of *Tōajiron* (East Asia Review),[15] Tōa Dōbunkai's association journal, appeared in December 1898. In that issue, Atsumaro expressed the stance of the association by reiterating the matter of its principles and purposes, and by criticizing the government's wavering attitudes. Additionally, he initiated work on the associations' planned activities and strengthened its structure by appointing Kuga Katsunan as general secretary as well as Tanabe Yasunosuke and Kashiwabara Buntarō as directors. To the newly created board of trustees he appointed House of Peer members Nagaoka Moriyoshi and Inukai Tsuyoshi, House of Representatives member Hoshi Tōru, and the non-official Kishida Ginkō. Soon after, the pioneering Ajia Kyōkai [Asia Association][16] was absorbed into Tōa Dōbunkai.

In April 1899, Konoe Atsumaro set out on an observation tour of Europe and America. His diary details his experiences. The trip was

---

15 *Tōajiron* [East Asia Review]. The official journal of the new Tōa Dōbunkai, it published just 26 issues over a thirteen-month period (December 1898–December 1899). It chiefly reported news of East Asia and organizational news.

16 Ajia Kyōkai [Asia Association]. This was the new name in 1883 of Kōakai [Revive Asia Society], founded in 1880 around the idea of "Asianism" (*Ajia shugi*). In 1900, Ajia Kyōkai was absorbed into Tōa Dōbunkai.

packed. Besides western countries, he visited India and other Asian countries, and stopped at various ports in China where he received many visitors. It is thought that this trip may have hastened the deterioration of his health, bringing on his early death. But this half year of travel was a high point of his life.

On October 29, 1899, Atsumaro arrived at Nanjing by way of Guangdong and Shanghai. There he met Liu Kunyi,[17] Governor General of Liang Jiang (the three provinces of Jiangsu, Anhui, and Jiangxi) and one of the most important reformers among Qing government leaders. The two men were of one mind that Japan-Qing interactions should be deepened and that western Power overtures should not be too taken too seriously. Atsumaro additionally brought up his interest in a Japan-Qing Alliance (Nisshin dōmeiron). Explaining the purposes of Tōa Dōbunkai and his hope to establish a school in Nanjing, Liu promised, "I will do everything I can to help."

Liu Kunyi

Atsumaro next visited Hankou, where he met Zhang Zhidong,[18] Governor General of Huguang (the two provinces of Hubei and Hunan) with whom he exchanged views on a broad range of topics. At Zhang Zhidong's strong request, the two agreed on two points related to educational exchanges: Qing (Shinkoku) students should go to Japan to study, and Japan should send teachers to Shinkoku. At one point,

---

17   Liu Kunyi (1830–1902). Born in Hunan province and holder of the highest *jinshi* examination degree, Liu served with great distinction in the Hunan Army suppression of the Taiping Rebellion, after which he was appointed to the high offices of governor of Jiangxi province, governor general of Liang-Guang (Guangdong and Guangxi provinces), and governor general of Liang Jiang (the three provinces of Jiangsu, Anhui, and Jiangxi). An advocate of Self-Strengthening, he supported the 1898 Hundred Days Reform. He counselled the Empress Dowager Cixi and advocated administrative modernization.

18   Zhang Zhidong (1837–1909). From a family with roots in Zhili (Hebei province today), he excelled in his studies and ranked near the top of his *jinshi* examination cohort. With support of the Empress Dowager Cixi, Zhang served as governor of Shanxi province, and governor general of Liang Guang (Guangdong and Guangxi) and of Hu Guang (provinces of Hubei and Hunan). Inside his jurisdictions, he promoted industrial production and railway construction. During the Boxer Uprising, he stood with Liu Kunyi against the court's anti-foreign extremism.

the subject shifted to Sun Yatsen. Zhang dismissed Sun, saying "He's nothing but a petty thief, not worthy of attention." Zhang showed little interest in international affairs. Atsumaro considered Zhang less sophisticated than Governor General Liu.

Whatever his private thoughts, Atsumaro started working immediately with Shinkoku leaders, preparing the way for Tōa Dōbunkai to engage in educational activities with both Governors General Liu and Zhang.

Looking after foreign students

Educational exchange agreements having been reached between Konoe and Governors General Liu and Zhang, Zhang Zhidong immediately sent thirteen students to Japan. To accommodate these students, Konoe in 1899 established a new school—the Tokyo Common Culture Academy (Tōkyō Dōbun Shoin). Interestingly, as the growing numbers of Chinese students found preferred residential locations in Tokyo, Tōkyō Dōbun Shoin itself relocated from one place to another: from Ushigome to Mizaki-chō to Akasaka Hinoki-chō to Kanda Nishiki-chō, and finally to Mejiro.

Tōkyō Dōbun Shoin in Mejiro (Tokyo)

In February 1901, Tōkyō Dōbun Shoin was placed under the jurisdiction of Tōa Dōbunkai, with Nezu Hajime as school director (*kantoku*). After Nezu assumed active headmastership of Tōa Dōbun Shoin in Shanghai, Tōa Dōbunkai director (*kanji*) Kashiwabara Buntarō took over as *kantoku* of the Tokyo school.

According to the "Tōa Dōbunkai Report" of October 1900, the educational policy of Tōkyō Dōbun Shoin was "to instill knowledge and the power of observation, making honest and capable youth." Courses included English (*Eibun*), mathematics, history, geography, physics, notetaking, translation (*honyaku*), reading (*dokuhon*), grammar (*bunpō*), beginning conversational Japanese (*shokyū kaiwa*), beginning math [for those who needed it], and Japanese language (*Nihongo*). Language teachers included Kanai Yasuzō, Shinmura Izuru—an editor of *Kōjien* [Japan's most authoritative dictionary]—and two others. According to Hosaka Jirō, a research specialist on the school, over time Tōkyō Dōbun Shoin included an array of outstanding teachers including Sugimura Kōtarō (English law), Katayama Masao (chemistry), Maeda Mototoshi (English composition), Kobayashi Mankichi (western art), Kameda Jirō (Japanese language), and also Miyazaki Tamizō (elder brother of Miyazaki Tōten).

The number of Chinese students in Japan increased dramatically after the Sino-Japanese War—and particularly after the Russo-Japanese War when the slogan "Study in Japan" drove up enrolments at Tōkyō Dōbun Shoin. Enrolments dropped sharply, however, after China's May Fourth Movement[19] in 1919 when anti-Japanese sentiment exploded. In 1922, Tōkyō Dōbun Shoin had to shut its doors.

Japan's victory in the Russo-Japanese War of 1904–05 hastened the mood for independence among the colonized peoples of Asia. In the French colony of Vietnam (French Indochina), the slogan "Study in Japan" brought a number of young Vietnamese to study at Tōkyō Dōbun Shoin. According to records at Japan's Ministry of Foreign Affairs, at its peak there were sixty foreign students at the Tokyo school. School director Kashiwabara and his wife cared deeply about these students who adored them as their "Japanese father and mother." The couple raised money for Vietnamese who had been expelled from their country, which inspired hard study and good grades among these students.

---

19   May Fourth Movement. On May 4, 1919, Beijing students gathered in large numbers at Tian'anmen Square to oppose the Treaty of Versailles which granted the "rights" of Germany in China to victorious Japan. Students demonstrated as well against Japan specifically, incensed by memories of Japan's humiliating Twenty-One Demands of 1915.

One of the Vietnamese students was Phan Boi Chau (1867–1940; in Japan from 1905–1908), a leader of the movement calling for independence from French colonial rule, whose thoughts were spreading to other students. Pressure from the French government on Japan forced the return of many of these students. Back in French Indochina, not just these students but their family members and friends were arrested, and about four hundred were thrown into prison.

In his account of the Vietnam students, Kashiwabara urged authorities to take a tolerant attitude toward those involved. After the Vietnam War [of the United States], researchers in Vietnam have continued to dig into this matter, shining light on how Kashiwabara, Tōkyō Dōbun Shoin, and also Asaba Sakitarō[20] of Shizuoka prefecture all assisted these Vietnamese students.

The education network of East Asia

Having obtained Liu Kunyi's agreement, Konoe set up one more educational enterprise: the Nankin Dōbun Shoin (Nanjing Common Culture Academy), in 1900. Before setting up this school in Nanjing, Tōa Dōbunkai had already supported a broad range of education initiatives.

The association newsletter, *Tōa Dōbunkai hōkoku* [Tōa Dōbunkai Report], published from 1900 to 1910, includes letters from members in the field regarding activities in Qing China (Shinkoku) and Chōsen (Korea). These reveal that Tōa Dōbunkai was moving in the direction of support for schools in Qing China, while also setting up or planning schools in Korea.

For example, the April 1900 issue carries reports from Ide Saburō in Shanghai, the Fuzhou branch in Fuzhou, Sawamura Shakunan in Xiamen [Amoy], Munakata Kotarō in Hankou, Shintō Yoshio in Pyongyang, Haraguchi Bun'ichi in Guangzhou [Canton], and Saeki Tatsu in Songjin [a newly-opened port; today, Kimchaek, in North

---

20 Asaba Sakitarō (1867–1910). Born in Shizuoka prefecture in Asahasa village (now Fukuroi City), Asaba Sakitarō was a medical doctor who supported the Vietnamese students in their independence movement, extending them his personal financial assistance. This brought French government pressure down upon him. Today, a commemorative monument to him stands in the old village of Asaba.

Korea]. The new Japanese language school in Pyongyang was singled out for praise. In Nanchang, Jiangxi, the Dōbunkai had supported the Meitatsu School and had sent two teachers, achieving an enrolment of more than forty students. However, certain individuals charged that "Dōbunkai is connected with Kang Youwei and Liang Qichao." This accusation forced the school to close. It should be noted, as background, that local Jiangxi officials wanted to make things difficult for new political parties [that might be anti-Qing] and for foreigners, so the whole matter can be seen as a kind of frame-up.

In the issue for May [1900], Munakata Kotarō in his Hankou report transmitted the local rumor that Empress Dowager Cixi had died, and he predicted that the Qing China would last only another three to six years. Meanwhile, Guangzhou and Shanghai filed reports on the numbers of teachers sent by Tōa Dōbunkai to various schools, and their situations. The Shanghai report spoke of how the *Tongwen hubao* [Shanghai Common News] could challenge the three existing Shanghai papers, and deliberated about how much the association should subsidize the Tōbun Gakudō (Japanese Language School) set up by Japanese in Huai'an. Besides these items, there were updates about the direction of things in Songjin, Wonsan, and Mokpo in Korea.

Educational exchanges were the very pillar of Tōa Dōbunkai, not only in Qing China but also in Chōsen. Toward this end, early field investigations had determined Pukchong in the north of Korea to be a prime site for a school. But local residents stubbornly objected, so that the school was set up instead in Songjin [also in the north]. The school's first head was Sasamori Gisuke. Born in Hirosaki domain in northern Japan, Sasamori was noted for his early exploration of Japan's Chishima (Kuril) Islands and the islands of the Ryukyus. By introduction of Kuga Katsunan, Sasamori had met Konoe Atsumaro, and through Tōa Dōbun Shoin he was commissioned to spread education in Chōsen. The basic course offerings at the school were moral cultivation,

Sasamori Gisuke

math, reading, Japanese language, composition, geography, and history, and its eighteen students were separated into Korea's two broad social classes of aristocrats and commoners. A Japanese language school was set up in Pyongyang that also taught biology, animal and plant husbandry, and physical education. Plans were also underway to support the Keijō (Seoul) Gakudō and also the Kannan [Southern Korea] Gakudō and Tatsujō Gakudō in Wonsan.

Thus one year before the establishment of Nankin Dōbun Shoin, Atsumaro's conception of a broad network of educational and cultural endeavors in East Asia, including the opening of schools for local students in Qing China and Korea with association assistance, and plans to assist with the publication of new and existing newspapers, had already reached the implementation stage.

To Shanghai from Nanjing

Nankin Dōbun Shoin was established as a kind of nucleus for an emerging network of educational and cultural endeavors in Asia. Conceived and implemented by Konoe, these endeavors were a tangible strategy for countering the west in Asia.

At the root of Nankin Dōbun Shoin's conception was "to take in Japanese and Chinese students, whereby Japanese students (*Nihon gakusei*) primarily study Chinese language (*Shinago*) supplemented by classes on real and appropriate matters of politics and economics, and Chinese students (*Shina gakusei*) primarily study Japanese language (*Nihongo*) supplemented by classes on scientific thought." Interested Chinese students immediately appeared, and because Tōkyō Dōbun Shoin was in operation, Chinese students (*Shinkoku gakusei*) were admitted there. Nanjing became the site for Japanese students.

In order to attract Japanese students, the existence of the Nanjing school had to be made known in Japan. Travelling to the different prefectures and metropolises (*fu-ken*), recruiters asked each to allocate local tax funds to support several students. Most prefectures had already fixed their budgets for the following year. Only the two prefectures of Kumamoto and Hiroshima, through special prefectural assembly sessions, decided to send students. Self-financed students and students funded by Tōa Dōbunkai brought the number to just over forty for that first year.

Students at Nankin Dōbun Shoin

As president of Tōa Dōbunkai, Konoe himself mounted a campaign around Japan starting in May 1900. He visited Hiroshima, Okayama, Kyoto, and Nagoya to explain the educational objectives of Nanjing Dōbun Shoin and to attract students. Konoe had been critical of clan politics, making it likely that there were prefectures that did not welcome his views. On the other hand, in the aftermath of the Sino-Japanese War, interest in China and in trade relations between Japan and China was at a high, and Konoe's campaign stops were all well attended. This reflected the fact as well that Tōa Dōbunkai branch offices had been opened in Hiroshima and Kyoto, and later in Hirosaki and Aomori; plans were underway for a branch in Nagoya.

Out of this experience grew nationwide speaking tours by five people including Tanabe Yasunosuke, Ogawa Heikichi, and Inoue Masaji. Ultimately, one municipality (*fu*) and sixteen prefectures (*ken*) budgeted to send forty-two funded students, six prefectures anticipated sending fifteen students, two prefectures were undecided, seven prefectures decided to send none, three prefectures sent four self-financed students, two prefectures anticipated sending someone, and one remained undecided as to numbers. Here taking shape was the Tōa Dōbun Shoin recruitment system of later times.

Nankin Dōbun Shoin offered a three-year program in two tracks, politics (*seijika*) and commerce (*shōmuka*). All students lived on campus. Required courses included Chinese language study (*Shinago gaku*), English language study (*Eigo gaku*), Confucian ethics (*rinrigaku*), geography, history, the law, economics, finance, Chinese administration and regulations (*Shina seido oyobi ritsuryō*), commercial practices (*shōgyō gaku*), and field research travel (*jitchi shūgaku ryokō*). Many sub-courses aimed at creating mutual understanding between Japan and Qing China and at giving students practical experience.

Unfortunately, headmaster Satō Tadashi fell ill and resigned his post. Nezu Hajime joined Tōa Dōbunkai and was named new headmaster of Nankin Dōbun Shoin, putting him in a position now to shape the school's future. The Boxer turmoil, meanwhile, was coming closer to Nanjing. To minimize its effects, Tokyo dispatched Tanabe Yasunosuke from Japan to supervise the students. With students unable to settle down, however, and fearing the worst in Nanjing, Nezu scrapped the idea of building a new campus there and shifted to Shanghai as the school's new base. Thus in 1901, the school opened its doors under the new name of "Shanghai Tōa Dōbun Shoin."

Chapter 4. Nezu Hajime: A Literary and Military Prodigy

A path to the military

Even as Konoe Atsumaro saw realization of a network of educational and
cultural enterprises in East Asia, he became agitated at Russia's encroachment in
Manchuria (Northeast China). Accord-
ingly, in September 1900 he formed the
National League (Kokumin Dōmeikai)
particularly to monitor Russia. Then, when
details of the secret Li-Lobanov Treaty[1]
[of June 1896] leaked, Konoe sounded the
alarm again and pressed the government to
adopt a Russia strategy. However, in 1903
Konoe's health declined, and the following

Nezu Hajime in his prime

January, at the young age of 40, he fol-
lowed Arao Sei to an early death. His warnings about Russia had proved
prescient for in February 1904, just one month after his death, the Russo-
Japanese War broke out.

If Arao Sei and Konoe Atsumaro had lived longer, would the
Russo-Japanese War and the later Pacific War have happened? History
does not allow for such what-ifs. But such a question at least makes
the death of these two highly accomplished men a matter of deep regret. The man who stepped forward to fill the gap left by these two
men was Nezu Hajime.

Nezu Hajime (1860–1927) was born in 1860 in Hikawa-mura in
Yamanashi-gun, Yamanashi prefecture (today's Yamanashi city), the
second son of Nezu Shōshichi. His wealthy family's ancestors had established the village, and for generations had held the title of *shōya* (village headman). His grandfather had managed a distillery business and
enjoyed a life of comfort until his profligacy lost him the business. His

---

1   Li-Lobanov Treaty or "Sino-Russian Secret Treaty" (*Ro-Shin mitsuyaku*). This
    secret agreement was signed in Moscow in June 1896 between Li Hongzhang
    (1823–1901) and Alexey Lobanov-Rostovsky (1824–1896). Should Japan attack
    either Russia or Qing China, the agreement read, each country would come to
    the defense of the other. The agreement also granted vast new rights to Russia in
    Manchuria, becoming a leading cause of the Russo-Japanese War of 1904–05.

father, seeking to restore the family fortune, emphasized simplicity and dependability, and Nezu grew up in that strict environment.

According to the book *Sanshū Nezu sensei den* [Biography of Nezu Hajime], at age ten Nezu became fascinated by Chinese classics, and pored over [the Confucian scholar] Rai Sanyō's *Nihon Gaishi* [Unofficial History of Japan] and *Nihon Seiki* [Records of Japan's Government]. A childhood friend recalls that at around age fourteen, "Nezu was reading the [Chinese classical Confucian texts] *Daxue* [The Great Learning], *Zhongyong* [Doctrine of the Mean], and *Mengzi* [Mencius] all from the *Sishu* [Four Books], and even the *Yijing* [Book of Changes]." The *Daxue* in particular never left Nezu's hands, and when friends came over they could expect a lecture on it. From these accounts we know that Confucianism (Ch. *Ruxue*; J. *Jugaku* 儒学) was an intimate part of Nezu's life from an early age.

Amidst the wave of westernization (*Ō-Bei ka*) of early Meiji Japan, at age seventeen Nezu decided he wanted to study in the West. He applied to and was accepted at the Normal School (Shihan Gakkō) in Yokohama where James Hepburn was an advisor. Hepburn, of course, was the same man who had recognized the special abilities of Kishida Ginkō. Nezu had now taken a big first step toward realizing his ambition. Unfortunately, he fell ill, dashing his dream of studying in America. This single illness helped decide the course of Nezu's life. If Nezu had stayed healthy and been able to study in America, he might have become a proponent of things western rather than an exponent of his anti-Westernism (*han Ō-Beishugi*). Such a scenario would have also changed the fates of Nisshin Bōeki Kenkyūjo and of Tōa Dōbun Shoin.

Just then, Japan was at the very beginning of its Meiji Ishin (Meiji Restoration) which advanced radical new reforms. The reforms pitted elements that favored a new structure of government against defenders of the old order led by *shizoku* (descendants of samurai). One outcome from this clash was the Seinan War [Satsuma Rebellion] of 1877, centered on the private academy of Saigo Takamori (1828–1877) of the former Satsuma domain. To deal with the threat, the government started recruiting new students for its Rikugun Kyōdōdan (Army School for Non-Commissioned Officers). From a pool of five hundred applicants, Nezu was one of just thirteen students admitted. His life's rudder now steered him down a military path.

Arguments with a German military instructor ... and withdrawal

Nezu Hajime was admitted to the Kyōdōdan Army School based on his excellent record. His military talents quickly manifested themselves. In November 1878, he graduated at the top of his class and was appointed to the rank of Army Sergeant First Class. Rather than being sent to the front in Kumamoto as he had hoped, the following year he was ordered to study at Rikugun Shikan Gakkō, Japan's top military academy. There he learned about cavalry, army engineering, and artillery, graduating in 1883.

During his Shikan Gakkō years, he formed an association called the "Yanakakai 谷中会" to cultivate the spirit (*seishin*) of fellow students. A year after Nezu's enrolment, Arao Sei entered the Shikan Gakkō. He attended Yanakakai, where the two met. Nezu was inspired by Arao's broad vision of "*Shina no hozen to kairyō*" [protection and reform of China], which awakened his own personal sense of mission. Nezu looked up to Arao, finding in him a kindred spirit, and the two became close friends. Thereafter, Nezu supported Arao's every endeavor from behind the scenes. The Yanakakai continued even after Nezu's graduation, producing numerous leaders. In the wars that followed, it also produced not a few martyrs.

Arao Sei graduated in 1882, followed by Nezu in 1883. In 1885, Nezu was assigned to artillery duty at the Hiroshima Garrison, while also entering the Rikugun Daigakkō (Army Staff College).[2] As far back as his Kyōdōdan years, Nezu had talked about world affairs and the importance of good governance (*keirin*). Among his ideas was "Establishment of an Army Staff College," a proposal he submitted to a magazine for publication. When ordered to enter the Rikugun Daigakkō, he vigorously protested that wars could not be won simply on the basis of book knowledge and theory. His strong views led to the following incident, which resulted in his being forced to withdraw from school in his second year.

---

2   Rikugun Daigakkō (1883–1945). Located at Kita Aoyama, Tokyo, its name was often shortened to Rikudai. It produced officers for the Imperial Japanese Army. Nezu attended briefly, but then withdrew.

The Japanese army invited Major Jacob Meckel (1842–1905) to serve as a military advisor the same year Nezu entered the Army Staff College, 1885. Meckel promoted reforms in military tactics, management, and hygiene, and encouraged a switch in overseas strategy. He planned a switch from the French army system still embraced by Japan to a German one.

Major Jacob Meckel

Standing at a class lectern one day, Meckel boasted that "If I were to lead a single German division, I could easily destroy the entire Japanese army." Nezu responded angrily, saying that this was an insult to Japanese officers. After that, every time Nezu attended a Meckel lecture they got into an argument. In his second year in an exam paper following a Meckel lecture, Nezu completely ignored Meckel's points about strategy, and proposed a strategy that he called a "Japanese system." Meckel was furious and decided to go back to Germany. Only the Staff College president's intervention managed to calm the situation. After this incident, however, the arguments continued, so that finally the Director of the General Staff asked for Nezu to withdraw. Meckel reserved harsh criticism for Nezu, saying that he was an officer not befitting a civilized country.

In his memoirs, Nezu mentions this incident but expresses no particular regrets. Rather, he recalls the college as the place he completed his exploration of an East Asia strategy, as promised to Arao Sei. With respect to Meckel, Nezu wrote that for the Japanese Army he was an *onjin* (deep benefactor), and Nezu praised Meckel saying that "Japan's victory in the Sino-Japanese War was due to him." Ultimately, this event shows Nezu's growing confidence as a military officer, his patriotism, and his passion for military strategy.

The Sino-Japanese War and nine deaths

After his withdrawal from the Army Staff College, Nezu Hajime was posted to the Sendai Artillery Regiment until, after just one week, he was transferred to General Staff Headquarters (Sanbō Honbu).[3] His withdrawal from the Staff College had closed off any path to promotion, but his interest in Qing China increased in a vein similar to that of Arao Sei. He continued his studies of ethics, politics, economics, composition, and military science, all the while deepening his research on Qing China through the China Section (Shina Ka) of General Staff Headquarters. Attached later to the Tokyo Artillery Regiment, he soon suffered beriberi (*kakke*)[4] which he overcame by going to hot springs in Hakone and Aizu Higashiyama for recuperation. His memoirs report that even here his desire to go to Qing China grew stronger.

Arao returned from Qing China to Tokyo in 1899. There he pursued his plan to quickly set up Nisshin Bōeki Kenkyūjo based on his experience with information gathering. Arao travelled to various places to recruit students, while Nezu took charge of finances. In 1890, having selected about 150 students, Arao returned to Shanghai despite the financial uncertainties the institution faced.

Nezu travelled to Qing China for the first time, where he served as school director (*kantoku*) of the new Kenkyūjo, travelling back and forth between Hankou and Shanghai. He began compiling the vast reports on Qing China gathered by Arao and the Hankou Rakuzendō, publishing them as *Shinkoku tsūshō sōran*, as noted above. In 1893, Nezu undertook an inspection tour of Central China, North China, Manchuria, and Korea, submitting an opinion report of his observations. Having done that, he left the military and began a life of seclusion in the vicinity of Nanzenji Temple in Kyoto. Nezu's seclusion began just as the curtain on a violent new era was about to open.

Nezu's memoirs report that when the Kenkyūjo was established, he felt a lack of personal knowledge and moral rigor. Feeling the need to cultivate these over several years, he obtained Arao's blessing to withdraw from public life. He began studying Zen under the priest [Imakita] Kōzen (1816–1892) at Enkakuji Temple in Kamakura near

---

3   Sanbō Honbu (General Staff Headquarters). Renamed Sanbō Honbu in 1878, it replaced the former Staff Bureau (Sanbō Kyoku) of the Ministry of War and was independent of the ministry. In 1888, an independent Naval Sanbō Honbu was also created.

4   *Kakke* (beriberi). Caused by a deficiency of Vitamin B1, it can lead to heart failure and damage of peripheral nerves. It occurred not infrequently among Shoin students and also among soldiers fighting in the Sino-Japanese War.

Tokyo. Sensing the benefits of this training, he continued his Zen studies under priest [Yuri] Tekisui (1822–1899) at Rinkyūji Temple in Kyoto. Nezu's actions almost suggest that he had a premonition about upcoming major events.

In 1894, the Donghak Peasant Uprising broke out in Korea. Japan and Qing China both sent troops to Korea,

Japanese forces landing at Port Arthur

precipitating the Sino-Japanese War. Nezu received a mobilization order from the General Staff Headquarters which sent him to Qing China to get a grasp on China's situation. To fill the information void created when Japanese government agencies were pulled out of China, Nezu went to Shanghai where he gathered information from Nisshin Bōeki Kenkyūjo graduates. The situation was very dangerous, and death never far from mind.

When Nezu returned to Japan, the emperor was on his way to Hiroshima, and Nezu went to Nagoya Station to see him off. Interested in Nezu's perspective on the situation, the emperor asked for information about Qing China. Thereupon, Nezu accompanied the emperor to Hiroshima, and for two and a half hours reported what he knew to the emperor. Given Nezu's sense of loyalty and patriotism, advising the emperor about China was the highest honor he could ever have imagined.

Perhaps because of Nezu's knowledge of Qing China, he was sent back to the battlefront, attached to the Second Army Command. Nezu saw active duty on the Liaodong Peninsula and in Jinzhou as a commanding officer who issued orders and strategized how to land Japanese forces. The battle experience was harrowing and dangerous, involving brushes with death.

In 1895, when Nezu returned to Japan, he again cast aside the military and re-entered a life of seclusion at the Jakuōji Temple in Kyoto. This time he devoted himself in earnest.

Days of Zen meditation and mourning

From October 1895, Nezu Hajime secluded himself at the Jakuōji Temple in a quiet, hilly expanse of Higashiyama in the east of Kyoto. He broke off all contact with the outside world and entered a life of quiet contemplation. The house where he stayed was on loan to him from the absent Arao Sei. Although today the area is a suburb with houses everywhere, more than one hundred years ago it was all farmland, and the house sat on a hillside to the east. It was a quiet space. A stone monument in front of the house [discussed below] connects the history of Arao and Nezu to today.

Nezu spent more than four years here. Every day he would make the trip of nearly eight kilometers to the Rinkyūji Temple where he practiced Zen meditation under priest [Yuri] Tekisui, mentioned above. Additionally, during two years from 1896, Ōtashiro Tōkoku (1834–1901), a Confucian scholar from the former domain of Morioka, invited Nezu to Kyoto to attend morning and evening lectures on the Confucian classics. This practice vastly expanded Nezu's learning and secured the spiritual foundations of Tōa Dōbun Shoin while it was under Nezu's watch.

Nezu's seclusion was not just about self-study and self-cultivation. In his heart, Nezu was mourning the young people and special friends who had lost their lives in the Sino-Japanese War. First, during the first half of the Sino-Japanese War, at Nezu's direction nine young braves (*shishi*), all graduates of Nisshin Bōeki Kenkyūjo or members of Hankou Rakuzendō, had gone into Qing China's interior to gather intelligence. Once caught, the nine lost their lives, something for which Nezu felt personally responsible. Not only did he pray in front of a Buddhist alter in one of his rooms, but he took on some of these men's orphaned children as pupils and raised them in his borrowed home. After consulting with Arao, he erected a stone monument right outside the house for repose of the souls of the Nine Martyrs' (Kyū Resshi 九烈士).

The Nine Martyrs Monument

Just before the memorial was erected, Arao Sei—the man whose aspirations had been most closely associated with those of Nezu—himself died in Taiwan. One can imagine Nezu's despair at losing his soul mate, something suggested by his extended self-seclusion. Yet his memoirs mention nothing about this episode. Arao's death may have simply hardened Nezu's resolve to pursue self-cultivation as a means of bringing about Arao's aspirations. Perhaps the event simply gave Nezu the strength to develop the Tōa Dōbun Shoin.

To commemorate the death of Arao Sei, Konoe Atsumaro built a large stone monument next to the Nine Martyrs memorial. In time, the words etched on the stone became moss covered and illegible. Several years ago, a graduate of the 42nd Shoin class, Mita Yoshinobu,[5] cleared away the moss and restored the inscription's legibility.

Nezu was not solely practicing Zen during this period of seclusion in Kyoto. Besides Chinese classics, he was reading books on history, politics, and economics. At the same time, he probed such matters as Japan-Qing relations in the aftermath of the Sino-Japanese War, the three Powers' intervention in the postwar settlement, the threat to Japan of Russian moves into South Manchuria, and Japan's Russia strategy.

Just about three months before Arao's death, Nezu married [Fujii] Eiko through the arrangement of Arao Sei. All the wedding attire was planned by Arao, to the surprise of Nezu's new wife. Nezu lived a simple modest life, concerned mainly about his many students. And whenever he went out, he wore the same frock coat. Even when he went out drinking, which he thoroughly enjoyed, he maintained a certain formality.

Then, in 1900, Nezu received a summons from Konoe Atsumaro.

Helping to avoid Qing China's collapse

In 1900, through a special envoy Takahashi Ken, Nezu was summoned to the capital by Konoe Atsumaro, thereby bringing him out of four

---

5   Mita Yoshinobu. A member of the 42nd entering class of Tōa Dōbun Shoin Daigaku, Mita played a leading role in the establishment of the Kanji test of the Japanese Language Research Center. He served as a consultant to the Ishikawa Kanji Tomo no Kai [Friends of Kanji Society] and was active in the study of ancient texts and in deciphering scripts on stone monuments.

years of seclusion. Nezu and Konoe had in fact met the year before in Kyoto, while Nezu was still in seclusion. At the time, Konoe was working on establishing Nankin Dōbun Shoin in Nanjing, whereupon Nezu expressed his personal preference to establish a real school in Shanghai. Konoe had agreed on this point. This exchange led to the subsequent founding of Shanhai Tōa Dōbun Shoin.

Nezu, now age 41, was suddenly swamped with assignments from Konoe. Soon after the establishment by merger of Konoe's new Tōa Dōbunkai, Nezu was named *kanjichō* (secretary general). Then, he was named headmaster (*inchō*) of the new Nankin Dōbun Shoin and advisor (*sewa yaku*) of the Tōkyō Dōbun Shoin, even as he traveled nationwide to recruit students. He then managed the opening ceremony of Nankin Dōbun Shoin. Nezu managed this mountain of roles and duties with smooth aplomb.

The Boxers after entering Beijing

That same year, Nankin Dōbun Shoin had to be moved to Shanghai due to disruptions related to the Boxer movement that had first erupted in distant Shandong. The Qing government in support of the Boxers had declared war on the [western] Powers, and the Powers retaliated by sending an allied expeditionary force into Beijing which led to real fighting. Worried that the Qing might collapse, Nezu sent a proposal to the Japanese government, "Policy to Protect the Qing" (*Shinkoku hozen saku*). The government would send troops to attack and occupy Beijing.

Governor General Liu Kunyi at Nanjing sent a telegram to Konoe condemning the Japanese government action. Konoe replied that the Japanese troops who rushed to Beijing ahead of the allied forces had prevented the Powers from doing more damage and had minimized the destruction to the Qing. Liu seemed to accept this point, and his favorable view of Japan led to his later support of Tōa Dōbun Shoin. Nezu's "Protect the Qing Policy" had worked. After the fighting, Nezu submitted his "Plan to Reform the Qing" (*Shinkoku kaikaku an*) to the two Governors General Liu and Zhang, who forwarded the plan in a joint memorial to the Throne. Some of Nezu's suggestions are thought to have been implemented.

Meanwhile, Russia had used the Boxer Incident to move an additional 100,000 troops into Manchuria (China's Northeast) and refused to withdraw its forces after the end of the fighting. The situation remained unchanged even after the signing of the Anglo-Japanese Alliance of 1902. Russia even proposed to the cabinet of Itō Hirobumi that Manchuria and Korea be split up between Russia and Japan. At about that point, the Li-Lobanov Secret Treaty of 1896 came to light. To Nezu, all this maneuvering seemed to accord with the strategy known as the "China Offensive" (Shina Kōryaku ron) of Russia's Deputy Chief of Staff. These developments prompted Nezu to help organize the Tai-Ro Dōshikai (Anti-Russia Society) [August 1903], an organization anchored by Konoe Atsumaro. Konoe travelled around the country warning of the Russia threat. Since this campaign overlapped with the recruitment of Shoin students and the Japanese government was promoting cooperation with Russia, the government used the threat of withdrawing its financial support for the school to contain Konoe's activism.

However, the argument for war against Russia gathered strength in Japan, and just one month after Konoe's death, negotiations between the two countries broke down and Japan and Russia went to war. The Shanghai Tōa Dōbun Shoin had only recently been founded, and Nezu was busy with its planning. Despite this, he undertook an inspection tour of Manchuria behind the lines. He proposed establishing schools in various regions, a suggestion that became a reality in some places. After the war with Russia, Nezu would apply his experience as a military strategist to running Tōa Dōbun Shoin.

Aspirations for more equal relations with China

This chapter concludes with a discussion of Nezu Hajime's understanding of Qing China. As previously mentioned, since childhood Nezu had loved reading Chinese Confucian classics such as *Daxue* [The Great Learning]. That love had shaped his personal bearing and life attitudes. At one point he had flirted with things western, but illness had prevented further pursuit of this interest. Instead, he switched to a military path based on more traditional martial arts in a period when the Meiji government was adopting a new military system. He studied practical military strategy and directly experienced the gory battlefield of the Sino-Japanese War of 1894–95.

At the Army Military Academy, he had come to know Arao Sei, and encountered Arao's ideas on protecting and reforming Asia including Qing China. Nezu was convinced that to achieve such ends Japan-China trade should be expanded and that methodologies (*hōhōron*) for mutual economic development could be devised. At Konoe Atsumaro's recommendation, he assumed the positions of secretary general of Tōa Dōbunkai as well as headmaster first of Nankin Dōbun Shoin and then of Shanhai Tōa Dōbun Shoin. The course of his life shifted thereby from a military world to the world of economics, education, and culture.

Although Nezu advanced the worldviews of Arao Sei and Konoe Atsumaro, he possessed his own ethical views rooted in his childhood love of Confucian learning. There were thus distinctions in his methodology (*hōhōron*) from Arao and Konoe.

In the aftermath of the Sino-Japanese War of 1894–95, Nezu pondered how to achieve real cooperation (*teikei*) between Japan and Qing China. As a first step, he proposed the dissemination of information in China through modern newspapers and encouraged the invitation of Qing China officials, teachers and business leaders to see Japan with their own eyes. He also proposed that Chinese students come to Japan for study, and that a College of Confucian Classics (Keika Daigaku 経科大学) be founded in Qufu, Shandong province, the birthplace of Confucius. The Qufu school could both train teachers and accept Japanese students, he proposed.

When the Republic of China was established after the 1911 Revolution, Nezu offered his views to the two leaders, Sun Yatsen in the south and Yuan Shikai in the north, about a number of issues: the reorganization and development of fiscal systems, military affairs, education, currency, weights and measures, monetary matters, transportation, and industry. Although these suggestions were appreciated, little was accomplished because of ongoing chaos and division.

Interestingly, in 1909, two years before the 1911 Revolution, Nezu who was then president of Tōa Dōbunkai proposed that the mission statement of Tōa Dōbunkai strike out the phrase "Protect China" (*Shina o hozen su*)—a phrase inserted in 1898 when Konoe Atsumaro merged the old Tōakai and Dōbunkai. Considerable debate ensued, but in the end the motion was adopted.

This episode, only recently came to light through primary materials compiled by Ozaki Masanari[6] in *Tōa Dōbunkai shi: Shōwa hen* [A History of Tōa Dōbunkai: Shōwa edition] (2003). Nezu's reasoning was that in the context of changed international relations between Japan and Qing China, the phrase "Protect China" was "a perspective that really looks down on China" and "lacks the sense of two countries with friendly relations." From the perspective of internationalization, the

Ozaki Masanari, editor of *Tōa Dōbunkai shi: Shōwa hen*

phrase made little sense, he argued. Such a stance would also have opposed Japan's Twenty-One Demands [of January 1915], unilaterally imposed upon China to strengthen Japan's special interests.

This one example shows Nezu as an "international person" (*kokusai jin*) with a basic awareness of countries as equals. Such thinking reflects the stance of Tōa Dōbunkai, in the same way that it served as a pillar of the *seishin* (spirit) of Tōa Dōbun Shoin for the fifteen years that Nezu was headmaster.

6　Ozaki Masanari (1922–2022). Born in 1922 in Shiga prefecture, Ozaki entered Tōa Dōbun Shoin Daigaku in the 42nd entering class, then graduated from Aichi University after repatriation to Japan. A career diplomat, he served as Japanese ambassador to Romania and Mongolia. For many years he was Managing Director of Kazankai, where he took charge of compiling and writing *History of Tōa Dōbunkai: Shōwa Period*, published by Kazankai in 2003 (1272 p.).

Chapter 5. In the International Metropolis of Shanghai

The campus at Guishuli in Gaochangmiao

Our discussion above of the character, thoughts, and actions of Arao Sei, Konoe Atsumaro, and Nezu Hajime showed how these various factors converged to shape Tōa Dōbun Shoin. All three men were in fact deeply involved in the founding of this Shanghai school.

At the very beginning, Arao Sei's *shijuku*-style private academy in Hankou grew into his Nisshin Bōeki Kenkyūjo in Shanghai. Then, under Nezu's planning and administration, Nezu brought closer the realization of Arao's conception of a genuinely modern school (*gakkō*) also in Shanghai. Meanwhile, Konoe Atsumaro was pursuing the dream of establishing a school in Nanjing—a political center of China—as an educational and cultural enterprise of his new Tōa Dōbunkai. Toward this end, he personally traveled to China. In China he obtained the cooperation of the two powerful Governors General Liu Kunyi and Zhang Zhidong. The new Nankin Dōbun Shoin was established at one corner of the Buddhist Temple Miaoxiang'an, and in 1900 started admitting students.

Had all gone well, the Nanjing school might have developed alongside the school being planned by Nezu in Shanghai. However, soon after the establishment of the Nanjing school, the Boxer Rebellion that had broken out on the Shandong peninsula started to spread south toward Nanjing. In August, Nankin Dōbun Shoin was moved out of Nanjing to Shanghai. Its

The campus at Guishuli in Gaochangmiao

provisional site in Shanghai was the Xiyangguan 西洋館 (Western Hall), site of the former Nisshin Bōeki Kenkyūjo on Tuisheng Road near the racetrack—a revival of sorts.

Shanghai at the time was a fast-developing port city at the mouth of the vast Yangzi River that flowed past Nanjing and Hankou far upriver. It was also the financial and economic center for western capital flooding into China. Konoe agreed to proceed with the concept long discussed by Nezu: a school based at Shanghai. The new school was called Tōa Dōbun Shoin, and the students from Nankin Dōbun Shoin were absorbed into it. A big challenge was securing a site in Shanghai for a larger campus. Kageyama Chōjirō, a graduate of Nisshin Bōeki Kenkyūjo and member of the preparatory committee helped with the search. In 1901, members of the 1st entering class (*ikkisei*) of Shanhai Tōa Dōbun Shoin were welcomed though affairs moved forward on an ad hoc basis.

The site selected was on the left bank of the Huangpu River at Guishuli in southern Gaochangmiao across the river from the French Concession and one or two kilometers from the Chinese city. Several buildings were available. (Its location was near the extreme southwest portion of the site of the 2010 Shanghai Expo.) The area was surrounded by farmland. One night, Headmaster Nezu who reached the riverbank after dark, led a group of new students around for nearly an hour before finding their school.

Tōa Dōbun Shoin's first campus came to be known as the "Gaochangmiao Guishuli campus." Just to its south along the Huangpu River was the Qing dynasty's famed Jiangnan Arsenal (Jiangnan Jiqi Zhizao Zongju), a sprawling military factory complex.

The dream of studying abroad

Nezu, who had achieved a measure of success as headmaster of Nankin Dōbun Shoin, had traveled all over Japan to recruit students. Now in response to the Boxer upheaval he undertook another grueling nation-wide recruiting campaign. He managed to recruit 51 publicly-funded (*kōhisei*) students financed by their local prefectures and municipalities and another 58 privately-funded (*shihisei*) students. On April 25, 1901, all gathered in Tokyo at the Peers Club (Kazoku Kaikan, formerly

The admission ceremony at the Kazoku Kaikan in Tokyo

the famed Rokumeikan) for their admission ceremony to Tōa Dōbun Shoin, a school that would become Japan's very first *senmon gakkō* (vocational or specialized higher school) established outside of Japan.

At the ceremony, Tōa Dōbunkai president Prince Konoe enumerated the reasons for establishing Tōa Dōbun Shoin, and implored these students while in China to "put your studies first, uphold your honor as Japanese, never give into youthful impetuousness, and care for your health...."

After touring Tokyo Imperial University and the Yokosuka Shipyard, this 1st entering class of the school went by ship from Yokohama to Kobe. En route, they visited Osaka Castle, the Osaka Commercial Museum (Ōsaka Shōhin Chinretsujo), the Osaka Arsenal (Ōsaka Hōhei Kōshō), and various newspaper offices. Finally, they departed from the port of Kobe for Shanghai under the watchful eye of Nezu. Starting in 1906 with the sixth entering class, in addition to the Imperial Palace in Tokyo, students visited historic Kyoto, Ise Shrine [Japan's most sacred imperial shrine], and industrialized Nagasaki [for its modern shipyards and munitions factories]. The entrance ceremony in Tokyo, followed by tours of major sites in Japan, became a set tradition for every class, from first to last.

Japan at the time was in the early stages of its capitalist economy and remained primarily an agricultural country. Most Shoin students were products of old-style middle schools or commercial schools outside of urban areas. It was therefore incumbent that before going to live in the international city of Shanghai, they acquire a fuller awareness of their own country. The students stayed at top-tier *ryokan* (Japanese inns) in city centers of Tokyo and Osaka and visited cutting-edge industries in other Japanese cities, evidence that Headmaster Nezu had absorbed much international awareness from Arao Sei and Konoe Atsumaro.

The method of recruiting students for Tōa Dōbun Shoin was unique. Modeled after Nankin Dōbun Shoin, the method involved prefectures and municipalities selecting their own students whom they then supported at local government expense. Konoe himself had launched a recruitment campaign around Japan, explaining the importance of trade with Qing China as well as educational and cultural exchanges, and endeavoring to gain the understanding of prefectural governors and prefectural assemblies. This precedent having been set,

Headmaster Nezu conducted similar recruitment campaigns, while Tōa Dōbunkai directors divided Japan into regions where they undertook student recruitment trips.

Japan's victory in the Sino-Japanese war turned the attention of prefectural governors toward Qing China. More governors began selecting students, spreading nationwide the practice by prefectures and municipalities of sending one or two or students to Tōa Dōbun Shoin. This recruitment method not only supported Dōbun Shoin financially but provided a consistent source of top students—killing two birds with one stone.

At the time in Japan, pursuing studies beyond middle school (*chū gakkō*) was a financial burden for even the best of students. Trade-related (*bōeki kankei*) schools provided a new option in addition to teachers' colleges (*shihan gakkō*) and military academies (*gunkankei no gakkō*) [both heavily subsidized]. But a school like Tōa Dōbun Shoin was truly epoch-making. It opened up an entirely new avenue for advanced education. Through it, many young Japanese realized their dream of studying in East Asia's greatest international city—Shanghai.

A fateful campus move

On May 26, 1901, an elaborate inauguration ceremony was held at the Guishuli campus in Gaochangmiao, Shanghai. Sixty-eight students from Japan and 11 students from Nankin Dōbun Shoin attended. Japanese dignitaries included Viscount Nagaoka Moriyoshi, the vice-president of Tōa Dōbunkai representing its president Prince Konoe, Japanese consul-general in Shanghai, captains of the battleships *Fusō* and *Akashi*, and many other Japanese officials. Chinese dignitaries included Shanghai *daotai* Yuan representing Governor General Liu Kunyi; Shanghai magistrate Liu representing Governor General Zhang Zhidong; Sheng Xuanhuai,[1] founder of Nanyang Gongxue (Nanyang Public School or

---

1   Sheng Xuanhuai (1844–1916). Born in Jiangsu province, Sheng worked closely with high imperial official Li Hongzhang (1823–1901) to carry out modernization projects related to Self-Strengthening. In 1895, Sheng founded the Beiyang Gongxue (Beiyang Public School, later Beiyang University, and today Hebei University of Technology) in Tianjin. Then in 1896, he established by edict of the Guangxu Emperor the Nanyang Gongxue (Nanyang Public School or College [for Chinese and Western Learning]) in Shanghai—later renamed Shanghai Jiaotong University

College, later Shanghai Jiaotong University); Chief Justice Wilkinson of the Shanghai High Court, and many others—altogether about five hundred attendees. The inaugural event concluded with fireworks and an elaborate banquet.

Viscount Nagaoka toured the facilities before the ceremony and was impressed. "The facilities were specially constructed, not unlike the Women's College (Nü Xuetang) established by the French," he observed. He marveled at the classrooms and dormitories, kitchens, bathrooms, and toilets, praising the flow of air and the sports facilities. He

Sheng Xuanhuai, a guest at the Shoin opening ceremony

noted the school was in no way inferior to schools in Japan, that meals featured six separate dishes, and that "their delicacy and beauty would be hard for Japanese to imagine."

According to *Tōa Dōbun Shoin Daigaku shi* [History of Tōa Dōbun Shoin University] (1982), this campus was a complex of four Chinese-style rental buildings constructed by Jing Yuanshan (1841–1903), head manager (*zongban*) of the Imperial Shanghai Telegraph Administration (Shanghai Dianbao Ju), built close to his home. Used for school buildings from the start, these facilities were now rented out to Tōa Dōbun Shoin [where the school remained until July 1913]. In its first year, Shoin used two two-story buildings for student dormitories, one one-story building for two classrooms, and the fourth building for Headmaster Nezu and faculty and staff. The facilities were better than the buildings in Nanjing or on Tuisheng Road [site of Nisshin Bōeki Kenkyūjo] in Shanghai, but there were no electrical lights, telephones, or pipes for running water, and the well water had maggots in it—as recalled by Negishi Tadashi, a faculty member at the time.

While I have searched fruitlessly for an image of this school as of 1901, Ishida Takuo, PhD, a researcher at our Tōa Dōbun Shoin Memorial Center at Aichi University, discovered some fascinating

---

and subsequently focused on engineering. Because he advocated nationalization of China's railways, Sheng sought refuge in Japan at the time of the Wuchang Uprising in 1911.

facts about the lineage of the Guishuli school site through the use of contemporary maps. In 1893, Jing Yuanshan (mentioned above), an influential member of the Shanghai business community, a Self-Strengthener, and a supporter of the Guangxu Emperor, invited Liang Qichao and other intellectuals to serve as teachers at his new Jingzheng Xueyuan (Jingzheng School). In 1896, Sheng Xuanhuai [founding *zongban* of the Telegraph Administration in Shanghai in 1880] established his Nanyang Gongxue (Nanyang Public School) on the site of Jing's school. The two schools merged under the name of Nanyang Gongxue (Nanyang College in English). Two years later, in 1898, Jing Yuanshan founded a western-style school for girls on this same site. Vice-president Nagaoka's notes hint at these changes.

Jing Yuanshan, a supporter of the Hundred Days' Reform [of 1898], fled to Macau after the collapse of that endeavor. Then, after the closure of Jing's girls' school, the progressive scholar Luo Zhenyu (1866–1940) who in Japan had studied Japanese language and also western-learning-through-Japanese-translations, opened his Japanese Language School (Dongwen Xueshe) on this site, a school said to have had Japanese teachers on its faculty. In 1901, lured by Governor General Zhang Zhidong and Sheng Xuanhuai, Luo moved to Wuchang and closed his Shanghai school. Thus, this historic site became available for Tōa Dōbun Shoin.

Considering that Sheng Xuanhuai, founder of Nanyang Gongxue, and a representative of Zhang Zhidong both attended the inauguration ceremony of Tōa Dōbun Shoin, we can conclude that both men approved of and cooperated with the establishment of this school. In its final years [up to 1945], Tōa Dōbun Shoin occupied the campus of Shanghai Jiaotong University—the name of Nanyang Gongxue's successor institution since 1921. That the start and end, the alpha and the omega of Tōa Dōbun Shoin's history, should be associated with educational institutions with ties to Sheng Xuanhuai is a fascinating twist of fate.

An exhaustive education in languages and practical studies

The founding of Tōa Dōbun Shoin at its Guishuli campus in Shanghai at the dawn of the twentieth century began to give substance to the dreams of Arao Sei, Nezu Hajime, and Konoe Atsumaro. Guiding the new school were two mission statements [compiled in October-November 1899 at meetings between Konoe and Governors General Liu and Zhang—hence their conspicuous attention to China]: "Essentials of Higher Learning" (*Xingxue yaozhi* / J. *Kōgaku yōshi* 興学要旨) and "Content of Education" (*Lijiao gangling* / J. *Rikkyō kōryō* 立教綱領). "Essentials" opens with the statement: "Our mission is to develop superior talent among Japanese and Chinese students [Nisshin *no gakusei*] by providing them with practical learning (*jitsugaku*) useful both at home and abroad; to nurture the 'wealth and strength' (*fukyō*) of Qing China (Shinkoku); to build cooperation between Japan and China (Nisshin); and to bring about the security of both Shinkoku and greater East Asia (Higashi Ajia)." "Content of Education" specifies first that Shinkoku students will be taught Japanese language and literature along with practical aspects of western leaning. Japanese students, on the other hand, will be taught Chinese and English language and literature along with both foreign and domestic organization, law, commerce, and industry. The fundamental goal is an education that trains talent (*jinzai* 人材) useful for both countries. [Trans. note: After China's defeat by Japan in 1894–95, Governor General Zhang was obsessed with China training men of real talent (*rencai* 人才).]

Both mission statements, written in Classical Chinese (Kanbun), were lengthy. "Essentials of Higher Learning" was more than 1600 Chinese characters in length, and "Content of Education" was about 1200 characters. Composing these in Classical Chinese enabled them to be widely read by both Qing leaders and educated Chinese. In fact, it is apparent that both Governors General Liu and Zhang agreed with and supported their purposes. [Trans. note: Liu and Zhang's secretarial staffs surely drafted both statements, but in close consultation with Konoe.]

The opening ceremony at the Tōa Dōbun Shoin

As for the training of Chinese students, Shinkoku students were sent at first to Japan to enter the Tōkyō Dōbun Shoin. Later, a Chinese Student Division (Chūka Gakusei Bu) was created inside Tōa Dōbun Shoin in Shanghai. But over time, Japanese students were the mainstay of the school.

In its first year of operation, Tōa Dōbun Shoin had a mere eight faculty members, plus Headmaster Nezu and four staff members. Its faculty included Negishi Tadashi mentioned above, the head teacher (*kyōtō*) Kikuchi Kenjirō, and Mori Shigeru. Language teacher Obata Masubumi was the friend of Arao from his Kumamoto Garrison days who had taught Arao both Chinese language and Chinese affairs. In addition there were Chinese teachers of Shinago (spoken Chinese), and a Britisher who taught English. Yamada Junzaburō who later supported Sun Yatsen served on the staff. Junzaburō's older brother Yoshimasa, a teacher of Chinese language and a staff member at Nankin Dōbun Shoin, had joined the revolutionary movement of Sun Yatsen in the wake of the Boxer Rebellion. As previously mentioned, Yoshimasa lost his life during Sun's Huizhou uprising of 1900, the year before the school's move to Shanghai.

Tōa Dōbun Shoin was a three-year school under the Japanese education system with an impressive curriculum. Gradually building towards a capacity of three hundred students, the school offered two specialty programs of study: business (Shōmuka) and political science (Seijika). The vast majority of students enrolled in business. Courses common to both specialties included ethics (*rinri*), spoken Chinese (Shinago), English (Eigo), newspaper reading, Classical Chinese (Kanbun), prose and letter writing, legal studies, civil law, commercial law, economics, and Chinese organizational systems (Shina *seido*). Shōmuka also included practical courses for commerce and trade such as commercial studies, commercial mathematics, bookkeeping, business practices (*shōgyō jissen*), product studies, Chinese commercial geography (Shina *shōgyō chiri*), and Chinese commercial customs (Shina *shōgyō kanshū*). Seijika or political science also included modern economic history of Europe, public and private international law, administrative law, finance law, and the political geography of China (Shina *seiji chiri*).

Both specialty tracks strongly emphasized the study of language. In all three years, students studied Shinago for eleven hours per week, and English for seven hours. Besides language, students took basic courses essential to the practice of commerce and trade in Qing China, which related to the economy, administrative systems, and law. Seen from today's perspective, Tōa Dōbun Shoin was Japan's very first modern business school (*bijinesu sukūru*). From the year 1907, the Big Trip (*dai chōsa ryokō*)—the research travel at the very heart of student life—was added.

After World War II, Tōa Dōbun Shoin gained a reputation as a "military spy school" (*gun no supai gakkō*). However, based on the school's early development and curriculum, no support can be found for such a claim.

The publication of *Shina keizai zensho* (1907–1908)

Tōa Dōbun Shoin in Shanghai had taken the first big step to train experts in trade. But because of shaky finances, the school's educational environment was less than ideal. Back in Tokyo, Tōa Dōbunkai's budget allotments went first to Tokyo, then to different parts of Korea and China for school operations and for general support, and even extended to newspaper publication and distribution. Tōa Dōbun Shoin received merely one quarter of Tōa Dōbunkai's total budget. Headmaster Nezu, while struggling to raise money for Tōa Dōbun Shoin, had taken on the role of president (*kaichō*) of Tōa Dōbunkai, itself facing growing pressures from tensions between Japan and Russia. Overcome by day-to-day duties, Nezu went so far as to ask Sugiura Jūgō[2] to stand in as Shoin headmaster.

Behind the scenes toiling tirelessly was brilliant young scholar Negishi Tadashi [discussed below]. On the Shoin faculty from the institution's start in Guishuli, Negishi took charge of the courses on economics and commerce. In order to understand Qing China and the actualities of its commercial practices (*shō torihiki*) and customs (*shō kanshū*), Negishi conducted investigative research (*chōsa kenkyū*) in

---

2 Sugiura Jūgō (1855–1924). Born in Ōmi (Shiga prefecture, near Kyoto), Sugiura studied in Britain from 1876 to 1880 on a Ministry of Education scholarship, concentrating on chemistry and agriculture. Back in Japan he served as administrator of government schools and wrote many thought pieces on Japanese identity and nationalism (*kokusui shugi*) for the newspaper *Nippon* and the magazine *Nihonjin*. His tenure as Tōa Dōbun Shoin headmaster was so brief that he never travelled to Shanghai.

Shanghai itself. Beyond that, he had his Shoin students make observations about local commerce, training them in research skills. Toward that end, Yamada Junzaburō, Obata Masabumi, and Sawara Tokusuke worked alongside students, giving them practical guidance in their use of Shinago (spoken Chinese).

In order to provide Shoin students with increased opportunities to observe Qing China, new students were taken around Jiangnan just outside Shanghai, while upper class students were taken on more distant study trips (*shūgaku ryokō*) to the cities of Tianjin, Beijing,

Cover of Vol. 12 of the *Shina keizai zensho*

and Hankou. Students said, "We want more trips," but financially more trips were beyond the school's means.

Behind these study trips was the wise hand of Negishi Tadashi. According to his reminiscences, Negishi organized student participants into small teams (*ban*), assigned them various research topics, and had them write up their research as graduation theses (*sotsuron*). The format of the later Big Trip research projects (*dai chōsa ryokō*) grew out of these early trips. A combined report (*hōkokusho*) submitted by two early research teams was fairly exhaustive. Published as a monograph under the title "Trade Practices and Currency Matters in Qing China," the report was praised for shedding light on the complex traditional commercial practices and financial matters of Qing China.

Energized by his successes, Negishi began assigning students topics meriting further research that could be investigated on longer trips. Over a period of several years, he systematically compiled the draft reports of students. Then, starting in 1907, he began publishing the twelve-volume *Shina keizai zensho* [China Economy Series] (1907–1908). Totaling more than 10,000 pages, it was published by Maruzen, a noted publisher.

In terms of content, the volumes began with agriculture and land-holding rights. They continued with the topics of labor, capital, prices of goods, people's lifestyles, finance, commerce, patents, compradors (middlemen traders), guild halls and public offices, union rules, customs tariffs, water transport, warehousing, Shanxi banks, commercial administration, trade goods exhibition halls, commercial usages, and bookkeeping methods. Finally, the series carefully classified and described specific industries. Literally an "encyclopedia" (*hyakka jiten* 百科事典) of the economy and commerce of late-Qing China, the name of Tōa Dōbun Shoin became much better known after its publication.

Based on the investigations and reports students produced, Negishi praised Shoin graduates highly saying that "graduates are now able to deal directly with Shinajin [Chinese people] without having to go through comprador middlemen."

During the Cold War, the accomplishments of Tōa Dōbun Shoin were ignored by Japanese. In the Republic of China (Taiwan), however, scholars began to notice this research and to reprint it. Lin Mingde[3] at Academia Sinica (Zhongyang Yanjiuyuan), for example, has praised Shoin publications saying that the research reports of the South Manchurian Railway Company (*Mantetsu chōsa hōkoku*) were uneven and patchy, whereas the *Shina keizai zensho* and the eighteen-volume, province-by-province *Shina shōbetsu zenshi* [Comprehensive Gazetteer of the Individual Provinces of China, 1917–1920] were systematic and exemplary.

Negishi Tadashi and his practical research

Negishi Tadashi (1874–1971), the man who compiled student field-research reports (*jitchi chōsa hōkokusho*) on commerce and economics in the twelve-volume *Shina keizai zensho* [China Economy Series] (1907–1908), was the educator who in Shoin's inaugural period most closely embodied its practical educational (*jissen teki kyōiku*) goals. He was also the first Japanese scholar to thoroughly analyze China's commercial society and its structure for the outside world. Thus, he deserves closer attention.

---

3   Lin Mingde. Born in Taiwan with a Ph.D. from University of Tokyo, Lin is a researcher at Academia Sinica (Zhongyang Yanjiuyuan) in Taiwan. His research specialty is Modern China-Japan Relations, and includes research on both Tōa Dōbun Shoin and Tōa Dōbunkai.

Negishi was born in 1874, the eldest of a former samurai of the Kishū domain, which is Wakayama City today. As a middle school student, Negishi had heard Arao Sei lecture on his Nisshin Bōeki Kenkyūjo. This sparked Negishi's interest in China and led to his later deep involvement with Tōa Dōbun Shoin. In 1895, Negishi enrolled at Tokyo Higher Commercial School (Tōkyō Kōtō Shōgyō Gakkō), majoring in trade (*bōeki*). For his graduation thesis (*sotsuron*), he conducted research related to water transport in Qing China. Just before Tōa Dōbun Shoin opened in 1901, he was sent to China as a travel student where he ended up a young teacher at the new school. As part of his courses on bookkeeping and accounting, Negishi investigated the wholesale rice business in Shanghai, conducting informal interviews. He then integrated his findings on business practices (*shō torihiki chōsa*) into his classroom teaching.

Negishi's teaching method emphasized the necessity of fully grasping the commercial realities of contemporary Qing China. Besides the previously mentioned *China Economy Series*, he separately compiled the *Qing China Trade Handbook* (*Shinkoku shōgyō sōran*) (1906). In five volumes, the handbook's contents included general business and commercial bookkeeping, commercial geography focused on railroads and waterways, currency and banking, and a catalog of commercial trade products.

Negishi Tadashi, editor of the *Shina keizai zensho*

After seven years at Tōa Dōbun Shoin, Negishi's health deteriorated and in 1908 he returned to Japan. There, he became head of the Research Department (Chōsa Bu) of Tōa Dōbunkai and founded its biweekly magazine of China news and analysis, *Shina* ("The China Review," 1910–1945). In 1914, he was named executive secretary (*kanji*) of Tōa Dōbunkai, and in 1921 after participating in the Washington Naval Conference, he was appointed a director (*riji*). Meanwhile, he became a guest writer for the influential *Asahi Shimbun* newspaper in 1911, and in 1916 became a teacher at his alma mater, Tokyo Higher Commercial School, where he lectured on "Economic Conditions in the East," a course that in fact gave substantial attention to Japan's China policies.

When the Manchurian Incident occurred in 1931 intensifying China's anti-Japanese activities, Japan's military gained power and Negishi stopped his overseas research trips, concentrating instead on academic research. In 1932, starting with his *Studies of Guilds in China* (*Shina girudo no kenkyū*), Negishi published one article after another, reporting the results of earlier on-site research on folk and ethnic organizations such as commercial organizations and community-based groupings (*kyōdō dantai*). In 1954, he was honored with the prestigious Japan Academy Prize (Nihon Gakushi'in Shō) for his work *Guilds of China* (*Chūgoku no girudo*) (1953).

Negishi's studies of China ranged broadly across urban and rural China. He was particularly interested in the Chinese family based on blood lineage and rural land ownership, and in the functions of urban merchant guild organizations. These were the foundational structures of Chinese society, he concluded. Negishi's also floated the notion of "societal Chinese" (*shakaiteki Chūgokujin ron*) in his work, a theory that proposed understanding Chinese people through the values manifest in their thought and daily activities. His research has been highly praised.

Negishi was the single most outstanding China research scholar to pass through Tōa Dōbun Shoin. Negishi's research findings were entirely based on on-site field work (*genchi chōsa*), something that made his work convincing, farsighted, and inspiring for a new generation of researchers of the Chinese economy and society. Negishi's achievements inform even our current understanding of modern China.

Moving the campus after the big fire

Tōa Dōbun Shoin at the Guishuli campus gradually increased its enrolments and extricated itself from financial difficulties, to its great relief. Meanwhile, Nezu Hajime, headmaster of Tōa Dōbun Shoin and secretary general (*kanjichō*) of Tōa Dōbunkai, continued to teach ethics (*rinri*) at the school. His so-called headmaster lectures (*inchō kōwa*), essentially guides for Shoin students and graduates about how to how to interact with people and comport themselves in society, gained notoriety.

We briefly step back to the opening of this book. Two student teams (*han*) on their research trips were caught up in China's 1911 Revolution, as the sentiment "Annihilate the Qing, Revive the Han" espoused by revolutionary troops during the Wuchang Uprising spread throughout the country. Then, in 1912, Yuan Shikai arranged for the child emperor Xuantong to abdicate, closing the curtain on nearly three hundred years of Qing dynasty rule. The new Republic of China (Zhonghua Minguo) was born, with Sun Yatsen serving as provisional president at Nanjing. Yuan Shikai was elected to the post of permanent president as part of efforts to bring the North into the new order. As Yuan's rule became more autocratic, however, Sun Yatsen and southern forces raised troops to overthrow him, and the country was plunged into civil war once again.

One of the fiercest battles of this so-called Second Revolution of 1913 occurred in Shanghai in the vicinity of the Jiangnan Arsenal just to the south of Tōa Dōbun Shoin. The southern forces of Chen Qimei[4] had occupied the arsenal during the 1911 Revolution, and southern forces took it again in July 1913. Yuan Shikai, leader of the northern forces, opened fire from gunboats in the Huangpu River, and wiped the occupiers out. Unfortunately, one shell landed directly on a building of the Guishuli school, and the whole campus went up in flames. Staff and students had already retreated to the French Concession so were safe. But the school was reduced to ashes, a total loss.

Nezu Hajime, then at Izu in Japan recovering from an illness, was devastated. But he insisted, "To retreat now would be bad for both countries," and he pledged to rebuild the school. Just then, new Shoin students were being welcomed. First- and second-year students were moved to temporary quarters in Nagasaki, the Niji'in temple in Ōmura and the site of the family grave of Tōa Dōbunkai president Marquis Nabejima Naohiro (1846–1921; last daimyō of the Saga domain, 1861–71). Here, classes were held. Still in the middle of their Big Trips in China, third-year students would return to Shanghai in the fall, and a temporary school had to be secured for them, too.

According to Nezu's autobiography, for three years he stopped drinking—a habit he loved—while a new Shanghai campus was be-

---

4   Chen Qimei (1878–1916). Chen Qimei went to Japan in 1906 to pursue academic studies and study business. There he met Chiang Kaishek (Jiang Jieshi, 1887–1975), joined Sun's Tongmenghui (United League), and became a revolutionary. He participated in the Shanghai uprising as part of the 1911 Revolution. When the movement for an independent Shanghai failed, he took refuge in Japan. Later, he was assassinated in a Shanghai hideout.

ing built. In the mean-
time, his health recovered. In
October of 1913, the school
moved from the southeast
of Shanghai (Guishuli) to
its northwest, Haskell Road,
just outside the International
Settlement. There, the school
rented former factory and
warehouse buildings of the
British-American Tobacco

The temporary Shoin campus on Haskell Road

Company, and the students at Ōmura in Japan were able to move to
Shanghai.

At the opening ceremony of this new campus, Headmaster Nezu
downplayed any regrets he may have had about the fruits of thirteen
years' work being wiped out in a single morning. He pledged anew,
"Tōa Dōbun Shoin exists where education exists, and we must not rest
for a single day. Now that [China's] domestic affairs have settled down,
I want to build a truly close relationship between China and Japan."

As it turned out, the temporary campus at Haskell Road proved
too small to accommodate Shoin needs. Moreover, in 1914 an
Agriculture and Industry Program (Nōkōka) was added as a third track.
Construction of a larger new campus became an urgent order of business.

The new campus on Hongqiao Road

Construction on Tōa Dōbun Shoin's third campus began in September
1915. The site selected was Hongqiao Road in Xujiahui (or Ziccawei, in
Shanghai dialect) at the western edge of the French Concession, west
of the Bund along the Huangpu River.

The first campus had been in a southern suburb of Shanghai, just
north of the Jiangnan Arsenal, but it had been destroyed by fire during China's Second Revolution. The second utilized a factory site
at the northern edge of the International Settlement, which proved
too small. The third campus was situated in the suburbs just outside
the French Concession. Just inside the concession amidst a forest
of buildings rose a Roman Catholic cathedral visible from the new

campus. Later, beginning with construction in 1928, the expansive Shanghai Natural Sciences Institute (Shanghai Ziran Kexue Yanjiusuo)[5] would move into the area. To the northeast was Nanyang Gongxue (renamed Shanghai Jiaotong University in 1921) founded by Sheng Xuanhuai, with its French-style buildings. At the western edge were agricultural fields and a canal, at one corner of which the new campus was built.

The new campus on Hongqiao Road in Xujiahui and contractor Kuwano Tōsaburō

Unlike past campuses, no buildings were available for rental, so the campus consisted of all new buildings and facilities. At its center was a large main building with administrative offices, research offices, a library, and large lecture hall. Separately there were classroom buildings, the Agriculture and Industry Program experimentation buildings, student dormitories, a dining hall, a club building for students, a bath house, an infirmary, faculty and staff housing, and personal residences. A recreation field was built on the far side of the canal, where sports clubs could hold track and field activities and ball games. Later, a new building was constructed for use of the Chinese Student Division (Chūka Gakusei Bu). But back then, the Shoin campus buildings stood out magisterially, starting with the main building.

Criss-crossed by canals, Xujiahui was a distribution center for rice and other crops at the time. Today, Xujiahui is a busy Shanghai center

---

5   Shanghai Ziran Kexue Yanjiusuo (Shanghai Natural Sciences Institute) was a sprawling modern research facility constructed beginning 1928 using Japanese Boxer Indemnity Funds and initially jointly run by Japanese and Chinese. The Institute opened in 1931 with two faculties: a Medical Faculty with three specialty departments and a Science Faculty with four specialty departments. It was founded partly to appease the anti-Japanese movement that was part of Chinese anti-foreignism in the wake of the May Fourth Movement of 1919. But after the Jinan Incident [of May 1928], China reduced its participation and the institution became overwhelmingly Japanese in make-up.

lined with skyscrapers; the Catholic cathedral is all that remains of the original landscape.

According to *History of Tōa Dōbun Shoin University*, at the point where basic construction work was nearly complete, the contractors attempted to abscond with the funds for construction. In a difficult position, Headmaster Nezu contracted with a concrete company where Kuwano Tōsaburō, a student previously under his care at his home, was employed. The 24-year old Kuwano wrote later, expressing his sense of indebtedness, that "I pushed myself day and night … until completion of a magnificent campus at Xujiahui."

The spires of the Catholic church are visible. The church remains today, but it is surround-ed by tall buildings.

The determined young Kuwano strove to create buildings not in-ferior to the buildings of the nearby French Concession or to the Nanyang College campus. Later postcards of Shanghai include photos of the Shoin campus, demonstrating that its architecture was indeed impressive for its time. On the strength of this achievement, Kuwano Tōsaburō went on to design the Japanese Consulate General in Shanghai, the Jiaxing and Hangzhou railway stations, Japan's Army bar-racks in Shanghai, and many other buildings in mainland China. After the war, Kuwano returned to Japan where he founded the Asahi Eizō Construction Company (later, Kyōwa Eizō Construction Company). His use of the term *eizō* (Ch. *yingzao* 営造) rather than *kensetsu* in his company name gives it a Chinese flavor.

Once again, Nezu struggled financially with the new campus. Chinese compensation for the burning of the Guishuli campus fell short, so that to raise money, Nezu traveled to Manchuria, Beijing, Tianjin, Jinan, Qingdao, and Hankou seeking donations from Shoin graduates. Thus, the new Shoin campus represented both the graduates' strong regard for their alma mater and their belief in Headmaster Nezu. The school was about to enter a new period of maturity.

The Agriculture and Industry (Nōkōka) Program

The year 1917 saw completion of the new Xujiahui campus, providing once again a core locale for education. Students enjoyed a full schedule of study and research, club activities, and campus life. In 1918, a new China Research Division (Shina Kenkyūbu) was established, setting the school on a path oriented toward China-centered research. At the same time, the Shoin established a Chinese Student Division (Chūka Gakusei Bu) and from 1920 admitted Chinese students to the school, realizing the founders' original vision of a school for students from both Japan and China.

The experimental building at the Nōkōka.

On Sundays, students would ride the street cars, and enjoy walking around Jing'an Road and Nanjing Road, which ran through the French Concession from east to west. As the number of Japanese in the northern Hongkou district[6] increased, Japanese food became more

---

6   Hongkou District (formerly spelled Hongkew). In the northeastern part of Shanghai, Hongkou took shape in 1863 within the International Settlement after merger of the British and American enclaves. In 1873, with construction of the Japanese Consulate, more and more Japanese settled in Hongkou, drawing businesses as well. A Japan Town (Ribenren Jie) with residences, shops, and schools formed in the early twentieth century. By the 1940's, one hundred thousand Japanese lived

readily available. During the same period, the number of Shoin graduates working in Shanghai increased, and older alumni would take their juniors out to eat and out for conversation. Students became enamored with life in the big international city of Shanghai.

Just before full completion of the new Xujiahui campus, the buildings of the Agriculture and Industry Program were finished. This epoch-making event broadened the scope of education and research beyond the social sciences. Based on an applied sciences framework and divided into two sections, Agriculture and Horticulture along with Mining and Metallurgy, the program admitted twenty students, all of them Japanese. The curriculum also included Chinese language (*Chūgoku go*), Chinese affairs (*Chūgoku jijō*), and commercial practices (*shōgyō jisshū*). The program was unique in that it combined courses required for Business Program students with technical courses, in what might today be called an integrated arts and sciences program.

World War I was a period in which the costs of war were ballooning while western influence in China was declining. Chinese capital and industries moved in to fill the gap. The Agriculture and Industry Program was an expression of faith in the ability of Japan to scientifically develop China's raw material resources while at the same time rapidly training Chinese people of ability.

However, the timing of Nōkōka's establishment was simply bad. After about 1920 and graduation of the program's fourth entering class, the postwar recovery of western manufacturing was waning while the world economy was contracting. Japan was not immune to these trends. On top of that, employment opportunities for graduates were scattered. According to the research of Takei Yoshikazu at Tōa Dōbun Shoin Memorial Center of Aichi University, four career paths opened up to graduates of this program: natural resources development, institutions that extended loans to Chinese, the Shandong Peninsula [German rights had been transferred to Japan in 1919], and trading companies. Grappling with the downturn, in 1920 Tōa Dōbunkai stopped recruiting students for the Agriculture and Industry Program. For a while, a plan was proposed to reorganize the Nōkōka as the Shanhai Kōgyō Kenkyūjo (Shanghai Industrial Research Institute) attached to the

---

in the Hongkou area.

78

school, but circumstances were unfavorable. Takei's research reveals that recruitment for this project was also halted.

Students at the time also went out on strike against this plan. The small magazine *Koyū* [Shanghai Friends; the semiannual publication of Koyūkai, the alumni association of Tōa Dōbun Shoin] (November 1957–), later reported that Business Program students complained that "the money being eaten by Nōkōka is causing us to be forgotten," whereas Nōkōka despaired that "the other students at Shoin despise us." The controversy around the Nōkōka persisted, but after 1922, once the decision was made to establish the Chinese Student Division, all traces of Nōkōka disappear.

Nezu Hajime's "Shoin Spirit" (*Shoin seishin*) endures

The year 1917 that saw Tōa Dōbun Shoin's new Xujiahui campus completed also saw the birth of the Soviet socialist government in Russia. In its aftermath, Comintern[7] influences spread inside China, while the US and Japanese economies foundered at the end of World War I in 1918.

Then, the May Fourth Movement in China [ignited by angry student demonstrations against the transfer of German rights to Japan under the Treaty of Versailles of 1919], spread beyond Beijing to the rest of the country. A surge in anti-Japanese sentiment among Chinese caused the Big Trip of 1919 to be postponed. Chōsen (Korea), colonized by Japan in 1910, launched its March First Movement[8] (1919) against Japanese authoritarian rule. Back in Japan, in mid-1918 there had been Rice Riots[9] over the growing gap between rich and

---

7 Comintern. The Comintern [Communist International; 1919–1943] was founded in 1919, two years after the Soviet Union. Its purpose was to spread communism to other countries under the leadership of the Soviet Union and to raise the profile of communism.

8 March First Movement (Korea, 1919). Inspired partly by US President Woodrow Wilson's "Fourteen Points" (January 1918), Korean activists assembled in Seoul on March 1, 1919 and announced their Declaration of Independence. Between March 1 and April 11, more than 1500 public demonstrations followed, many put down brutally by the Japanese military with thousands of Koreans killed, wounded, and arrested. For a while, Japanese authorities introduced more lenient policies, but these were reversed in the 1930s with approach of the Second Sino-Japanese War. In 1949, the Korean government designated March 1st a national holiday.

9 Rice Riots (Japan, July to September 1918). When rice prices spiked during post-

poor. These monumental changes took Tōa Dōbun Shoin into new directions. Things began to change, even for Headmaster Nezu.

The construction of the Xujiahui campus coincided with a China economic boom during World War I. Any shortfalls in construction funds were made up by donations from Shoin graduates employed in China. Still, Headmaster Nezu always struggled with funding challenges. Without the spiritual strength developed during his youth, he could not have surmounted the many troubles of the period.

Nezu Hajime in his later years

Each time Nezu returned to Japan from Shanghai he would seek donations. He raised 300,000 yen which solidified the financial foundations of Tōa Dōbun Shoin. Then he tackled a dream of his: reforming Shoin education around "spiritual education" (*seishin kyōiku jigyō*) at a new ethics center—Seimei Gakusha 誠明学社. Unfortunately, prices of goods soared after the end of World War I, though the Shoin was able to manage, thanks to its endowment. Meanwhile, Nezu's health deteriorated and he was forced to abandon his dream of a Seimei Gakusha. In his reminiscences Nezu writes that abandoning this dream was his greatest regret.

Amidst all this, in October 1920, a joint celebration was held at the new Shoin campus to commemorate twenty years of Tōa Dōbun Shoin history and to celebrate Headmaster Nezu's 60th birthday. Student recruitment had stopped for the Agriculture and Industry Program; new students were enrolling in the long awaited Chinese Student Division; the China Research Section published its first issue of *Shina kenkyū*

---

war inflation, housewives in the small fishing town of Uo'zu, Toyama prefecture, called for the lowering of prices by rice delivery vessels. Their call of July 23 spread nationwide, and escalated to demonstrations, riots, strikes, looting, and incendiary bombings of police stations and government offices. Many protestors were arrested and convicted of crimes, while on September 29 Prime Minister Count Terauchi Masatake (1852–1919) and his cabinet resigned, taking responsibility for the collapse of public order.

[China Research]; and the Shoin was elevated to a prestigious Higher Specialized School (Kōtō senmon gakkō) status, with its program of study increased to four years. For Headmaster Nezu these were all matters to celebrate.

The celebration of Nezu's 60th birthday began in grand style. Congratulatory messages of guests praised Headmaster Nezu for his industriousness and tireless *seishin* (spirit). Baron Makino Nobuaki (1861–1949; second son of Satsuma leader Ōkubo Toshimichi, adopted out into the Makino family), formerly Minister of Foreign Affairs and now vice president of Tōa Dōbunkai, declared that "Headmaster Nezu's wholehearted efforts on behalf of the country and on behalf of Dōbun Shoin are the exertions of a high-minded man worthy of our admiration and respect." Makino went on to pledge his full support as next president of Tōa Dōbunkai. In response, Nezu expressed his profound gratitude for "the heartfelt support of alumni, faculty, staff, and students through the trials and tribulations of the past twenty years that have continued right up until today."

In 1923, Tōa Dōbunkai took on the legal status of a corporation (*hōjin*). Konoe Fumimaro, son of Atsumaro, assumed the position of vice president. Nezu, for his part, stepped down as headmaster of Tōa Dōbun Shoin. His *Shoin seishin*, however, would continue, infusing the life of his school.

Chapter 6. The Big Trip

The Anglo-Japanese Alliance creates an opportunity

Tōa Dōbun Shoin was born a business school with a dual educational focus. First was language study, which was embedded in the curriculum. The study of Chinese language (alternatively called Shingo 清語, Shinago 支那語, or later Chūgokugo 中国語) would allow dealings directly with local producers, bypassing those Chinese middlemen known as *maiban* or compradors.

Second was travel to all parts of China in order to gain an understanding of the real conditions (*jittai*) of China, something first called Qing China, and then after 1912, the Republic of China. The materials gathered by Arao Sei and compiled by Nezu Hajime into the three-volume *Shinkoku tsūshō sōran: Nisshin bōeki hikkei* [Commercial Handbook of China: Essentials of Japan-China Trade] (1892) provided an understanding of overall conditions in Qing China. But the conditions in local areas and the real facts about local business practices, customs, and products remained virtually unknown. In order to advance trade, it was essential to obtain accurate information.

Local research trips (*shūgaku ryokō*) in the vicinity of large cities enabled students to gain a modest understanding of the realities of Qing China. To this end, the young professor Negishi Tadashi formed students into small teams (*ban*), assigned them themes for field investigations centered around urban commerce, and compiled their reports into the twelve-volume *China Economy Series* (*Shina keizai zensho*; 1907–1908) distributed by Maruzen, which was widely praised. From its very beginnings, then, the school was anything but idle in efforts to gain an understanding of Qing commerce and trade. Even so, there was growing student demand to explore not only China's cities but to learn about rural China and China's uncharted interior. Meanwhile, Tōa Dōbunkai, the parent organization of Tōa Dōbun Shoin, lacked the financial resources to meet the school's needs and the many desires of students.

Some students during their summer holidays used remittances from home to get together with classmates and set off on trips up the banks of the Yangzi River or by foot into rural areas. This demonstrated their passionate desire to learn more about Qing China.

In 1905, five students from the 2nd entering class (*nikisei*) were summoned by Headmaster Nezu immediately after their graduation.

Nezu stunned them by saying, "I want you to head into China's western regions (Xiyu 西域) and investigate Russian penetration of that area."

This development requires some explanation. In 1902, Japan and Great Britain had signed the Anglo-Japanese Alliance.[1] For Japan, this was a moment of exaltation: Great Britain, a western superpower, had revised its unequal treaties with Japan and admitted Japan as a member of the international community of nations. Britain needed Japan's cooperation against the common threat posed by Russia which had taken advantage of, first, the Sino-Japanese War of 1894–95 and then the Boxer Uprising to pursue a "southward policy" of encroaching and occupying Chinese territory in Manchuria (Northeast China). Prince Konoe, as mentioned above, had come to the conclusion that "war with Russia is inevitable" in light of Russian movements into Korea in the wake of its incursions into Manchuria.

Battle of Mukden as featured on Ema plaque (1907)
Housed at Toyohashi City Museum of Art and History

With the guarantees of the alliance in place, the Russo-Japanese War would later begin. However, in the meantime, Great Britain re-

---

1   Anglo-Japanese Alliance (1902). Signed on January 30, 1902, the Anglo-Japanese Alliance was renewed in 1905 and 1911 and allowed to expire in 1923. The Alliance was a means for Britain to contain Russia after Russia failed to withdraw its troops from Manchuria following the Boxer Rebellion. During the Russo-Japanese War in 1904–05, Britain helped to check the Franco-Russian Alliance. Nominally neutral, Britain also managed to supply Japan with crucial intelligence information.

quested Japan's Ministry of Foreign Affairs to conduct an investigation of Russian encroachment in China's western regions [adjacent to British-claimed territories]. The Foreign Ministry lacked any network of information gatherers in western China. What came to mind instead was Headmaster Nezu and his Tōa Dōbun Shoin.

Investigating China's western regions

Of the five graduates summoned by Headmaster Nezu, one had to be replaced. All the others readily accepted the opportunity for a big trip offered by their esteemed headmaster.

Even to Han Chinese, China's western regions were a world of non-Han nomads who sometimes attacked them. But the regions were even more unknown to Japanese at the time. The jades and gemstones and leather goods and grapes of China's west were richly alluring, but the region itself was remote and hard to reach. What the Japanese knew about this world was encapsulated in the Shōsoin in Nara, a treasure house that preserves precious objects acquired by Japanese envoys to the Tang dynasty [618–907] and brought back from the Tang capital of Chang'an [Xi'an today], such as Arabesque-patterned cloth, masks, and glass articles. Japanese tourists have travelled in numbers to the

Four students from 2nd entering class who headed west to do research. Sakurai is not featured, but Hayashide, Hatano, Miura, are in back left. Kusa is on the far right.

Silk Road regions, as the area is now commonly called, only in the past twenty years or so.

The five Shoin graduates who accepted this assignment were Hayashide Kenjirō, Hatano Yōsaku, Kusa Masakichi, Miura Minoru, and Sakurai Yoshitaka. Hayashide and Hatano travelled together from Yili [Ili] westward toward Dihua (today's Urumqi), and Sakurai headed for Kobdo and beyond, all in Xinjiang. Kusa and Miura went to Kulun (now Ulan Bator) and on to Uliastai, taking on the assignment of Outer Mongolia. The group left Beijing together in July 1905, amidst the Russo-Japanese War. Those going to Xinjiang reached Urumqi at the year's end. In 1906, field investigations continued. By the time it was over, this great adventure had lasted a full two years.

We know the particulars of one itinerary from Hatano Yōsaku who kept a detailed travel journal (*nisshi*). Immediately after leaving Beijing, Hatano contracted malaria, missing about a week of travel. His journal makes frequent reference to recurring fevers. He traveled both by cart and on foot. But the roads were bad and sitting in the cart aggravated

Routes taken by five members of 2nd entering class in their investigation of western China commissioned by the Ministry of Foreign Affairs (1905–1907)

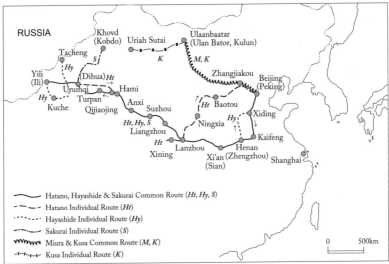

(Created from Hatano's diary, Hayashide's memoirs, and Tōa Dōbun Shoin's official history.)

his hemorrhoids—so he walked most of the way. His travels took him to Lanzhou, and from there through the Hexi Corridor westward to the Tianshan mountain range. Using Urumqi as his base, he traveled to Yili and Tacheng. Unfortunately for him, early in his travels the Russians had spotted him. They tailed him, and otherwise obstructed his progress. This forced him to hide when he was in towns and villages. Also, to avoid the oppressive heat of the desert by day, he often moved at night, guided by the stars and the moon.

In towns and villages, Hatano recorded the populations of both locals and foreigners from various lands, and carefully investigated the language, associations, shops, land, products, and road conditions in each area. The report that he submitted to the Ministry of Foreign Affairs also included information about race and ethnicity, local products, trade conditions as applied to merchants of different ethnicities, and transportation networks. This report, along with the other four reports, represented the first serious effort by Japanese to research China's western regions. On the road home, Hatano had the advantage of being able to travel on frozen rivers, even as high fevers reminded him that death lurked. At one point, he encountered a missionary named Hunter who miraculously saved his life.

Hayashide Kenjirō travelled over nearly the same route as Hatano. On his way back, he met Major Hino Tsutomu[2] of the Japanese Army with whom he shared information about China's far west. The major was struck by the high quality of research by this Shoin graduate, and this chance meeting became the impetus for Hino's popular book, *Iri kikō* [Travels in Ili] based partly on Hayashide's reports. After returning to Japan, Hayashide was invited by the Qing government to return to Xinjiang—this time as a schoolteacher.

These five men's adventures had been rough going, but the trip had been a major success.

---

2   Hino Tsutomu (1866–1920). Hino was born in Iyo (Ehime prefecture, Shikoku). In 1906 the Japanese Army sent Major Hino on a reconnaissance mission to Xinjiang in far western China and on to India, a trip that would last one and a half years. Hino met Hayashide Kenjirō who was on his way back to Shanghai, and collected more information about Xinjiang. After returning to Japan, Hino published his book *Iri kikō* (Travels in Ili) in 1909.

The Ministry of Foreign Affairs' monetary reward

Students back at Tōa Dōbun Shoin had been hoping for a major success in their five colleagues' great adventure (*dai bōken ryokō*), and gave them a rousing welcome on their return. At the same time, students begged the school to allow them a similar *bōken ryokō*. Financial difficulties at the school, however, prevented their demands from being met.

As things turned out, Japan's Ministry of Foreign Affairs keenly appreciated the reports from these investigations and awarded 30,000 yen to Tōa Dōbun Shoin. Suddenly in possession of an unimagined amount of money, school authorities had no choice but to acquiesce quickly to student demands. The plan that emerged was to spend 10,000 yen per year over three years to support independent student "big research trips" (*dai chōsa ryokō*). Now there was a solid financial base for Professor Negishi Tadashi's research on the commercial realities (*shōgyō jittai chōsa*) of China.

Thus, in 1907, Shoin's 5ᵗʰ entering class (*gokisei*) embarked on the school's very first formal *chōsa ryokō*. Its time frame of five months involved hurried planning and preparation at the end of June, departures in early and mid-July, and finally, return to the campus in October. Students were organized into teams (*ban*) of two to five or six. The themes for research and travel destinations, along with the route itself, were planned by students in consultation with Negishi. The names of the teams—all ending in the word "route" (*xianlu* 线路)—derived from their travel itineraries.

Shoin students leaving school in vehicles are sent off by their classmates

In 1907, the 5th entering class was broken into seven travel teams (*ryokō ban*) and assigned to the Beijing-Hankou Railway Route, the Huai-Wei River Route, the Zhejiang-Jiangxi-Hunan-Guangdong Route, the Fujian-Zhejiang-Macao-Hainan Route, the Wuhan-Guangzhou Railway Route, the Henan-Shaanxi-Hubei Route, and the Shandong Province Route. In addition there were "residence teams" (*chūzai ban*) that chose to reside variously in the eight cities of Shanghai, Hankou, Guangzhou, Hong Kong, Yingkou, Zhifu [Chefoo], Tianjin, and Beijing. Possibly due to hasty preparations, the number of students in "travel teams" was only about half of the total, making the number of residence teams carrying out research on cities larger than that of later big trips. Students may also have been divided into teams based upon whether or not they were good walkers.

Looking at the 6th entering class—the second travel team (*dai nikai ryokō ban*) of 1908—one sees eleven travel teams and just one residence team. The eleven travel teams [their name now abbreviated to *xian* for "route" or line] were the Kou-wai Lama Temple Rehe [Jehol] Route, the Shanxi-Mongolia Route, the Shanxi-Henan Route, the Tianjin-Pukou Railway Route, the Henan-Hubei-Guangdong Route, the Hubei-Sichuan Route, the Chu-Yue Hubei-Guangdong Route, the Jiangxi-Fujian-Guangdong Route, the Liaodong Coastal Route, the Yangzi River Route, and the Wan Jiang River Route. The single residential team stayed in Beijing. The names of the various routes were based on Chinese abbreviations or poetic names for provinces, adding an element of romance to students entering worlds unknown to them.

The research topics of these travels turned into graduation theses (*sotsugyō ronbun*). Student observations from the first and second travel teams [1907 and 1908] were published in two issues of *Tōa Dōbun Shoin Alumni Association Bulletin* under the titles of "Breakthrough Travels" and "Lands of Emperor Yu and Phoenix Claws." From the third travel team onward [1909–], student reports were published by the school no longer in the bulletin but as stand-alone books. Edited by students, the documents serve as a comprehensive record of each travel team's experiences. Meanwhile, reports of about one hundred pages in length suddenly turned into massive volumes of four hundred pages or more. In addition to group photos of each team and maps of their itineraries, the books featured written contributions by Headmaster Nezu and by prominent Chinese.

Main cities on routes taken by 6th entering class

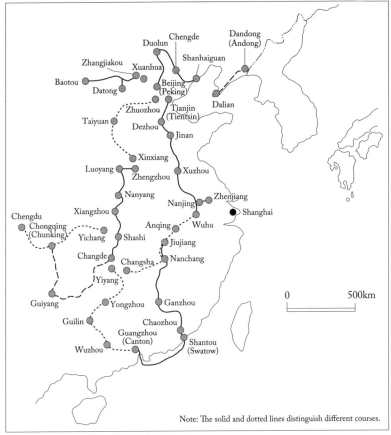

Note: The solid and dotted lines distinguish different courses.

(One group stayed in Beijing.)

Thereafter, digest versions of travel team journals (*nisshi*)[3] and other accounts were published annually. The content and quality of student research reports (*chōsa hōkoku sho*) exceeded all expectations. Duly impressed, Shoin administrators decided to continue the trips beyond the

---

3   Travel records (*kiroku*) of Shoin students. Each year, digest versions drawn from travel journals (*nisshi*) were collected and published. Published each year except for years when incidents or events intervened, thirty-three annual volumes of *nisshi* were published. These provide a lively record of both research findings and the routes of travel.

first three travel teams. Continuing for nearly half a century, the Big Trip (*dai ryokō*) opened windows not just onto China but also onto Southeast Asia.

Getting to know the bare realities of China

The Big Trip of Dōbun Shoin students was integrated into the curriculum and remained the most important event of a student's final school year.

China, like Japan at the time, was an agricultural country. To get to their travel destinations, students mostly had to travel on foot through rural villages in what their journals called *lu xing* 陸行 (overland travel). When they were able to travel by boat along the Yangzi or Yellow Rivers, limited funds required them to travel as "deck passengers" just like local Chinese—and to get wet when it rained.

The students in fact always travelled under the same conditions as Chinese, which led to special insights. For example, when going down the Yangzi River, each time [Chinese] passengers disembarked some would pilfer other passengers' goods, until by the end of the journey more than half of student belongings might have disappeared. Not understanding how things worked in local areas and unfamiliar with the thinking of Chinese on

Surrounded by curious locals, students from 16th entering class cook their own food

board ship, disembarking students were also able to observe firsthand the various mechanisms in place for taxation and bribery of local officials.

Unlike today where hotels and inns are options, students would often have to stay at horse stables in villages when stopping for the night. The travelers would spread out a mat on floorboards, happy if they could avoid attack by even a few of the insects known as *Nankin mushi* ("Nanjing bugs"),[4] that is, bedbugs. They also stayed in farmers'

---

4   *Nankin mushi* 南京虫 ("Nanjing bugs"; bedbugs; *tokojirami*). Bedbugs survive through hematophagy, ingestion of their victims' blood. Preferring low light conditions, they are nocturnal. *Nankin mushi* were common in China during this period,

huts or even slept outside, which could be dangerous. In county seats, students would find a cheap room and negotiate a price, directly experiencing this bare reality of Chinese life.

For food, the person in charge for the day would make the rounds to farm families in the morning, buy up ingredients, and prepare food for the road. They might also stop at roadside stalls for such items as steamed buns (*mantou*), congee (*xifan*), and eggs, fresh off the stove. All this led to considerable contact with farmers, something students did not mind since many came from rural backgrounds themselves. Not a few Shoin students felt an attachment (*aichaku*) to Chinese farmers and rural life, and thereby came to love China itself.

Even amidst the chaos of the 1911 Revolution, it was necessary for students to stop and greet local magistrates when passing through their districts. Indeed, it turned out that not a few of the magistrates had studied in Japan. There were cases of guards being assigned for their protection in areas infested by bandits (*hizoku* 匪賊),[5] and on certain occasions farmers and horses would transport student belongings. One thing students resented was being awakened at night by police demanding to inspect their passports or to check their luggage. At the time, it was routine practice to monitor outsiders in villages and especially foreigners, a practice that continues to this day.

As the number of Shoin trips increased, locals came to expect students each new year. A line would sometimes form outside student lodgings with people asking for medications carried in their luggage. The main interest was in Jintan 仁丹 [a breath and sore throat medicine]. Student journals also record that sometimes pregnant women would appear in search of treatment. These accounts give some idea about the state of health care in villages at the time.

As travel routes became longer, thieves (*hizoku*) and horse bandits (*bazoku*) turned up more often. In one case, guards hired to protect a student team turned out to be bandits in disguise. The head bandit charged toward the students brandishing a traditional Chinese sword,

---

and Shoin students frequently suffered from them even in their dormitories.

5   Bandits (*hizoku* 匪賊). Peasant farmers who lived downstream in the flood plains of the Yangzi River would often go hungry and turn to thievery. This occurred most often in the provinces of Jiangsu, Anhui, and Shandong. After 1911, it was warlords (*gunbatsu* 軍閥) who occupied many areas, disrupting public order. During this period, ex-soldiers and peasant bandits both spread around the country.

and team members feared for their lives. Seeing that the chief had an eye problem, one team member thought, "I'm going to die anyway" so handed the man his precious eye medicine. The leader was so grateful he let them off with their lives, but stripped them of everything including their clothes.

Danger was a constant companion during these trips—but not a single student died. Meanwhile, students got to know the bare realities of China (*hada de Chūgoku o shiru*).

Research waiting to be seen by the rest of the world

The Big Trips of Tōa Dōbun Shoin students continued until 1943 when it appeared increasingly likely that Japan might lose the Pacific War. Altogether, a total of about 4500 students had followed about seven hundred different travel routes. Centered on the Chinese mainland, the research territory covered an area that also extended in the north to Manchuria (Northeast China) and Vladivostok, and south into colonial Southeast Asia. Research trips on such a scale over such a long time period—a period of nearly one half century—are unparalleled in world history. The high quality of research by these students is evident in the twelve-volume *Shina keizei zensho* [China Economy Series, 1907–1908]. These volumes preserve the tradition thoroughly instilled by Professor Negishi Tadashi of *ideology-free observations and on-site investigations* [emphasis added].

The object of investigation changed over time from the study of commercial practices, economic activities, and production conditions to education, human character, culture, famine, population, transportation, cities, and rural China. Indeed, the curriculum developed into what is known today as Area Studies (*chi'iki kenkyū*).[6] Taking charge of research trips after Negishi Tadashi was Baba Kuwatarō,[7] himself a Shoin gradu-

---

6 [Trans. note: See Reynolds, Douglas R. "Chinese area studies in prewar china: Japan's Tōa Dōbun Shoin in Shanghai, 1900–1945." *The Journal of Asian Studies* 45, no. 5 (1986): 945–970. This article analyses Tōa Dōbun Shoin's curriculum, including its emphasis on language study and field work, and compares it with postwar Area Studies programs in the United States.]

7 Baba Kuwatarō (1884–?). A member of the 5th entering class of Tōa Dōbun Shoin, Baba became a professor at his alma mater in 1916 where he taught economic geography and commodity studies and supervised the Big Trip. He headed Shoin's

Courses taken on mainland China by students
from 5th entering class to 23rd entering class

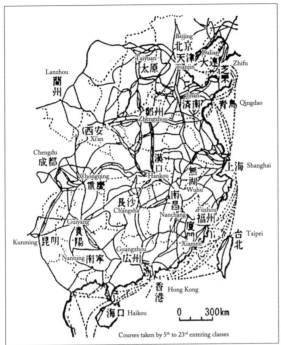

Courses taken by 5th to 23rd entering classes

ate and faculty member responsible for economic geography (*keizai chi-rigaku*). Perhaps related to Baba's long involvement with economic geography education, the content of field research became more academic in orientation as students undertook more comprehensive research on China and Southeast Asia. This focus strengthened the case for moving the Tōa Dōbun Shoin up in rank to university status.

During the Pacific War, American strategic studies of Japan gave rise to Area Studies,[8] an approach coinciding with the rise of the aca-

---

Shina Kenkyūbu [China Research Division] from its founding in 1918. When Tōa Dōbun Shoin was elevated to university status in 1939, Baba was appointed head of the Preparatory Division. He published many important studies including *Shina keizai chirishi* [China's Economic Geography] (2 vols.; 1922).

8   *Chi'iki kenkyū* 地域研究 (Area Studies). During World War II, the US launched a new avenue of research on non-Western countries employing multidisciplinary perspectives that encompassed both the humanities and social sciences. Ruth

demic field known as Cultural Anthropology. Yet in terms of research methodology, Tōa Dōbun Shoin had been employing Area Studies methods decades before the U.S. After the war, China dogmatically criticized Tōa Dōbun Shoin as a vanguard of imperialism. Certainly, by the end of the war the content of Big Trip reports had subtly changed due to the rise in formal status of Tōa Dōbun Shoin and to worsening relations between Japan and China. But today, China has started to see the Big Trip research results as a valuable resource that fills in some of the gaps of modern Chinese history.

Sun Yatsen's informal inscription on a Big Trip report

According to my own extensive research, the Big Trip (*dai ryokō*) can be broken down into four periods. **Period One** is the "period of expansion." During this period, students chose to travel to areas unknown to Japanese and scrambled to expand knowledge about these areas. For example, travel teams (*ban*) might take the name of a province such as the Shandong Team (Shandong *ban*), the Guizhou Team, and the Sichuan Team. The Sichuan team did not limit its investigations to Chongqing, Chengdu, and Emei Mountain but headed further west into the Tibetan plateau, and even visited Wenquan (epicenter of the massive 2008 earthquake) and Songpan located at the edge of a major glacier. The most important goal for students of course was to come up with superior findings that could be turned into a fine graduation thesis (*sotsuron*). In fact, however, it was curiosity about particular regions that seems to have determined the travel routes selected. It was not uncommon, as seen in the following example, for members of the judo club

Benedict's *The Chrysanthemum and the Sword: Patterns of Japanese Culture* (1946) was representative of that genre of research. After the war, this methodology was applied to research on Central and Latin America and Africa. Cultural Anthropology emerged from within Area Studies as it took shape. [Trans. note: Fujita's original has not been altered here.]

員　委　備　御　行　旅

馬　　香　　佐　　馬塲　　石　　大　　小
　　　々　　教
川　　木　　授　　田　　脇　　山

Baba Kuwatarō, center, one of the coordinators of the Big Trip (1928)

with strong physiques to form a team and travel together to remote areas of China's interior such as Sichuan, Yunnan, Shaanxi, and Gansu.

Besides publication of the graduation theses, each year's observations and experiences were sometimes published in pamphlet form around selected themes. The beginning of each volume would open with an address from a Japanese dignitary such as the president of Tōa Dōbunkai, the school headmaster, or a noted general of the Japanese Imperial Army such as Fukushima Yasumasa. On the Chinese side, Tōa Dōbun Shoin went to great lengths to get renowned figures such as Sun Yatsen, Li Yuanhong, Dai Tianqiu [Dai Jitao], Zhang Binglin, or top warlords such as Wu Peifu and Cao Kun to contribute brush-ink characters in their own hand.

Trekking to the far corners of the mainland

Period Two of the Big Trips was the "period of maturation" which lasted about a decade, through the 1920s until the Manchurian Incident of 1931. This was a full and satisfying period for Tōa Dōbun Shoin. In 1917, the Xujiahui campus had been completed and in 1918 the China Research Division (Shina Kenkyūbu) was established. On its twentieth

Armed group comprised of local peoples of Qinghai Province

anniversary the school was elevated to a prestigious four-year Higher Specialized School (Kōtō Senmon Gakkō), and a Chinese Student Division (Chūka Gakusei Bu) had been founded. These developments together created an excellent educational atmosphere and helped make the business school's course offerings appropriate to the more complex environment of the times.

By 1920, the Big Trip had already covered more than two hundred different travel routes. Routes were chosen increasingly according to topics for research rather than geography. From the time of the 19th class's research trip of 1921 [for third-year students about to graduate], teams separately compiled members' travel journals (*nisshi*) in addition to the standard research reports (*chōsa hōkokusho*). These journals contain more ordinary observations and experiences, which raised the value of the travel journals. These accounts also served as a kind of "guidebook" for future student travelers.

During Period Two, research travel to Southeast Asia increased sharply. One team travelled to Annam (French Indochina, now Vietnam), and one member offered this advice to his juniors at the end of his journal: "The French are arrogant not only to the locals but also to us Shoin students. If you want to talk to them as equals, master French."

The 19th entering class was organized into twenty teams (now called *chōsa ban* or investigation teams). These included the Gansu-Ningxia Sheeps' Wool and Leather Investigation Team, the Han and Jialing River System Economies Investigation Team, the Manchuria Investigation Team, the South Seas Maritime Trade System Investigation Team, the Manchurian Stock Exchange Investigation Team, and the Zhili-Shandong-Shanxi-Henan Cotton Economy Investigation Team. The objects of inquiry are clearly reflected in team names: They include both the geographic area of travel and the topics to be investigated.

In the case of the Gansu-Ningxia Sheeps' Wool and Leather Investigation Team, the group travelled from Shanghai to Hankou, Loyang, Xi'an, Pingliang, Lanzhou, and Xining, after which they visited Qinghai Lake on foot. The return trip took them down the Yellow River through Ningxia and Baotou, then overland to Beijing, Tianjin, and Qingdao, and finally back to Shanghai. This lengthy trip of 152 days was matched only by the 1905–07 exploration by Hatano Yōsaku of China's western regions. It was a grand expedition.

Qinghai Lake[9] is at the northeastern corner of the Tibetan Plateau just beyond the Sun-Moon Pass. The Pacification Commissioner who resided in Lanzhou made his rounds of the region about twice a year, visiting tribal leaders in the area and carrying out a ceremonial exchange in a tent to reassert his authority. The actual ceremony is recorded in an account by a Shoin student who observed it firsthand. At the southwestern edge of the vast Tibetan Plateau, still outside the jurisdiction of the Republic of China government, was a grassland extending from Sun-Moon Pass to Qinghai Lake. Interestingly, student records note that at points the vegetation was so tall as to lose sight of team members on horseback in the distance ahead. If you visit the area today, the vegetation is shorter, as economic development has altered the appearance of China's interior grasslands.[10]

Separately, according to Southeast Asia travel accounts, many resident Japanese were engaged in all manner of agriculture, commerce, and itinerant trade, winning the respect of local peoples. The war initiated by Japan [after 1941] ignored these favorable conditions and resorted to the use of brute force. To this day, that war casts a dark shadow over Japan in this region.

---

9   Qinghai Lake. This beautiful lake high up in Qinghai province is the largest lake in China's vast interior. After Liberation in 1949, Han Chinese flocked to the lake and overfished the Emperor Fish. Local Tibetans were outraged. Since then, a conservation movement has been underway.

10   [Trans. note: Fujita speaks here from personal experience. His fascination with student research trips marks him as an "adventurous" geographer-explorer in the mold of early Shoin students. He has traveled to China's interior countless times.]

Unending adventures and dangers

Every one of the seven hundred Big Trips is fascinating. But I want to introduce several grand trips that have become legendary among Shoin graduates.

Clothing of minority group as depicted by Anzawa Takao

One is the *chōsa ban* (investigative team) of seven people from the 25th entering class known as the Yunnan-Burma Economy Investigative Team. Its planned course was to travel from Hong Kong to Haiphong and Hanoi; then to Kunming and Yunnan; and finally south to Burma (Myanmar today). The routes were exceedingly difficult. They were then to head north into Sichuan province passing through Chengdu, with the idea that the team could retrace its steps back to Shanghai.

By the time the team reached Kunming, however, the 1928 Jinan Incident in Shandong[11]—a military clash between Japanese army troops and revolutionary Northern Expeditionary Forces of Chiang Kaishek— had occurred, and anti-Japanese feeling was running high. Chinese bandits (*hizoku*) meanwhile had been proliferating at China's provincial borders. The team received notice the Yunnan provincial government and the Japanese Consul in Chengdu had issued orders for the team to turn back. The team, however, sensed something strange about the

---

11   Jinan Incident (1928). After the Northern Expedition Armies of Jiang Jieshi (Chiang Kai-shek) reached Jinan in Shandong province, on May 3, 1928 an armed conflict broke out with the Japanese Imperial Army bent on "protecting Japanese people and defending Japanese rights."

message. Before the Incident it had promised to meet a group of young Tibetans in Tibet, and the team suspected that officials were trying to block this. Without warning, it changed plans about going to Burma and hurriedly headed westward toward Tibet.

Yunnan-Burma course

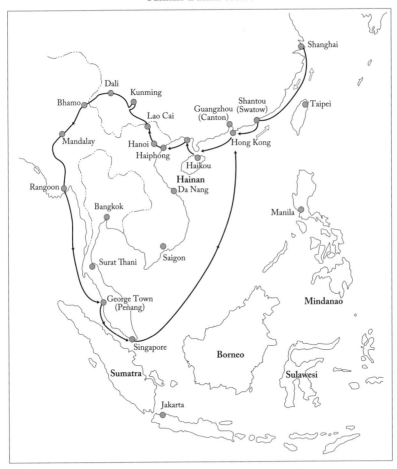

When the students arrived at Anning to the west, they were captured by government troops and taken back to Kunming. Provincial authorities placed them under surveillance, which was reported in the press, and it was said that tears of regret poured down team member faces.

Some kind Chinese stepped in to help the team, whereupon its members switched into Chinese clothing and divided into two groups. Group One traveled on foot southward to Dianchi Lake, while Group Two concealed itself in a ship's hull to get to the opposite shore. Finally, they were rid of Kunming! By following side roads and village paths, they reached the town of Chuxiong. Then, after arriving at the Buddhist city of Dali, they travelled along the north-south ridge of steep ravines toward the southeastern edge of the Tibetan Plateau, followed by hiking along a jagged east-west mountain range on trails little more than rough and dangerous footpaths. They found themselves on a grueling hiking course where to navigate precipitous ravines they had to grasp cables and straps high above rushing waters.

I interviewed one of these team members, Anzawa Takao, who also gave a lecture at Aichi University on the occasion of his one hundredth birthday. Mr. Anzawa recounted how at one point they had bought two horses and hired a driver to help on a steep stretch. Climbing up and down steep slopes, the luggage tilted and started cutting into the horses' flesh. It bothered the team to see blisters forming on the animals. Meanwhile, the driver had stolen some clothing from the luggage and sold them to purchase opium—whereupon the team fired him. Mr. Anzawa took on the role of horse driver, his first such experience. He talked about getting splattered with mud from the horses' hooves and his irritation at the horses' constant farting. What an interesting, hard trip this turned out to be!

While on the road, Mr. Anzawa researched prices and gathered information for his graduation thesis. In areas with ethnic minorities, as soon as the team stopped to rest a crowd would gather. This gave team members a chance to ask about prices for products and materials. When I analyzed these materials, it turned out that there were significant disparities in prices. The reason for such disparities, interestingly, was that the region was vast and rugged, and people and their livelihoods were cut off from each other by the topography.

Mr. Anzawa enjoyed social dancing until age one hundred. He also enjoyed painting in the Nanga style. Approaching the level of a "pro" (*puro*), he even held a one-man exhibition at an art gallery in Ginza.

War shatters a student passion for learning

Period Three of the Big Trips was a "period of restriction" lasting from 1931—year of the Manchurian Incident[12]—to 1939 when Tōa Dōbun Shoin was elevated to university status. The Manchurian Incident occurred on September 18, 1931, just as the 28th entering class was wrapping up its Big Trip which had started in June. For the next two years, the government of the Republic of China refused to issue research travel permits to Shoin students.

As a result, the geographical area for the Big Trips of the 29th and 30th entering classes was restricted to Manchuria (Northeast China). The 29th class, which was scheduled to travel into China's interior, was deeply disappointed by this change. Twenty-two of the twenty-four *ban* [Trans. note: The labels *ryokō ban* and *chōsa ban* have been dropped, replaced by a simple *ban*; this huge downgrade from a research focus leads Fujita to call this a "period of restriction"] were rerouted to various parts of Manchuria. The remaining two groups were the Taiwan and Hong Kong teams. Both headed up the Yangzi River then on to Changsha under very trying circumstances. The twenty-two *ban* in Manchuria, because of hasty planning, kept running into each other.

Students of the 30th entering class were assigned responsibility for individual *xian* (counties or districts) in the newly established state of Manchukuo.[13] Many of the students of the 31st class continued investigations of those same *xian*. After two years, teams had carried out

---

12 Manchurian Incident (1931). The Manchurian Incident came three years after the June 1928 assassination of Marshall Zhang Zuolin (1875–1928), the Chinese warlord of Manchuria, when the Japanese Kwantung Army officers blew up his train. The 1931 incident, known to Chinese as the "September 18 Incident" and also as the Liutiaohu or Mukden Incident, was similarly the work of militarists in the Kwantung Army. On September 18, 1931 they exploded a bomb near a South Manchurian Railway track at Liutiaohu near Mukden (Fengtian; today Shenyang). The Japanese Imperial Army accused Chinese dissidents of the act and made this the pretext for Japan's seizure of the whole of Northeast China (Manchuria).

13 Manchukuo (Manshūkoku). After the Manchurian Incident of September 1931, the Kwantung Army declared its Manshū Occupation Plan which it changed in February 1932 to its Manshū State Plan under Japanese supervision. The latter was formalized by the Japan-Manchukuo Protocol of September 15, 1932. The new head of state was Puyi (1906–1967), the last emperor of the Qing dynasty. A great show was made of the ideals "harmony amongst the five ethnic groups" and "dominion by a virtuous king." Industry and infrastructure developed dramatically until 1945, when Soviet troops invaded Manchukuo and destroyed it.

Photo taken by a student from 30th entering class
of a Japanese warship crossing the Songhua River

investigations of nearly one hundred individual districts. This body of
research at the district level provides an understanding of the basic
foundations of the Manchurian state at the time. There are differences
in strength in the various Manchukuo districts immediately after their
formation, and also differences in the quality of student *xian* reports.
Later, Datong Xueyuan (Datong Academy, an educational institution
for training higher officials with some Shoin graduates also enrolled)
was established in Manchukuo. It tried to duplicate the Big Trip of Tōa
Dōbun Shoin, though its investigations were limited to places inside
Manchuria.

Travel permits were issued once again for the 33rd entering class.
Except for one team that went to Southeast Asia, the other twenty-
eight teams (*ban*) spread throughout China. The 34th class left on
their trips in June 1937 ... but in July the Lugouqiao [Marco Polo
Bridge] Incident[14] occurred, starting the Second Sino-Japanese War.
Immediately after, students received telegrams from Dōbun Shoin or-
dering them to return to the school. This brought the travels of the
twenty-three *ban* of the 34th class to a halt.

Meanwhile, fighting intensified in Shanghai and the students who
had returned to the campus were evacuated to temporary quarters in
Japan, in Nagasaki. Just prior to this, Headmaster Ōuchi Chōzō had
agonized over demands from the Japanese military for students to serve

---

14   Marco Polo Bridge Incident. On July 7, 1937, at Lugouqiao (Marco Polo Bridge)
      in the southwestern part of Beijing, Japanese and Chinese forces clashed. This brief
      incident (*jiken*) triggered the Second Sino-Japanese War, known among Japanese as
      the Shina Incident (Shina Jihen).

for half a year behind the lines as military interpreters (*tsūyaku jūgun* 通訳従軍). Seventy-nine students volunteered for this service.

Worst of all, on November 3, 1937 the unthinkable happened. Chinese troops looted and set fire to the Xujiahui campus.[15] About 300,000 pages of original Big Trip documents went up in flames. From 1938, Tōa Dōbun Shoin took over the campus of Shanghai Jiaotong University where many refugees had sought safety. [Trans. note: Jiaotong faculty and students had already fled Shanghai for Kunming in the far southwest, where they spent the war years].

From the time of the 35th entering class [of 1935] up to the 38th and 39th entering classes—the end of the era of "old" Tōa Dōbun Shoin—student trips were confined to territory under Japanese occupation and were shortened in time to a single month.

Period Four was the "period of extinction." In 1939, the school was elevated to university status under the name of Tōa Dōbun Shoin Daigaku (Tōa Dōbun Shoin University). The Big Trip research topics, now under the direction of a [pure academic] seminar professor began with a three-week survey of the Yangzi Delta, after which students could scatter. Under these new arrangements, the 42nd entering class worried whether the Big Trip could continue, as it became more and more atomized or individuated (*shiteki* 私的). Some students even participated in *qingxiang gongzuo* (mopping up operations)[16] under the Japanese army aimed at village pacification. Graduation began to be moved forward. The 43rd class (of 1943) and its individuated trips were the last of the real Big Trips.

When Tōa Dōbun Shoin was elevated to a university, some favored maintaining Shoin traditions. In 1943, a new Senmon Bu (Specialist Division) was created [meant to preserve "traditions" from the past], and in 1944 students in their second year traveled to Inner Mongolia.

---

15 [Trans. note: This act of wanton destruction may have been tit-for-tat, at least in part. For in July 1937, Japanese warplanes and the Japanese Imperial Army targeted and destroyed about two-thirds of the campus of China's noted Nankai University in Tianjin, deliberately burning its library and looting its museum treasures. The Chinese public was outraged at this senseless act of barbarism.]

16 Mopping up operations (*qingxiang gongzuo*). This term referred to the "rural pacification" policies of Wang Jingwei 汪精卫 (Wang Zhaoming 汪兆铭 1888–1944) and his Nanjing government after 1941. Its aim was to exterminate bandits (*hizoku*) and to annihilate the communist Eighth Route Army (Ba Lu Jun).

But with these new initiatives the Big Trip tradition dating back to the 5th entering class ended. Originally fueled by passion for learning and burning curiosity, student dreams were shattered by the war.

Two hundred thousand pages ... collected on foot

The Big Research Trip (*dai chōsa ryokō*) of Tōa Dōbun Shoin began in 1907 with the 5th entering class and continued nearly half a century up to the 43rd and 44th classes under the new Senmon Bu. The trips had covered some seven hundred travel routes over a vast area centered on China but also extending to Manchuria (Northeast China) and down to Southeast Asia. How could such an enormous quantity of information be assembled and then published?

In late fall, when students returned to campus from their research trips, they began to write up their research reports (*chōsa hōkoku sho*) around individual topics on thin *Mino washi* paper. They worked on these until the following spring. Student observations, inquiries, and research results along with local primary materials were then submitted as their graduation theses (*sotsugyō ronbun*). Printed on one side of the *Mino washi* paper, the reports of all students combined could total more than four hundred pages. Considering that these fieldwork materials were collected largely on foot, the results were no small feat.

Beginning from the 19th entering class, students formally submitted copies of their *nisshi* 日誌 (travel journals) which contained vivid descriptions of local life. While the overall quality of the journals was uneven, not a few rivalled their graduation theses. A student editorial committee (*henshū i'inkai*) looked through each team's journals, excerpted the best material, assigned titles, and then ultimately published them in thirty-three volumes.

I looked at duplicate copies of handwritten originals [Trans. note: Students submitted copies to Tōa Dōbunkai in Tokyo, and also to the Ministry of Foreign Affairs; thus, only the originals were lost in the Shanghai fires]. I then excerpted the most lively entries from the whole of China, and published them through Taimeidō under the umbrella title of *Tōa Dōbun Shoin China Field Research Trip Records* (*Tōa Dōbun Shoin Chūgoku chōsa ryokō kiroku*) (4 vols; 1994–2002). The fifth and final volume, published by both Taimeidō and Fuji Shuppan (2011), was entitled *Running Around Manchuria* (*Manshū o kakeru*). It is exhilarating to get a firsthand sense of what things were really like back then.

The twelve-volume *China Economy Series* (*Shina keizai zensho*; 1907–1908) compiled by Professor Negishi Tadashi used a similar method. This work was followed by the eighteen-volume province-by-province *Shina shōbetsu zenshi* [Comprehensive Gazetteer of the Individual Provinces of China; 1916–1920], based on student graduation thesis findings and published by Tōa Dōbunkai. Compilation work for the latter centered on main editor Ōmura Kin'ichi, a professor of political geography, and each provincial gazetteer featured prefatory greetings and poems. For example, Headmaster Nezu contributed the preface

Cover of Vol. 1, "Guangdong Province" of *Shina shōbetsu zenshi*

for Volume One, noting that more than one thousand students had produced more than two hundred thousand pages of reports, now published for the benefit of the world. Nezu hoped, he said, that this body of work would make a major contribution to research on China.

Volume One focused on Guangdong province, and was based largely on the reports of nine students from the 5th to 13th entering classes. It was a massive volume of 1,200 pages that covered the sections such as overview, open markets, trade, cities, transportation and the transport of goods, postal and telegraph services, climate, manufacturing and industry, commercial practices, cooperatives and wholesalers, warehousing, and currency and financial systems. The subsequent volumes without exception were massive and systematically organized, each about one thousand pages in length.

More than twenty years later [during the war years], Tōa Dōbunkai began publication of a planned twenty-two volume update, *New and Revised Comprehensive Gazetteer of the Individual Provinces of China* (*Shinshū Shina shōbetsu zenshi*; 1941–44). More detailed in content, its

All 18 volumes of *Shina shōbetsu zenshi*

lead editor was Shoin graduate Yonaiyama Tsuneo[17] who had travelled extensively around China while employed by the Ministry of Foreign Affairs. In the preface to Volume One, Tōa Dōbunkai president Prince 近衛文麿 Fumimaro [son and successor of Atsumaro] wrote, "This work clarifies much about actual conditions on the mainland, and I hope that it contributes to the coexistence and coprosperity (*kyōson kyōei*) of the peoples of Asia."

Unfortunately, the war intensified so that publication had to be halted with Volume Nine. Still, both the original and the new *Comprehensive Gazetteer* series paint a close-up portrait of China in the first half of the twentieth century. Their value is substantial, and scholarly appreciation of the work is likely to grow.

What student travel records say about the real China

I have devoted nearly thirty years to the study of Big Trip journals (*nisshi*) and reports (*hōkoku sho*) of Tōa Dōbun Shoin students. Besides the journals, which I edited and published in five volumes mentioned above, I have published such monographs as *Regions of Modern China as Portrayed by Tōa Dōbun Shoin Students* (*Tōa Dōbun Shoinsei ga kiroku shita kindai Chūgoku no chi'iki zō*) (Nakanishiya Shuppan, 2011) and *Studies of Tōa Dōbun Shoin China Field Research Trips* (*Tōa Dōbun Shoin Chūgoku dai chōsa ryokō no kenkyū*) (Taimeidō and Aichi Daigaku

---

17   Yonaiyama Tsuneo (1888-1969). Yonaiyama was a member of the 8th entering class of Tōa Dōbun Shoin. He had worked in a Chinese consular office [no mention where or for how long] and had supported Sun Yatsen. He traveled all over China—north, south, east, and west—and became an expert in stone monument inscriptions, and published many books. He was widely recognized as a *Shina tsū* (Old China Hand).

Bun'gakkai, 2000). I would like to reflect on insights that can be gleaned from these student accounts.

In the first half of the twentieth century, when Tōa Dōbun Shoin students were travelling all over China, the country was in a period of revolution, war, and general chaos. Student accounts faithfully record revolutionary upheavals and the determined struggles of warlords while at the same time describing the beginnings of modernization in various regions.

Maps of currency usage and language usage created by students imposed on each other (Fujita's map)

Speaking generally, traditional Chinese society did not widely recognize the value of public space (*kōteki kūkan*). Student accounts emphasize the lack of hygiene everywhere. Rural villages, towns, and roadways were extremely cramped and narrow, garbage and filth were strewn everywhere, and water-and-sewer systems almost nonexistent. As one example, one student travelled from the [foreign] island-enclave of Gulangyu across a narrow strait from the [Chinese] coastal city of Xiamen [Amoy] and was amazed at the filth of the Chinese side. Xiamen, he wrote, is "the filthiest city in China." To the south of Xiamen along the coast were the cities of Shantou [Swatow] and Guangzhou [Canton], both of which were redeveloping their streets with plans to introduce water-and-sewer systems. It is likely that urban improvement plans of individual warlords, the return to China of successful overseas Chinese bringing their experience from colonized cities of Southeast Asia, and the modern British-style city development of Hong Kong all had their influences. Indeed, the streets of Xiamen were probably filthy because westerners and overseas Chinese refused to live there, residing instead on the upscale island enclave of Gulangyu.

Students who visited Sichuan province in around 1930 recorded how astonished they were not only at Chongqing and Chengdu but at secondary cities, where they watched the ongoing construction of broad roads with sidewalks, and large Ford-style buses starting to operate. The work was all being carried out under direction of a warlord army. One account notes that, "In Deyang Park [in the city of Deyang] there are flower gardens, teahouses, and a library. The area just to the north is under the jurisdiction of Tian Songyao of the 29th Army." In towns such as Wenchuan and Maoxian in the mountains that ring the Sichuan Basin, motor roads, recreation grounds, and libraries were under construction. Accounts indicate that books in the various libraries had been ordered from Shanghai.

Student accounts report that in Sichuan, local warlords competed with each other to invest in public projects in areas under their jurisdiction. This is reminiscent of China today in which provinces compete with each other to invest in public projects. The top warlords had studied in Japan and followed Japanese models of modernization in their projects. Shaanxi and Shandong provinces, where wars had broken out, also had warlords. These jurisdictions too devoted themselves wholeheartedly to the modernization of China's public spaces.

Intriguing insights could be gleaned from student research reports. The 12th entering class investigated language and currency in different regions of China. Areas sharing a spoken language constitute a "culture sphere," and areas having a common currency an "economic sphere." If we superimpose the two spheres on a map, the areas where the two overlap indicate areas that are most fiercely independent. This map has some explanatory power even with respect to China today.

Chapter 7. In the Eye of a Storm

Makino Nobuaki's spirit of liberalism

Let us briefly turn back the hands of time.

In 1923, Nezu Hajime, known as "the patron saint (*kamisama*) of Tōa Dōbun Shoin" and beloved by faculty, staff, and students alike, resigned as headmaster. In 1927, he died. With Nezu's death, the third of the great men responsible for the conception and founding of Tōa Dōbun Shoin—along with Arao Sei and Konoe Atsumoro— had passed away. Nezu was not only the longest serving of all Shoin head-masters, but he had overcome financial difficulties, had philosophically culti-

Makino Nobuaki, who main-tained a liberal atmosphere at the school

vated the school's relationship with China, and had given the institu-tion its basic structure. He also served for a time as secretary-general (*kanjichō*) of Tōa Dōbunkai. Through a combination of practical ability and a keen sense of responsibility, he both managed the school and shaped its educational mission.

In 1922, the year before Nezu's retirement as headmaster, Tōa Dōbunkai was incorporated as a nonprofit foundation (*zaidan hōjin*). This change formalized its regulations regarding donations, and estab-lished the posts of president, vice-president, and chairman of the board. It also decided the role of directors and regularized membership and advisory meetings. Long-time president Marquis Nabeshima Naohiro[1] became executive director, Viscount Makino Nobuaki the new presi-dent, Prince Konoe Fumimaro the vice-president, and Shiraiwa Ryūhei, a graduate of Nisshin Bōeki Kenkyūjo, China entrepreneur, and China

---

1   Nabeshima Naohiro (1846–1921). Nabeshima Naohiro was the eleventh-generation head (*daimyō*) of Hizen (Saga) domain. From 1871 to 1882, he studied in Britain, and served as Japanese Minister to Italy. Back in Japan, in 1884 he received the peerage rank of Marquis. He was advisor to the Meiji and Taishō Emperors, presi-dent of the prestigious Genrō'in (Chamber of Elders), and personally close to the imperial family—one daughter and one granddaughter through marriage became imperial princesses.

hand, the chairman of the board. The number of Tōa Dōbun Shoin graduates serving as advisors (*hyōgi'in*) also increased.

Makino Nobuaki accepted the post of president subject to one main condition: that Tōa Dōbunkai follow the principle of "limiting itself to purely educational and cultural matters." This coincided with vice-president Konoe's advocacy of the principle of remaining "non-political." Now a *zaidan hōjin*, Tōa Dōbunkai embarked on a clearer [non-political] course. More specifically, Tōa Dōbunkai devoted itself to investigative surveys, research, publications, and to educational endeavors such as the Tōa Dōbun Shoin in Shanghai and the Tianjin China-Japan Academy (Tianjin Zhong-Ri Xueyuan; Tenshin Chū-Nichi Gakuin). Initially for Chinese, the Tianjin school also admitted Japanese middle and high school students from 1931. After publishing the eighteen-volume *Shina shōbetsu zenshi* (1916–1920) Tōa Dōbunkai continued plans to publish the *Shinshū Shina shōbetsu zenshi* (1941–44) in twenty-two volumes. In fact, the organization published an enormous number and variety of publications. I have estimated the number of publications to be about 250.

Makino Nobuaki was born in 1861, second son of famed samurai Ōkubo Toshimichi of Satsuma (Kagoshima today). At a very young age he was adopted into the family of Makino Kichinojō where he was raised and educated. Worth noting is that at age ten, he accompanied his birth father Ōkubo and others on the famous Iwakura Mission to Europe and America (1871–73).[2] In the U.S. where he studied briefly in a middle school, Makino developed an international perspective. Back in Japan, he enrolled in Dai Gakkō (later, Tokyo Imperial University), which he left to enter the Ministry of Foreign Affairs. In later years, he served variously as the governor of Fukui and Ibaraki prefectures, as ambassador to Italy, then as Minister of Agriculture and Commerce and as Minister of Foreign Affairs. After World War I, he participated in the Paris Peace Conference as deputy plenipotentiary.

2　Iwakura Mission to Europe and America (1871–1873). Led by Prince Iwakura Tomomi (1825–1883), the Iwakura Mission consisted of more than one hundred people ranging from top leaders in government to students heading for study abroad. Its goals were to promote friendship with America and Europe, to explore preliminary negotiations for the revision of unequal treaties, and to bring back observations of western culture. The mission's observations in fact spurred the rapid modernization of Meiji Japan.

Attending the same conference was Konoe Fumimaro. Makino, a moderate advocate of liberalism (*jiyū shugi ron*), from 1925 to 1935 was appointed Lord Keeper of the Privy Seal, where he helped prevent the Imperial Household from becoming ultra-nationalistic.

Makino's prominence would prove consequential. Militarism (*gunkoku shugi*) was on the rise, leading to the attempted military coup—the February 26 Incident[3]—of 1936, while Makino was staying at a hot springs resort at Hakone. Junior military officers plotted to assassinate him, but a police guard and a granddaughter managed to foil the plot. This granddaughter was Asō Kazuko, the daughter of Yoshida Shigeru (1878–1967), Japan's postwar prime minister.

Makino's policy was to preserve Tōa Dōbun Shoin as a school with a liberal tradition. This set it apart from more tightly regulated schools inside Japan. Using the February 26 Incident as a pretext, he resigned as president of Tōa Dōbunkai, to be succeeded by Prince Konoe who basically maintained Makino's liberal posture.

The creation and demise of the Chinese Student Division

In 1918 the Tōa Dōbun Shoin decided to move ahead with its plan for a Chinese Student Division (Chūka Gakusei Bu) that was parallel to the Japanese division. Originally, the education of Chinese students had been managed in Japan at the Tōkyō Dōbun Shoin. However, after Japan issued its Twenty-One Demands in 1915 seeking to expand its rights and interests in China, an anti-Japanese movement arose and the numbers of Chinese students going to Japan plunged. As a result, the Tokyo school closed. The establishment now of a Chinese Student Division meant that an original dream of Tōa Dōbun Shoin—Japanese and Chinese students studying together—was brought to fruition.

Thereafter, a Tianjin Tongwen Shuyuan (Tenshin Dōbun Shoin) was opened in 1921 and a Hankou Tongwen Shuyuan (Kankō Dōbun

---

3   February 26 Incident (Ninīroku Jiken 二・二六事件). On February 26, 1936 young officers of the 1400-member Kōdōha (Imperial Way Faction) of the Japanese Imperial Army carried out a coup that lasted for three days. Although its goal to establish a military government failed, Japan's Prime Minister, Finance Minister, and Keeper of the Privy Seal were all assassinated and the cabinet was toppled. Hereafter, the country moved down the road of militarism (*gunkoku shugi* 軍国主義).

Shoin) was started in 1922, expanding educational opportunities for Chinese students. Tōa Dōbun Shoin's Chinese Division was established with the agreement of the Guomindang government. Enrolment was limited to 50 Chinese students. In the first year, students took a special preparatory course of Japanese and English language study. The final three years were spent with Japanese students pursuing a common curriculum.

As luck would have it, the establishment of the new division coincided with the start of the May Fourth Movement [of 1919] in Beijing and with the rise of anti-Japanese sentiment all across China. In the first two years of planning, first Professor Shimizu Tōzō and then Professor Baba Kuwatarō travelled throughout China to recruit students. The result was thirty-five students enrolled in the first year, half of them publicly funded at the recommendation of national and local governments, and the other half self-financed. Tuition for Chinese students was less than at national Chinese universities or at western mission schools, which enabled Chinese middle school graduates of limited means to enroll and later be able to travel to Japan. The year 1921 is also when Tōa Dōbun Shoin was elevated to a Higher Specialized School (Kōtō Senmon Gakkō), after which graduates of the Chinese Student Division qualified for admission in Japan at schools such as Kyoto Imperial University, Tohoku Imperial University, Osaka Commercial University, Waseda University, or Nihon University. Not a few graduates joined influential Japan-China business enterprises.

The 1920s was a decade of truly momentous change in China. The Chinese Communist Party (CCP) was organized in Shanghai in 1921. Students in the Chinese Student Division, strongly influenced by developments around them, started to use school dormitories—out of reach of Chinese authorities—as a base for political activism.

Chinese Student Division on the new campus

Student Mei Dianlong[4] formed a communist cell which he led, while anti-imperialist agitation swirled around such issues as the Educational Rights Recovery Movement (aimed against foreign-run schools) and the Anti-Christian Movement. Professor Shimizu Tōzō had to intervene repeatedly to secure the release of Shoin students who had been arrested, no easy task. On top of this, Chinese Student Division head Ōmura Kin'ichi, author of the lyrics for the Shoin school song, died, to be succeeded by Sakamoto Gikō.

The radical thought and actions of Chinese Division students gradually seeped down among Japanese students, who formed their own Communist Youth League. Shoin students Nishizato Tatsuo,[5] Anzai Kuraji,[6] and Nakanishi Tsutomu (Kō)[7] became involved in anti-war activities, and were later arrested for distributing anti-war flyers to Japanese Navy marines in 1930 and to Imperial Army forces in 1932. The base for all these activities was the Chinese Student Division which, in 1934, was shut down by Tōa Dōbun Shoin. Nearly five hundred Chinese students had enrolled at the Chinese Student Division,

---

4   Mei Dianlong. Mei Dianlong was a student in the 1st entering class of the Chinese Student Division in 1921. Having absorbed influences of the Chinese Communist Party (formed in Shanghai on July 1, 1921), he became a leader of a socialist movement at the school and formed a party cell.

5   Nishizato Tatsuo (1907–1967). Born in Kumamoto prefecture, Nishizato was a member of the 26th entering class of Tōa Dōbun Shoin. At the school, he organized the Nisshin Dōsō Dōmei [Japan-China Struggle Alliance] and created an incident by handing out anti-war fliers to Japanese Navy marines in Shanghai. After the war, he was active as party secretary of the Kumamoto branch of the Japanese Communist Party.

6   Anzai Kuraji (1905–1968). Member of the 27th entering class, Anzai was born in Dalian and sponsored by the South Manchurian Railway Company. Together with Nishizato and Nakanishi Tsutomu, Anzai helped create a Shoin cell of the Chinese Communist Youth League. He too was arrested for distributing anti-war fliers. He was expelled from Tōa Dōbun Shoin for participating in the 1931 school strike. After 1949, as part of Japan's Pro-China Faction he travelled back to the land of his birth.

7   Nakanishi Tsutomu (Kō) (1910–1973). Born in Mie prefecture, Nakanishi belonged to the 29th entering class. At Dōbun Shoin he took part in the same activities as Nishizato and Anzai. After graduation, he joined the Mantetsu Chōsa Bu (Research Division of the South Manchurian Railway) and demonstrated in his research that China's war resistance capacity was growing in strength. After the war, he served in the Upper House representing the Japanese Communist Party. Like Anzai, Nakanishi strayed from party orthodoxy.

but as a result of the complexities of the Japan-China relationship only about one-tenth ever graduated.

In the early 1990s, research on graduates of the Chinese Student Division by Mizutani Naoko led her to observe that the student communist leader Mei Dianlong was a quiet hard-working student. In oral interviews, other graduates had the following to say about the school: "Dōbun Shoin was a good school," and "For its time, Dōbun Shoin ... was an educational institution both unique and ideal. In today's era of peace, such a school with students of both countries studying together without nationalistic ambitions would be great."

Lu Xun, an inspiration for Shoin students

Famous people occasionally visited Tōa Dōbun Shoin. Among Japanese, Admiral Tōgō Heihachirō[8] and General Nogi Maresuke,[9] the two officers most responsible for Japan's military victory in the Russo-Japanese War of 1904–05, paid a visit in 1911. And in 1929 visits were made by future prime minister Inukai Tsuyoshi and by Tōyama Mitsuru, a founder of the [ultra-nationalist right-wing] Black Dragon Society (Kokuryūkai). The views of Inukai and Tōyama differed from each other, but the two were united in their early support for Sun Yatsen.

In terms of Chinese visitors, Hu Shi (1891–1962) visited the Shoin in 1927, to be followed by Lu Xun (1881–1936) in 1931. These two intellectuals were representative of the age. Hu Shi had studied at two major American universities [Cornell and Columbia] where he became interested in pragmatism. He advocated the use of *baihua* (vernacular or spoken Chinese) in literature and criticized Marxism-Leninism. When the Chinese Communist Party unified China, he moved to the United States. [In 1958, Hu Shi moved to Taiwan as head of Academia Sinica (Zhongyang Yanjiu Yuan).] Lu Xun, in contrast, was sent to Japan

---

8   Tōgō Heihachirō (1848–1934). Sometimes called "the Nelson of the East," Admiral Tōgō as Commander-in-Chief led the Imperial Japanese Navy to decisive victories over China in 1894–95 and over Russia in 1904–05.

9   Nogi Maresuke (1849–1912). A general in the Imperial Japanese Army, he became a national hero during the Russo-Japanese War for his bloody five-month siege of Port Arthur. Famous for his devotion to samurai loyalty and self-sacrifice, he carried out ritual suicide (*seppuku*) on the day of the funeral of the Meiji Emperor, September 13, 1912, as an act of piety.

for his education, where he studied medicine at Sendai School of Medicine (later,
the Medical School of Tohoku Imperial
University). He subsequently turned to literature as his means of "saving" the Chinese
people. His *Diary of a Madman* [a short
story published in 1918] and later works
laid the foundations of modern Chinese literature.

Lu Xun

Hu Shi's lecture at Tōa Dōbun Shoin
was entitled "The Anti-Scientific Thought of
Various Individuals," covering the years from
1000 to 1600. This was the age of *lixue*
[School of Principle of Neo-Confucianism],
Hu explained, followed by a period of reaction called anti-*lixue*. As
examples, Hu Shi cited Gu Yanwu[10] and three other major thinkers.
Lu Xun, for his part, lectured on the theme of "*Liumang* [Rogues] and
Literature." Notes on the lecture and student reflections have survived.
One student, Kasabō Otohiko, took the following notes on this lecture.

China has two *liumang* (rogue) traditions. One was that of the
Ruzhe followers of Confucius, and the other that of chivalrous men
who followed Mozi. In the beginning, both types were benevolent.
But as their thinking degenerated, many of them degraded into *liumang* (rogues), in the analysis of Sima Qian.[11] According to Sima
Qian's account, both Confucianists and chivalrous men generated a
kind of poison. If these *liumang* spotted an opportunity, they turned
into monsters. If a political system was weak, *liumang* swooped
down to expand their power and overthrow the government, not infrequently taking power for themselves. Well known examples from

---

10   Gu Yanwu (1613–1682). Gu Yanwu was a Confucian scholar at the end of the
     Ming and the beginning of the Qing dynasties. He travelled widely across China,
     using geography and history for evidentiary research—known also as empirical or
     pragmatic studies (*shiyong xue*).
11   Sima Qian (ca. 145–ca. 86 BCE). Known as "the Father of Chinese history"
     [China's Herodotus], Sima Qian was author of the foundational study *Shiji* [Re-
     cords of the Grand Historian] completed during the Early Han dynasty (202
     BCE–9 CE).

Chinese history [according to Lu Xun's lecture] included Liu Bei,[12] a *liumang* later called a gentleman; Liu Bang;[13] and Zhu Yuanzhang [1328–1398, founder and first emperor of the Ming dynasty], all of whom began as *liumang*.

How is all this related to literature (*wenxue*)? Following the success of the Northern Expedition [in 1927], the Guomindang set out to eradicate China's new literature [of the post-May Fourth era]. It seized power just like *liumang* and gradually bankrupted contemporary literature. Once the new (*xin*) was exterminated, all it could do was bring back the old (*jiu*). Before the Guomindang came to power, it had advocated the latest new culture (*xin wenhua*).[14] But once in power, it revived the old. This method is no different from the sophistry of the Confucianists and the intimidation of Mozi's chivalrous men. In this connection, five young writers of left-leaning publications like *Benliu* [Running Currents] were rounded up and shot or buried alive [by the Guomindang]. This act is worse than the notorious Qin Shihuang [259–210 BCE; the First Emperor of China, who "burned the books"]....

This lecture of Lu Xun's has never been published. His voice of resistance to oppression and his indictments stirred the souls of his audience. Regarding his invitation to speak at Dōbun Shoin amidst tense Japan-China relations, Kasabō recalls that Lu Xun frequently visited Uchiyama Shoten[15] [in easy walking distance of Lu Xun's residence; both are tourist landmarks today] where he would listen to conversations between owner Uchiyama Kanzō and Shoin students looking for

---

12   Liu Bei (161–223 CE). A military aide to Zhuge Liang (181–234 CE), Chancellor of the state of Shu during the Three Kingdoms Period (220–280 CE), Liu Bei founded and ruled as first emperor of the Shu Han dynasty (221–223 CE).

13   Liu Bang (256–195 BCE). Liu Bang, born into a peasant family, rose to become founder and first emperor of the Early Han dynasty (202 BCE–9 CE).

14   [Trans. note: Chinese to this day refer to the May Fourth Movement as the "New Culture Movement" (Xin Wenhua Yundong). Lu Xun has this in mind.]

15   Uchiyama Shoten (Uchiyama Bookstore). Uchiyama Bookstore was run by Uchiyama Kanzō (1885–1959). Born in Okayama prefecture, Uchiyama first went to China in 1913. He opened this bookstore in 1917 and expanded it into a more serious bookstore in 1924. It gradually became a meeting ground for Japanese and Chinese intellectual types where cultural exchanges could still be enjoyed.

books. His invitation to speak came most likely from Professor Suzuki Takurō.

Upgrade to university status in the midst of war

In November 1937, tragedy struck (discussed briefly in Chapter 6) when the Hongqiao Road campus of Tōa Dōbun Shoin was destroyed by fire. This occurred toward the end of the Second Shanghai Incident, when Japanese military forces clashed with a Chinese army division fortified with German weapons. The Chinese forces, in retreat, headed westward from the International Settlement to the outer edge of the French Concession—right in the path of Tōa Dōbun Shoin. The troops invaded the campus. After looting various commercial samples, books, and equipment, they set the buildings ablaze. Over a period of three days and three nights, fire consumed the gorgeous structures, 100,000 books, 100,000 commercial samples, and 300,000 pages of Big Trip reports. Just prior to this tragedy, geographer Tanaka Keiji[16] had visited the campus to research its huge collection of Big Trip reports. He is said to have wept on getting news of their destruction.

The campus after the fire

---

16   Tanaka Keiji (1885–1975). Born in Tokyo, Tanaka became a leading geographer. After graduating from Tokyo Higher Normal School, he studied in Europe and then took a faculty position at his alma mater. Later, he was appointed to the position of special professor of geography at Tokyo Liberal Arts and Sciences University (now the University of Tsukuba). Through fieldwork, he achieved great success in his research on gazetteers (*chishi* 地誌).

Tōa Dōbun Shoin faculty and students took refuge temporarily in Nagasaki to await rebuilding of the Shanghai campus. However, funds were hard to come by. Meanwhile, the nearby campus of Jiaotong University [whose staff and students had fled from Shanghai in 1938 to escape Japanese aggression] had filled with war refugees. By agreement with the Japanese military government, Tōa Dōbun Shoin was granted temporary use of the Jiaotong campus. Although Shoin's wartime occupation of the campus was never authorized by Jiaotong University, the two institutions are now talking. Kazankai 霞山会, the postwar successor of Tōa Dōbunkai (Kazan was the literary name for Konoe Atsumaro) took the lead. Thanks to the efforts of Kazankai chairman Kitagawa Fumiaki and standing director Hoshi Hiroto, researchers from Jiaotong University and Aichi University have since 2004 been carrying out joint research on the history of Tōa Dōbun Shoin.

With the goal of building a new campus, the Shoin initiated a donation drive and book collection campaign. In addition to buying new books, many donations of books came from Shoin graduates, Japanese and Chinese companies, publishing companies, research institutes like the South Manchuria Railway Research Division, philanthropists, and other universities. Early on, about 60,000 books had been assembled, a number which would swell to 250,000 titles. To this day, the receipts for these books are preserved at Shanghai Jiaotong University.

At the same time, headmaster (inchō) Ōuchi Chōzō along with teachers and staff, alumni, and students began a coordinated call for the school to be upgraded to a university. Proponents argued that as a top-level educational institution, this school could train talent to participate in the governance [keirin 経綸—a favorite code word of the day] of China and Asia, and to conduct China-related research. After all, Tōa Dōbun Shoin had already accumulated mountains of research on China and had an enviable record of achievements. In 1940, new president (gakuchō) Ōuchi Chōzō applied to the Shanghai Special City Land Bureau to secure land for the newly elevated Tōa Dōbun Shoin University, a clear indication of intent to build a new campus.

President of Tōa Dōbunkai at the time was Prince Konoe Fumimaro, a position he had held for three years. From 1926 to 1931 he had also served as headmaster of Tōa Dōbun Shoin. During those years he occasionally visited Shanghai and offered admonitory advice to faculty and students. Konoe also served as prime minister in 1937, in 1940, and again in 1941, when he thrust the country into the morass of the Pacific War.

In 1938, as president of Tōa Dōbunkai, Konoe had submitted a university-status application to Foreign Minister Arita Hachirō. [Trans. note: Because Tōa Dōbun Shoin was located overseas, it fell under the jurisdiction of Japan's Ministry of Foreign Affairs rather than under the Ministry of Education.] In recognition of the success of the Shoin model of academic excellence infused with practical learning, the Diet approved the application in January 1939 and announced its decision in the Cabinet Official Gazette of December 26, 1939. Thus, the school was reborn as Tōa Dōbun Shoin Uni-

Konoe Fumimaro around the time when he became the headmaster of the Tōa Dōbun Shoin

versity under Japan's University Code, with headmaster Ōuchi serving as first president. That year, one hundred sixty students enrolled in the first preparatory class (*yoka*), while the school had eighty faculty and staff.

President Ōuchi Chōzō had maintained Tōa Dōbun Shoin University as a *riberaru* (liberal) school not subject to military training. But in May 1940 he had to resign on account of illness. Succeeding him as president was Yada Shichitarō, a director of Tōa Dōbunkai. In December of 1940, the university's future (and last) president, Professor Honma Ki'ichi, assumed the post of head of the preparatory division (*yoka chō*).

As a university, the school had separate preparatory (*yoka*) and college (*gakubu*) divisions, along with a seminar-based (*zemi*) research program. But as the war worsened, graduation was speeded up, students were conscripted, and labor mobilization mandated. Wartime orders engulfed the institution. The Senmon Bu (Specialist Division) newly established in 1943 opened on a campus in eastern Shanghai,[17] but after

---

17   Senmon Bu (Specialist Division). This division in 1943 utilized buildings of the American Baptist-run Shanghai College (later, Shanghai University) not far from the Huangpu River. After six months, buildings in Xujiahui were completed so

half a year relocated to the main campus. In fact, from the second year as a university onward, students operated under very difficult circumstances until August 1945, which brought an end to the war.

Schools inside China operated by Tōa Dōbunkai

Finally, I want to mention briefly the schools operated by Tōa Dōbunkai inside of China—other than Tōa Dōbun Shoin.

Tōa Dōbunkai initially reached an agreement with Qing China to develop educational and cultural projects and exchanges. At first, Qing students were enrolled in Japan at Tōkyō Dōbun Shoin but, as mentioned in Chapter 3, the number of interested students plunged after the May Fourth Movement of 1919.

This did not mean that Tōkyō Dōbun Shoin just stood by with folded arms. In fact, in 1921, the year before its closure, the Tianjin Tongwen Shuyuan Zhongxue Bu (Tianjin Dōbun Shoin Middle School) was opened in the Chinese coastal city of Tianjin. In the following year in 1922, the Hankou Tongwen Shuyuan Zhongxue Bu (Hankou Dōbun Shoin Middle School) was established in the central Chinese city of Hankou. This provided Chinese children a chance to receive a standard Japanese middle school education that opened the way for the most outstanding students to a higher education in Japan with public funding. Toward that end, the schools set up courses in Japanese language and Japanese culture in addition to the standard lower-level curriculum that could help move students forward in the Japanese higher educational system. Preparing students first in the three lower-middle grades and next in the three upper-middle grades allowed graduates to be sent to Japan as overseas students.

However, the May Fourth Movement increased Chinese antipathy toward foreign-run schools, including mission schools [largely run by western Protestant missionaries]. This brought about rise of the nationalistic Educational Rights Recovery Movement. The Tianjin and Hankou schools were strongly impacted by these winds of change, so that incoming student numbers dwindled and drop-outs among existing

---

that the 44th to 46th entering classes for both the preparatory and college divisions, numbering altogether more than five hundred students, were able to study in Xujiahui.

students increased. At that point, with regard to Tianjin, Tōa Dōbunkai sent director Ōuchi Chōzō (later headmaster of Tōa Dōbun Shoin and president of Tōa Dōbun Shoin University) to Beijing University to confer with Professor Zhou Zuoren [1885–1967; younger brother of Lu Xun, and a brilliant essayist and translator of Japanese literature educated at Rikkyo University in Japan] and others. In order to move from a school solely run by Tōa Dōbunkai to one jointly managed by Japan and China, five professors from Beijing University were invited to form a China-Japan Educational Committee (Zhong-Ri Jiaoyuhui). All the facilities of the Tianjin school were placed under the new committee, accounts were assigned to Tōa Dōbunkai management, and the name was changed to Zhong-Ri Xueyuan (China-Japan Academy). The new school began operations in 1926.

Distribution of schools run by the Tōa Dōbunkai in China

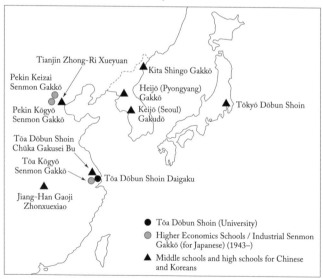

But the times were inauspicious, yet again. The May Thirtieth Incident [of 1925] intensified student political activism, resulting in frequent school closures. After 1940, because of a sharp reduction in the number of western-run schools [in Japanese-occupied China] and the increase of Japanese in China, Chinese student enrolments in Japanese schools increased, and job prospects for graduates were good.

The Hankou Dōbun Shoin was similarly brought under joint management of a Japan-China board of directors, and its name changed to the Jiang-Han Gaoji Zhongxuexiao (The Yangzi-Hankou Upper Middle School). Meanwhile, the Japanese Ministry of Foreign Affairs initiated a "Supplemental Overseas Study System" whereby in 1931 at Zhong-Ri Xueyuan and in 1932 at Jiang-Han Middle School, nearly twenty Japanese students were funded to study at each of the two schools. When the Chinese Student Division of Tōa Dōbun Shoin opened, students from both these schools could move up.

However, after the China Incident of 1937 [followed by Japan's full-scale invasion of China], the Jiang-Han Middle School in Hankou closed and its Japanese students transferred to the Zhong-Ri Xueyuan in Tianjin. In 1944, Jiang-Han reopened, only to close for good the following year when Japan lost the war. Clearly, the war had a devastating impact on Jiang-Han Middle School.

The 1937 burning of the flagship Tōa Dōbun Shoin during the Second Shanghai Incident was a devastating blow. The reconstruction of its campus became the first order of business. As a first step, already mentioned, efforts were made to acquire land for a new campus. Tōa Dōbunkai, in response to the new situation in China, saw the need for educational institutions capable of producing talent that could further East Asian culture, develop China's natural resources, and contribute to a lasting peace. With its eye on Beijing, it submitted an application to the Japanese Ministry of Foreign Affairs for a comprehensive Tōa Dōbun University (Tōa Dōbun Daigaku) in Beijing, along with three other ambitious institutions: a Tōa Dōbun College of Agriculture and Industry (Tōa Dōbun Nōkōgyō Shoin), a Tōa Dōbun College of Manufacturing (Tōa Dōbun Sangyō Shoin), and a Tōa Dōbun Women's College (Tōa Dōbun Joshi Shoin). The idea for locating major parts of Tōa Dōbun Shoin in Beijing may have first surfaced here.

With regards to these proposals, very briefly, the idea of a comprehensive Tōa Dōbun University was fulfilled to some extent with the elevation of Tōa Dōbun Shoin in Shanghai to a university in 1939. With respect to the other proposals, in 1943 the Japanese government and the Greater East Asia Ministry (Dai Tōashō; November 1942–August 1945) commissioned Tōa Dōbunkai to found a new North China Higher School of Industry (Kahoku Kōtō Kōgyō Gakkō); to operate the Beijing College of Economics (Pekin Keizai Senmon Gakkō) as successor to the Beijing Asia Development College (Pekin Kōa Gakuin); and in 1942 to operate the East Asia College of Industry (Tōa Kōgyō Gakuin) as successor to the British-founded Henry Lester Institute of Technical Education in Shanghai. These projects realized Tōa Dōbunkai's plans for new educational institutions that would expand and broaden the scope of Tōa Dōbun Shoin's early commitment to agriculture and industry.

Three schools in Beijing and Shanghai thus came to be entrusted to the care and management of Tōa Dōbunkai. With regard to the Beijing College of Economics which succeeded Pekin Kōa Gakuin, Ishida Hiroshi, geography professor emeritus of Hiroshima University, gathered materials and interviewed graduates of the Pekin Kōa Gakuin including transfers to the Beijing College of Economics. Professor Ishida was invited by Aichi University's Tōa Dōbun Shoin Memorial Center to give a talk on his research. Attending the talk were not a few graduates of both Pekin Kōa Gakuin and Beijing College of Economics. Many graduates shared their experiences and provided a clearer picture of what the schools were like. The remembrances of graduates of Kōa Gakuin with its long history were especially vivid.

From the left, Ueo Ryūsuke, Ishida Hiroshi, Morishita Hiroshi, (1st entering class of Pekin Keizai Senmon Gakkō), and Takatō Saburō (41st entering class of the Tōa Dōbun Shoin)

Meanwhile, recruitment proceeded for the entering class of 1944. The preparatory school for Tōa Dōbun Shoin recruited nearly one hundred students; Dobun Shoin's Senmon Bu (Specialist Division) recruited about one hundred sixty students; the North China Higher

School of Industry about one hundred twenty students; and the Pekin Kōa Gakuin about one hundred new students. Applicants to these four schools took a common entrance exam available to students who had completed four years of middle school. The president of Kōa Gakuin, geographer Nakanome Akira, envisioned a rather liberal education for the school. However, as is well known, student military conscription frequently shortened their studies.

Chapter 8. Some Shoin Graduates Become Shining Stars

Opening a shipping line into Hunan Province

Nisshin Bōeki Kenkyūjo, established in 1890, operated for five years; Tōa Dōbun Shoin, founded in 1901, operated for forty-five years until its closure at the end of the war in 1945. Both schools together operated for fifty years and sent five thousand graduates out into the world. During the half century of upheaval between the end of the nineteenth century and the middle of the twentieth, what kind of career paths did graduates follow?

Student rosters and records in *History of Tōa Dōbun Shoin University* [*Tōa Dōbun Shoin Daigaku shi*] (1982) show that not a few of the graduates were astonishingly talented "shining stars" in their fields. Before the war, China was a place where Shoin graduates could really realize the mission upheld by their school, "coexistence and coprosperity" (*kyōson kyōei*) with China. Many started businesses to this end. After the war, exchanges between Japan and China stopped until diplomatic relations were restored [in 1972]. At that point, activities of Shoin graduates became very prominent once again. In this chapter, I want to introduce several graduates who helped in building ties between Japan and China.

Several graduates of Nisshin Bōeki Kenkyūjo, precursor of Tōa Dōbun Shoin, started their own enterprises rather than working for established institutions. Doi Ihachi[1] was one well-known example. But here, I want to focus particularly on Shiraiwa Ryūhei (1870–1942). Shiraiwa's name appears on a membership list for a meeting of Tōa Dōbunkai in 1900. Then, in 1908 the names of sixty-nine graduates of Nisshin Bōeki Kenkyūjo appear on another Tōa Dōbunkai membership list. That year, Shiraiwa gave a presentation at a Dōbunkai symposium entitled "Remarks on an Investigative Trip to Hunan." Here he reported on his travels to Hunan Province at the end of 1898 to February 1899, revealing some of the intriguing things he had seen there.

---

1   Doi Ihachi (b. 1868). A native of Ishikawa prefecture, Doi graduated from Nisshin Bōeki Kenkyūjo. Inspired by Arao Sei's Product Exhibition Hall (Shōhin Chinretsujo), he became involved in retail trade. After the first Sino-Japanese War of 1894–95, he gave his enterprise the poetic name of Ying-Hua Yanghang 瀛華洋行 (Japan-China Trading Company). His early efforts helped pioneer the development of Japanese trading companies (*shōsha* 商社).

Shiraiwa's report has some important background. After Japan's victory in the First Sino-Japanese War, a Japan-China Treaty of Commerce and Navigation was signed in 1896 that [forced] open the Yangzi River to more navigation by foreign vessels. Amidst this development, Shiraiwa explains the reasons for his interest in Hunan province as follows:

Shiraiwa Ryūhei, who opened up a shipping route to Hunan Province on the Yangtze

Hunan province has produced heroes like Zeng Guofan [1811–1872] and Zuo Zongtang [1812–1885] who helped to revitalize the Qing dynasty. The heads of some sixteen provinces, men of outstanding talent, were born in Hunan. [Mao Zedong was born there in 1893.] However, the province was very China-centered and insular, and opposed the spread of Christianity so that there were no churches there. Modernization had thus been extremely slow. In the capital of Changsha, the most prominent factory was a mere match factory.

Dongting Lake is right at the center of Hunan province. Depending on the season, the water level can rise and fall making river transport difficult. The region's plentiful agricultural products and mineral resources should be exploited. I had wanted to open a river route to Hunan in order to contribute to its modernization.

Route opened up by Shiraiwa Ryūhei from Shanghai to Hunan

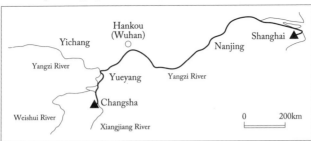

At age 26 [in 1896], Shiraiwa founded the Daitō Shinri Yōkō shipping company in Shanghai. Overcoming numerous obstacles, he opened tributary rivers one after the other to shipping traffic, sometimes in

collaboration with the British. In 1907, he merged Shinri Yōkō with Nisshin Kisen Kaisha [Japan-China Steamship Company] and opened up a direct river route to Changsha; he had fulfilled his dream. In 1920, Shiraiwa became a director of Tōa Dōbunkai and in 1923 its chairman. Nakamura Tadashi who has annotated Shiraiwa's diaries has labelled Shiraiwa an "Asianist entrepreneur" (*Ajia shugi jitsugyōka*).

Graduates who refused to give up

When I began investigating the history of Tōa Dōbun Shoin, I started interviewing Shoin graduates. The oldest living graduate was a man from the 6th entering class of 1906. I had promised to meet with him soon, but my busy schedule forced me to keep postponing our meeting. Then I got news of his death. His family wrote, "He was so looking forward to meeting you ... almost as if waiting for his lover (*koibito*)." This news was such a shock to me.

Immediately, I flew to Nagasaki to meet with the next oldest living graduate, a man over 90 from the 9th entering class. As soon as I stepped in the door, the first thing he said was, "I've been counting the days waiting for your visit. It's as if I had to calm down waiting for my lover (*koibito*)." Thrilled to hear this, it made me realize that the graduates were bursting with things they wanted to say, and that a single day of waiting was like a thousand years. After this, I began interviewing graduates intensively, and sent out questionnaires to all those still living.

When interviewing, I asked that the graduate's wife and family members be present. In most cases, Shoin graduates had kept their past lives to themselves, rarely opening up to their families. And greeted back in Japan by the hostile "Tōa Dōbun Shoin spy school" stereotype after the war, they simply kept their mouths shut. As a

Saitō Fumio, Nakatani Yoshinobu, and Suzuki Yasushi about to depart on their Big Trip

result, Tōa Dōbun Shoin earned the epithet of "a phantom-like famous school."

Family members who sat in on the interviews were astounded at what they heard. Wives began to regard their husbands differently, and grandchildren and great-grandchildren of about high school age listened in wide-eyed wonder.

Saitō Fumio was a student in the 9th entering class from Miyazaki Prefecture. Graduating in 1912 just after the 1911 Revolution, Saitō's classmates over time chose to work in trading companies, or with newspapers, the South Manchurian Railway, Japanese consulates, or as teachers in China. Saitō however chose to apprentice himself to a Chinese cotton firm where Chinese business practices were drilled into him. He went on to found the Dazhi Gongsi, a company that became a great success. At one point, under the guidance of Professor Negishi Tadashi, he investigated business practices of Qing China, further enhancing his value as a builder of ties between Japan and China.

Saitō married happily and his family settled in Shanghai. Learning from reports [in the 1940s] that the war situation was worsening, he evacuated his family to Nagasaki for safety. Nagasaki, unfortunately, was where the atomic bomb was dropped. Regretting his evacuation decision, Saitō became increasingly despondent.

Flat broke, Saitō returned to Japan after the war. Seeing the destruction in Nagasaki, he was sure his family was dead. But then, despondency turned to joy. He had found his family alive! They had been on a hill not far from the epicenter, and the hill had shielded them from the blast and the bomb flash. Although shards of glass had rained down on them, their lives had been spared. To survive in Nagasaki, Saitō began scavenging. He became friends with a policeman who happened to be out on the street. Before long, he began managing a paper shop that turned into a success.

Like Saitō, many Shoin graduates were destitute after the war, and ended up leading second—and completely different—lives. For this, they drew on the indomitable spirit (*tamashii*) they had gained from hiking through the Chinese countryside.

Talent that spreads across industries

Working in Japan was hardly the goal of Tōa Dōbun Shoin graduates. The early years of Tōa Dōbun Shoin in the late Qing and the beginning of the Republic after 1911 was a time when Japan had not yet made significant investments in China. But World War I weakened the business interests of western Powers in China. Seizing this opportunity, Japanese moved capital into China, and together with the Chinese, invested in trading companies and maritime shipping, textiles, oil refining, and mining. In the area of finance, western banks, preoccupied with Europe and European colonies, left an opening in the China market to such banks as the Yokohama Specie Bank and banks from [Japan's colonies of] Korea and Taiwan. It was against this historical backdrop that Shoin graduates were able to choose and pick their places of employment.

Like Shiraiwa Ryūhei and Saitō Fumio, many early Shoin graduates utilized their Shoin training to found their own small- and medium-sized companies, rather than working at large [Japanese] firms. In doing so, they were fulfilling the hopes of Headmaster Nezu Hajime to cultivate talent in support of Japan-China trade. Through their independent businesses, graduates became pioneers in Japan-China trade.

The *History of Tōa Dōbun Shoin University* emphasizes the independent entrepreneurial spirit (*dokuritsu kigyō seishin*) of Shoin graduates. Indeed, I could not help but notice this quality in my interviews when I was conducting my own research. The career path of Shoin graduates was truly unique. Tōa Dōbun Shoin was a "business school" (*bijinesu sukūru*) where students gained experience, knowledge, and self-confidence through studying actual business practice, a program supplemented by their Big Trip. Furthermore, Shoin graduates developed this superior "business sense [*sensu*]" during a period when capitalism in China was at its nascent stage. Their accumulated experiences and skills served them well even after the war in Japan.

There are several striking examples of Shoin graduate's business acumen. Ishizaki Ryōji of the 1st entering class became involved in the dairy industry in Shanghai. Starting with just three milk cows, he increased his herd to two hundred cows, while producing dairy products praised for their quality.

A student of the 2nd entering class, Ishizaki Kōjirō, after initially joining a shipping company, set up Ishizaki Yōkō Trading Company in Changchun [Northeast China] that traded in specialty products. Ishizaki went on to become a major player in Manchuria's economic sphere, holding key positions such as President of the Hsinking [J. Shinkyō; Ch. Xinjing ("New Capital"), name of Changchun as the new capital of Manchukuo after 1932] Chamber of Commerce and Industry; Chairman of the Manchuria Chamber of Commerce and Industry Federation; Standing Director of the Nichi-Man Jitsugyō Kyōkai [Japan-Manchuria Industry Association]; and Chairman of the Manchuria Special Products Trade Association. Another student of the 2nd entering class, Senami Senpei, began his career at the Yokohama Specie Bank, moved on to the Shanghai branch of Mitsui Bussan, and finally turned his attention to the textile industry in Shanghai. He established the Gongxing Ironworks that supplied machinery for textile production. Okamoto Hisao of the 6th entering class eventually became president of the Tianjin Chamber of Commerce and Industry. After a period of studying the locality, Okamoto established the Sanshō Yōkō Trading Company and later Sanshō Menka (Sanshō Cotton) that traded cotton, grain, and soybeans to Japan.

Murakawa Yoshimi from his days at Yaxiya Gangyechang along with his juniors. He is fifth from the left. Photograph courtesy of his family.

Numerous graduates began in trading then moved on to manufacturing. Kimura Kyūshirō of the 14th entering class founded Nihon Jinzō Sen'i [now Kitoku Shinryo], and Murakawa Yoshimi of the 16th class, after working at Kuhara Shōji and elsewhere, set up the Yaxiya Gangyechang [Asia Steel Works] in Shanghai, a large conglomerate with specialty factories producing cast iron, cables, cans, and electric furnaces. After the war, these iron works continued operations as Chinese state-run enterprises. Maeda Masuzō of the 26th class, based on his experience at Teikoku Mishin [Imperial Sewing Machines], founded Riccar Sewing Machine Co. and Janome Sewing Machine Co., employing a creative management style and competing against American and European products. In postwar Japan, Nobumoto Yasusada of the 40th class rose to the posts of president and chairman of the Akebono Brake Co. which developed the braking systems for Japan's high-speed Shinkansen trains.

These men were the results of the Shoin education and they made a substantial contribution to the modernization of commerce and industry in China.

Showing the road to "coexistence and coprosperity" (kyōson kyōei)

At the turn of the twentieth century, enterprises from Japan advancing into (shinshutsu) Qing China increased dramatically. And graduates of Tōa Dōbun Shoin became the shuryoku (main force) inside those companies making inroads into China.

The earliest Japanese trading company to go into Qing China was Mitsui Bussan (Mitsui & Co., Ltd.). Mitsui hired thirty-six graduates from just the first ten classes of Tōa Dōbun Shoin; from the 11th class onward, it hired an additional seventy graduates. The Ōkura Gumi [Ōkura Group], later Ōkura Shōji, which moved into China early, hired twenty-eight graduates from the 1st to 18th Shoin classes. Mitsubishi Shōji hired more than fifty graduates, Nisshō Iwai more than forty, and Furukawa Kōgyō fifty-seven. Many other graduates found employment at Sumitomo Shōji and also at Tōmen [Tōyō Menka Kaisha; now Toyota Tsūshō], Itō Chū Shōji (Itochu Corporation), Nichimen Jitsugyō, Marubeni, and Kanematsu Kōshō (formerly, Kanematsu & Co., Ltd.; later Kanematsu-Gosho).

The shipping industry hired many Shoin graduates starting with Shiraiwa Ryūhei's Nisshin Steamship Company and followed by Tōakai'un, Dairen Kisen, Nihon Yūsen, and Yamashita Kisen. In the textile industry, graduates found employment at Dai-Nippon Bōseki, Kanebō, Fuji Bōseki, and also at Tongxing Fangji [Tongxing Spinning Co.] that operated only in China. In the banking industry, graduates were hired of course by the Yokohama Specie Bank and by banks in [the Japanese colonies of] Korea and Taiwan. They also worked in the Japanese banks Nihon Ginkō, Sumitomo Ginkō, Mitsui Ginkō, Mitsubishi Ginkō, and the Manshū Chūō Ginkō. Graduates also found themselves in important jobs in Manchuria (Northeast China) as well as in the diverse geographies of Southeast Asia, Europe, North America, and South America.

In postwar Japan, during the difficult period when zaibatsu conglomerates were being broken up and companies being restructured, not a few Shoin graduates—who had opened up foreign markets previously ignored by most domestic Japanese firms—came to occupy pivotal positions in various businesses. It is no exaggeration to say that graduates of Tōa Dōbun Shoin who returned with an international perspective from China and Southeast Asia played a fundamental role in our country's rapid postwar economic growth.

By way of example, Sakaguchi Yukio of the 21st entering class was employed at Nisshin Seiyū in Dalian. This small-scale enterprise pressed oil from soybeans, corn, and sorghum. After Japan's defeat, the factory was taken over by the Soviets. Sakaguchi supervised its handover. Chinese employees were fond of Sakaguchi and are said to have thrown a farewell party for him. After his return to Japan, a group with Sakaguchi at its center set up Japan's largest oil producing factory [now The Nisshin OilliO Group, Ltd.]. Later, Sakaguchi looked for opportunities for technical cooperation with China. Rather than monopolizing profits, he pursued a path of coexistence and coprosperity (*kyōson kyō'ei*). Then, after assuming the posts of president and chairman, Sakaguchi rid the company of the [Japanese] practice of hiring academic elites and instead hired new employees based on proven ability. Sakaguchi clearly made the most of his prewar China experiences, and it is evident that his thoughts and actions were grounded in the "Shoin *seishin*" (Shoin spirit). Haruna Kazuo of the 36th class, who rose to become president of Marubeni, is another example of a Shoin graduate with a clear Asia strategy.

Oda Keiji enrolled at Tōa Dōbun Shoin Daigaku in 1943 in the midst of war. Immediately after the war's end, his last two

years of study continued in Japan at Aichi University, successor to Shoin University. Upon graduation, he joined the trading company Kanematsu. Placed in charge of the Petroleum Division in 1978 at the time of the Oil Shock, Oda patiently negotiated with China, managing to arrange imports of Chinese oil. Not only did this save Kanematsu, it substantially consolidated the company's position. After Oda assumed the positions of president and chairman, he made coexistence and coprosperity (*kyōson kyōei*) with China a pillar of the company's policies. Oda later served as president of Aichi University's alumni association. At enrolment and graduation ceremonies for students, he frequently spoke about how international sensibilities shaped his concept of management.

Oda Keiji, who became president and chairman of Kanematsu

Focusing on the *genba* … a Shoin tradition

When I took over as head of the Tōa Dōbun Shoin Memorial Center of Aichi University in 2011, Shoin graduates had donated more than ten thousand books and other items, and they were in the process of being sorted. These donated materials demonstrated that Shoin returnees remained interested and deeply engaged with China, and that they valued the education they had received at the institution.

Itō Kikuzō

One day I arrived at the Memorial Center to find a truck parked outside delivering about fifty mikan-orange-sized boxes of materials. When I looked to see who they came from, the name was that of Itō Kikuzō. A member of the 40th entering class, Itō had been a columnist for the *Chūnichi shimbun* (Tōkyō Shimbun). The boxes were stuffed with books and materials related to China. Kurai Ryōzō of the 28th class and a columnist for *Asahi shimbun* had also sent the center a large crate of books and materials from his family home in Kumamoto. These materials made me think that Shoin graduates who went into journalism could never really shake off China.

Itō had worked as special correspondent for *Chūnichi shimbun* in Hong Kong and also in Beijing, where he was in charge of selecting topics for coverage. His tenure in Beijing began in 1965, just one year after China first permitted Japanese correspondents to reside in Beijing. At that time, the other Japanese newspaper correspondents in China were also largely former students of Tōa Dōbun Shoin. There Itō witnessed the beginnings of the Cultural Revolution. He became suspicious of events around him at one point, reporting that ongoing demonstrations in support of Mao Zedong were actually a cover being used by Mao to criticize the Chinese government. Meanwhile, criticisms of plays that started in Shanghai were similarly aimed at something behind the scenes.

After failure of Mao's Great Leap Forward [1958–62],[2] Liu Shaoqi,[3] head of government of the People's Republic of China, had risen to prominence through popular support. Itō was quick to report that the new protests were really aimed at undermining Liu Shaoqi's position. For this and his other reporting, Itō was honored in 1967 with the Vaughn Award for International Reporting conferred on correspondents who had made a substantial contribution to reporting international affairs. Itō refused to be swayed by official government pronouncements and instead attempted to understand the real situation from realities-on-the-ground (*genba*). In this respect, he was simply carrying on the tradition of the Shoin Big Trip. Many foreign news agencies reportedly translated and published Itō's reports from China at the time.

The tradition of the Big Trip actually propelled many Shoin graduates into the world of journalism. As previously mentioned, during the late Qing period, Tōa Dōbunkai published newspapers in many

2 Great Leap Forward (Dayuejin 大跃进) policy (1958–1960). From 1958 to 1960, Mao Zedong implemented a plan to drastically increase agricultural and industrial production and ultimately to overtake the US and Britain. A poorly conceived "armchair theory," the plan was based on dubious technology and ultimately failed. More than twenty million people starved to death, and Mao gave up his post as State Chairman [while retaining his more consequential post of Party Chairman].

3 Liu Shaoqi (1898–1969). After failure of Mao Zedong's Great Leap Forward, Liu Shaoqi succeeded Mao as State Chairman of the People's Republic of China. He introduced some moderate policies but was forced from power during Mao's Cultural Revolution [1966–76] and hounded to death.

localities, and financially supported publications where they already existed. The most notable of these were *Hanbao* [Hankou News] and *Minbao* [Minnan News] published by Munakata Kotarō; the *Yadong shibao* [East Asia Times] published by Shiraiwa Ryūhei and his group; and the more than twenty publications of Tōa Dōbunkai including *Dōbun kohō* [Dōbun Shanghai News], *Zhoubao Shanghai* [Weekly Shanghai], *Dongfang tongxin* [Eastern Miscellany], *Zhina shibao* [China Times], *Qingdao shibao* [Qingdao Times], *Zhina wenti* [China Issues], *Shanhai taimuzu* [Shanghai Times], *Huang hui, Waijiao chunqiu* [Foreign Affairs], *Min'guo ribao* [Republic Daily], *Jiangnan wanbao* [Jiangnan Evening News], *Dalu xinbao* [Mainland News], and *Shengjing shibao* [Mukden Times]. Mainly Chinese-character publications, the papers used Shanghai as a distribution center while serving a readership that spanned the entire country, from the Chinese south up to the Manchurian north.

Many Shoin graduates found employment at various Japanese domestic newspapers such as the Asahi, Mainichi, and Yomiuri newspapers. After the war, many became more active in the media world of large regional newspapers such as the Chūnichi and Nishi Nippon group papers, at Kyōdō Tsūshin (Kyodo News), Jiji Tsūshin, and other news agencies, as well as at the national broadcaster NHK and local broadcasting stations. For example, Tanaka Kanae of the 25th entering class became president of Mainichi Shimbun after the war. Masuda Kenkichi, who worked as a columnist for the Nishi Nippon Shimbunsha, became widely admired by readers of his columns and by audiences of his live lectures. All of these individuals thoroughly lived and practiced the traditional Shoin educational principle of *genba*-ism (*genbashugi*)—the principle of embracing reality as it is on the ground.

Finely tuned international sensibilities

Many graduates of Tōa Dōbun Shoin's political science (Seijika) and business (Shōmuka) divisions aspired to become diplomats. During the late Qing dynasty, the Japan-Qing relationship had been strengthened and Japanese consulates opened all across China. It was natural that Shoin graduates proficient in the Chinese language and familiar with China's state of affairs (*jijō*) would find employment at consulates.

Later, after birth of the [Japanese puppet] state of Manshūkoku [in 1932], graduates were hired in large numbers as state officials.

However, as employees of consulates in China, graduates at most could hope for an appointment as a consul general, and a tendency existed to see Tōa Dōbun Shoin as a training ground for low-level diplomats. It took Ishii Itarō of the 5th entering class to dispel this prejudice, when he passed the national Diplomatic Service Examination in 1915. Thereafter many younger graduates followed his example and served not only in China but at embassies and consulates in countries all over the world.

Ishii Itarō, who became consul in Shanghai. In photo, he is welcomed by the alumni association. He is sixth from left in the second row.

In 1946, just after the war, Ishii resigned from the diplomatic service and wrote the book *My Life as a Diplomat* (*Gaikōkan no isshō*) (1950; also later reprints) based on notes from his daily journal. Ishii, who served twice as Shanghai Consul General and also as head of the East Asia Bureau of the Ministry of Foreign Affairs, candidly depicts the efforts of leaders of China and Japan as they groped toward peace in the midst of war.

In his book, Ishii worried that the Japanese military was damaging Japan-China relations by its autocratic behavior and by inserting itself into politics without sufficient international sensibilities (*kokusai kankaku*). While head of the East Asia Bureau, Ishii submitted two proposals, one calling for compromise and the other calling for mediation. He struggled painstakingly to put Japan's relationship with China on a more equal footing while avoiding direct confrontation, and to restore Japan's foreign relations to a state of normality. The inadequate influence of Japan's Foreign Minister combined with the obstinacy of the military ultimately led to the self-destruction of the military, a process Ishii portrays in some detail. In Ishii's account, we can discern a preference for balance as well as an international sensibility cultivated during his years at Tōa Dōbun Shoin.

Nakayama Masaru, although not formally a diplomat, also got caught up in certain diplomatic matters. A member of the 16th class, Nakayama enrolled in the political science division. He almost never attended class, but rather could be found reading on his own in the library. Given his free-spirited approach to learning, he was unable to graduate. Headmaster Nezu recognized his talent, however, and made an exception, awarding him a certificate of completion, as he had done for Tōyama Tatsusuke.[4]

After completing his program, Nakayama went to work for *Asahi shimbun*. He became ill, however, and returned to live with his family. Later, he became a *shokutaku* (part-time employee) of the Foreign Ministry. After the Manchurian Incident of 1931 he travelled widely around China and wrote assessments of Japan's China policies. In 1937, he met Konoe Fumimaro [Japanese Prime Minister from June 1937]. In the aftermath of the Marco Polo Bridge Incident [of July 1937], Nakayama wrote the draft of Konoe's speech at Hibiya Public Hall. Nakayama continued as a China analyst and speechwriter and became acquainted with others in Konoe's inner circle.

Perhaps because of such connections, Nakayama was invited in 1938 by Ishiwara Kanji (Ishihara Kanji) to become a professor at the newly established Kenkoku National University in the Manchurian capital of Shinkyō (formerly Changchun). There he taught a course on East Asian Political Theory which he based on classical Chinese philosophy. In November 1938, Nakayama wrote the draft of Konoe's November Proclamation [for a New Order in East Asia] and also helped bring about the escape of Wang Zhaoming [Wang Jingwei][5] from Chongqing

---

4   Tōyama Tatsusuke was the son of Tōyama Mitsuru [see footnote in Ch. 1; mentioned in Ch. 7].
5   Wang Zhaoming (Jingwei) (1883–1944). Wang was a political figure in the Repub-

at the same time. This son of Tōa Dōbun Shoin became one of Konoe Fumimaro's most trusted advisors.

Nakayama's written analyses of Japan-China relations before and after the war are sensibly balanced, and to this day remain a great aid to our understanding of Japan-China and Japan-US relations.

The Yamada brothers and Sun Yatsen

Tōa Dōbun Shoin produced many educators and researchers. Pioneering this group are the two brothers, Yamada Yoshimasa and Yamada Junzaburō. The elder brother Yoshimasa was born in 1868, and in 1900 he accepted a dual position at the new Nankin Dōbun Shoin as a professor and a director (*kanji*). Junzaburō, eight years his junior, enrolled at the new school and then followed it to Shanghai in 1901, where he served in the dual position of assistant teacher of Chinese and English as well as a member of the administrative staff.

The Yamada brothers were born in the Tsugaru Hirosaki domain. It was rare for people born in Northeast Japan (Tōhoku) to take an interest in China. But in the late-Tokugawa period, the Tsugaru domain had refused to join the regional coalition known as Ō'u'etsu Reppan Dōmei[6] which battled against the new Meiji government. Subsequently, Tsugaru enjoyed the favor of the new government compared with other Tōhoku domains. Kikuchi Kurō, uncle to the two brothers, founded the progressive Tō-Ō Gijuku academy which hired many foreign teachers to carry out its international educational curriculum. While the Yamada brothers were under the tutelage of their uncle, they also came under the influ-

---

lic of China who was pro-Japanese (*chi-Nichi ha* 知日派). During the anti-Qing movement and in the early Republic, Wang was a close confidante of Sun Yatsen (d. 1925). From 1938, when Chinese efforts to seek a peace settlement with Japan failed because of Japanese intransigence (Chinese operated through their Reformed Government based at Nanjing from March 1938), Chinese and Japanese together formed a new separatist government, the Reorganized National Government of the Republic of China, 1940–45 also based at Nanjing, with Wang Jingwei as president. Wang died in Nagoya in November 1944, before the war ended, while undergoing medical treatment for an assassination-attempt wound from several years earlier.

6   Ō'u'etsu Reppan Dōmei 奥羽越列藩同盟. A broad alliance of thirty-one Tokugawa-era domains in the northern provinces of Mutsu, Dewa, and Echigo. Formed during the Boshin War (1868–69) to resist the new imperial government, the military alliance was formed by members who had been refused pardon for anti-imperial activities.

ence of fellow student [and future influential nationalistic journalist] Kuga Katsunan (1857–1907), who lived just across the street. It was Yoshimasa who first took off for Qing China, and Junzaburō followed.

While still in Japan, Yamada Yoshimasa moved from working with the Suisan Denshūsho [Fisheries Training School] to the Hokkaidō Konbu Kaisha [Hokkaido Dried Kelp Company]. Thinking to expand his market, he crossed over to Shanghai where he came under the influence of both Nisshin Bōeki Kenkyūjo and Arao Sei. He proceeded to study Chinese and to familiarize himself with the current situation in China. In 1899 he returned to Japan and met Sun Yatsen, with whom he agreed on many things, in Tokyo. The next year, when Sun Yatsen organized the Huizhou Uprising [in his native Guangdong province in the far south] taking advantage of Boxer Uprising chaos [in the far north], Yoshimasa quit his posts at Nankin Dōbun Shoin and headed for Huizhou. He informed the local commander that Japanese weapons promised by Taiwan had been halted, after which he was not heard from again. Several years ago, a document unearthed at Academia Sinica in Taiwan appear to confirm Yoshimasa's death.

After the 1911 Revolution, Sun Yatsen erected a stone monument for Yoshimasa at Zenshō'an Temple in Yanaka, Tokyo that reads "Yamada Yoshimasa Memorial" to show his deep respect. Yoshimasa, a martyr to Sun's revolution, demonstrated a loyalty that transcended national identities or boundaries. Yamada Junzaburō, for his part, left Tōa Dōbun Shoin in 1904 to work as a translator in the Russo-Japanese War with a division of Japanese troops from his home area. After the war, he worked as a surveyor of natural resources in Manchuria [in areas under Japanese control, most probably]. After returning to teach at Tōa Dōbun Shoin, he moved on to the South Manchurian Railway Company.

After the 1911 Revolution broke out, Sun Yatsen hurried back to China from the west and was greeted in Hong Kong by [Sun's close friend] Miyazaki Tōten. They headed to Shanghai, where Yamada Junzaburō who had known Sun through his late brother met him again. Junzaburō now decided to support Sun, carrying out his brother's wishes. Later Junzaburō assisted Sun as a kind of secretary and obtained Sun's absolute trust.

Through Junzaburō, Sun Yatsen received substantial funds from the Japanese financial world to support his revolutionary activities, which

Yamada Yoshimasa

The younger brother Yamada
Junzaburō with Sun Yatsen

were ongoing. Sun, for example, was forced to yield the presidency
of China to Yuan Shikai, occasioning a Second Revolution by Sun to
overthrow Yuan. In order to obtain arms, Sun went so far as to propose
concessions in Manchuria to Japan. However, the Second Revolution
fell apart when Song Jiaoren, a supporter of Sun, was assassinated.
Making things worse, Sun's right hand man Chen Qimei was also assassinated, and Sun's relationship with the Japanese government broke
down, greatly destabilizing his position. In November 1924 in Kobe,
Sun gave his famous speech on "Pan-Asianism" (*Dai Ajia shugi*) which
proposed that Japan might best serve as "Asia's hegemonic leader" (*Ajia
no meishu*). Returning to Beijing, Sun died of illness in March 1925.
Yamada Junzaburō was at Sun's deathbed, just as he had always been
by his side. Of the many Japanese who supported the 1911 Revolution,
the contributions of the two Yamada brothers shine the brightest.

Building ties with China in the postwar period

After the war, diplomatic relations with China were cut off and Shoin
graduates had no direct way to engage with China. Nonetheless, not a
few graduates sought contact with China in Hong Kong, Taiwan and
other countries of Southeast Asia. At the same time, they played a tre-

mendous front line role that opened new international markets during postwar Japan's rapid economic growth.

After normalization of diplomatic relations between Japan and China in 1972 and after the start of China's policy of "reform and opening" (*gaige kaifang*) in 1978, many Shoin graduates sought to establish links with China. The postwar diplomatic break between Japan and China had lasted so long, however, that it was really only graduates after the late-1930s' entering classes who could be actively engaged.

The new activities were not limited to business. Many graduates desired deeper kinds of interactions that had been a hallmark of Shoin students. Here, I want to look at the case of exchanges involving Shanghai Jiaotong University (Jiaotong Daxue; Jiao Da).

As previously discussed, Tōa Dōbun Shoin had had a long and meaningful relationship with Shanghai Jiaotong University. Early on, when Tōa Dōbun Shoin moved to its Xujiahui campus on Hongqiao Road, Jiao Da which had started out as Nanyang College was in the Shoin's immediate vicinity. Students of the schools had frequent contacts through sports, clubs, and even fancy dress parades. Japanese research on Marxism—the results of which could be found at Tōa Dōbun Shoin—made their way from Dōbun Shoin to students of Jiaotong University. It is even said that as Japanese military pressure on China worsened [after the Manchurian Incident of 1931 and the Shanghai Incident of 1932], Shoin students provided guidance to Jiao Da students organizing anti-Japanese activities and organizations.

But the Second Shanghai Incident of 1937, ended the honeymoon when the Shoin campus was torched by Chinese troops and when [Japan's occupation of Shanghai] forced Jiaotong University to move to Chongqing and forced the French Concession to evacuate. Tōa Dōbun Shoin resumed classes in buildings borrowed on the Jiaotong campus, which had attracted large numbers of refugees. After the war's end, Jiaotong University accused Tōa Dōbun Shoin of illegally occupying its campus buildings, and the relationship further deteriorated.

In the 1980s, in the aftermath of China's reform and opening, some Shoin graduates feeling a sense of nostalgia and wanting to clear their name, approached Jiaotong University. As indicated previously, the Kazankai Foundation in the early 2000s helped establish a joint research project focused on Tōa Dōbun Shoin that involved the Office for Compiling the History of Shanghai Jiaotong University (represented by Professor Ye) and the Tōa Dōbun Shoin Memorial Center of Aichi University (represented by Fujita). As part of this project, Professor Mao Xingyun of Jiao Da presented a paper on the activities of Shoin graduates to promote Sino-Japanese Friendship (*Zhong-Ri youhao*) at a joint research symposium in 2007.

Based on Professor's Mao's paper, I want to introduce the activities of Shoin graduates after the war and particularly in the aftermath of China's 1980s reform and opening. Professor Mao focused specifically on six Shoin graduates.

The first individual was Miyake Masaru of the 43rd entering class. Starting in 1984, Miyake donated a cherry tree that he planted on the Jiao Da campus. Then in 1985 he organized a Japan-China Educational Association (Nicchū Kyōiku Kyōkai) of which he was president. In addition to extending annual invitations to Chinese students and leaders to come to Japan, Miyake introduced Jiao Da to Japan's Showa Women's University which in 1992 donated a high-rise library building to the Chinese campus. Miyake also mediated a relationship with Mitsubishi Motors, which resulted in the establishment of a new automotive training program at Jiaotong University.

Presenters at the Sino-Japan symposium
Takei, Imaizumi, Fujita, Ye, Su, Mao, Sheng, Ou, Sun from the left.

Mao's second featured individual was Akioka Ieshige of the 44th entering class. In 1967, Akioka became Bureau Chief of the Beijing office of *Asahi shimbun*, where he played an important role in the efforts of Prime Minister Tanaka Kakuei to normalize relations with China. He is also said to have met regularly with Chinese Premier Zhou Enlai. After his retirement from *Asahi shimbun*, he served in Japan as the representative (*dairi-nin*) for China's leading newspaper, *Renmin ribao*, and is praised for his great success at keeping lines of communication open between Japan and China.

Mao's third featured individual was Kurata Ayao of the 44th class. As a professor of Kobe Gakuin University, Kurata visited China dozens of times as the university's representative. He established educational exchange agreements with four Chinese universities including Jiaotong University, vigorously encouraged Japanese students to travel to China, and accepted many Chinese visiting students. Kurata's research and writings on the Chinese legal system have been well received, even in China.

Fourth was Maeda Seizō also of the 44th class. Raised in Shanghai, he worked as a translator and a guide, and later became known for his in-depth studies of the Chinese language at Jiaotong University.

Fifth was Yoshikawa Nobuo of the 45th class. Having visited Jiaotong University in 1981, in 1986 Yoshikawa organized the first delegation from Jiao Da to visit Japan. Yoshikawa later sponsored a Japan-China conference on the environment. Moreover, he founded a publishing company as a joint venture with Jiaotong University in order to publish a journal of information studies. After Yoshikawa died prematurely of colon cancer in 1998, China established a Yoshikawa Nobuo Sino-Japanese Exchange and Education Fund in his memory.

Finally, the sixth individual was Aichi University graduate Kitagawa Fumiaki of the 46th class. Kitagawa first visited China in 1985 in his capacity as vice president of Yamaichi Securities Co. There he lectured on such topics as securities and joint stock companies and finance, first at Jiaotong University and then throughout China. A strong advocate of education about China, he served as vice-president of the Japan-China Educational Association mentioned above, and in 2002 assumed the post of chairman of the Kazankai Foundation. A supporter of research exchanges between Shanghai Jiaotong University and Aichi University, he was instrumental in sponsoring the 2007 symposium.

Professor Mao highlights several commonalities among the six graduates. They all studied in a unique environment in which they directly experienced the changing relationships between Japan and China; they all developed unusually strong ties to China which they used positively to promote friendship between China and Japan; and all ably seized on China's reform and opening (*gaige kaifang*) to advance friendship. During the war, the Shoin graduates were unable to exhaustively engage with China. Thus the six [postwar] graduates described here (along with others like them) who built bridges with China in the post-war period are noteworthy.

Chapter 9. The Birth of Aichi University

Rebuilding an institution that loved China

The year the war ended and the one that followed witnessed the drama of rebuilding Tōa Dōbun Shoin University in Japan, even as Shoin University was closing in Shanghai. To begin with, in 1945, students of the incoming 46th entering class were unable to travel to China from Japan. Itō Chūbē, president of Kureha Textiles (then Kureha Airlines) in Toyama City and Kureha vice-president Kunugi Toraji, a Shoin graduate, generously lent the school a portion of one of its factories to serve as the "Kureha branch campus." School opening was delayed by uncertainties until July 25.

President of the Kureha branch campus was Saeki Mamoru, a Kanbun (classical Chinese) professor in Shoin's preparatory (*yoka*) division. A total of three hundred students enrolled that year in Shoin University, chiefly in the preparatory and the Specialist Division (Senmon Bu). On the faculty were thirteen teachers: Sakamoto Ichirō, Yamaguchi Sakuma, and Ikegami Tei'ichi all teaching Chinese language; Ōta Eichi teaching Principles of Economics; Ichi'en Kazuo teaching Law and Politics; Kamiya Tatsuo teaching International Law; and Wakae Tokuyuki teaching English. In addition, three people served on staff.

The Kureha brach campus in Toyama Prefecture

At first, about twenty-five students were scheduled to be evacuated from Shanghai to the Kureha campus. This suggests that Honma Ki'ichi, president of Shoin University, was at least considering moving his school to Kureha or elsewhere in Japan in the event of Japan's wartime defeat. In any case, the Japanese Residents Association in Shanghai and the Japanese military opposed this plan, so the number of students sent back was reduced by half.

Daily classes as well as labor-service mobilization did indeed begin at the Kureha branch campus on July 25. Immediately after, however, just before dawn of August 2, 1945 American B-29 bombers fire-bombed the city of Toyama, burning most of it to the ground. The bombing killed some three thousand people and wounded another eight thousand. Shoin students immediately organized relief teams and headed into town by truck. Inoue Masahiro, a member of the 46th class who lived in Toyama prefecture, described the scene: "Burnt, blackened corpses were piled up along the banks of the Shinzū River.... Crying mothers walked around carrying babies burned to a crisp.... It was a scene from hell. We helped to dispose of dead bodies, clear burnt ruins, and distribute food...." Only the Yamato Department Store and the Hokuriku Electric Power buildings remained standing, Inoue noted.

When the war ended, the Kureha branch campus closed and faculty and staff returned to their family homes. The branch school president and others appealed to Tōa Dōbunkai chairman Konoe Fumimaro and to the Minister of Foreign Affairs to allow the branch school to keep operating. In a memorandum to the government, they explained its ongoing significance:

> ... This school's founding mission lay in understanding and researching Chinese affairs (*Chūgoku jijō*) without bias (*fuhen no rikai* 不偏の理解), in the context of cooperation between Japan and China. Chinese familiar with Shoin graduates know this, and we must recognize the need to carry these things forward.... Tōa Dōbun Shoin has faced criticism that the school provided trained personnel for Japan's imperialist advance into the mainland. Actually, the finger should be pointed at domestic universities. The people who love China (*Chūgoku o aisuru mono*) and the people who understand China (*Chūgoku o shiru mono*), and moreover the commentators inside Japan who have played a major role in enlightening the public about China, are almost all graduates of Tōa Dōbun Shoin....

This memo captures the essence of Shoin as an institution of higher learning: its founding mission, its significance, and its independence from its counterparts in Japan.

Foreign Minister Yoshida Shigeru received this memorandum and approved the school's continuing existence. On October 15, another opening ceremony was held with one hundred fifty-eight students, reviving Tōa Dōbun Shoin yet again. However, Tōa Dōbunkai, the institutional sponsor of Tōa Dōbun Shoin chaired by Konoe Fumimaro, was shut down by GHQ [General Headquarters of occupied Japan]. One month later, Tōa Dōbun Shoin was closed yet again. Nonetheless, the temporary second revival made later developments possible.

Student records brought back from China

Just before and after the war's end, what was the actual situation around Tōa Dōbun Shoin University in Shanghai?

At the end of 1945, Shoin University President Honma Ki'ichi sent a report to Tōa Dōbunkai that anticipated the war's end. "Our troops caught in this unstable war situation are calling for a stubborn defense of Shanghai, and a concentration of soldiers.... Japanese civilian men and women have been organized into defense forces (*bōeitai*) under military command. Their 'bamboo gun' armaments are a sign of the coming end of this war...." It is this assessment that led Honma to contemplate evacuating students from Shanghai to the Kureha campus in Japan.

The report also revealed that the Shoin campus [meaning Jiaotong University] was being used to store freight for Japanese military units and as housing for itinerant troops. Division and brigade command headquarters were also set up there, so that whatever remained of the university was pressed into service of the military. President Honma urged women, children, and families to return to Japan. Some returnees would be treated as non-citizens, however. Times were hard for everyone.

In Japan, the cost of living skyrocketed, and prices rose by twenty times in just one year. Money transfers from Japan ceased, and the school had to withdraw funds from its reserves. Things got so bad that the school had to take down trees, walls, and bricks from its old campus nearby in order to buy food and other essentials. On top of that, it began to sell off plots of land from the old campus in exchange for gold bars and to purchase alternative sources of fuel. When the war ended, students, faculty, and staff returning to Japan also needed money for living expenses and salaries.

President Honma's actions demonstrate impressive foresight and reflect his personal experience as a foreign student living in post-World War I Germany, where he had lived through runaway inflation. In China, President Honma had a trusting relationship with Chinese who held gold bars for him—as recalled by Honma's daughter, Tono'oka Akiko.

Honma had come to Shoin University from Tōkyō Shōgyō Daigaku [Tokyo College of Commerce; now Hitotsubashi University] in the 1940s, having resigned from that university over a dispute called the Hakupyō Jiken [the "White Ballot Incident"] involving graduate thesis evaluations. (His colleague, Takagaki Torajirō,[1] well known as representative of the "research faction," also resigned.) Once installed, Honma was head of Shoin's large preparatory division. Appointed to the position at the recommendation of the Monbushō (Ministry of Education),

Honma invited Takagaki and a succession of noted scholars to join him, raising the level of instruction as well as the academic level of students. Yada Shichijirō, then-president of Shoin University, adamantly opposed these Monbushō efforts, and eventually forced Honma to leave Shanghai for Beijing. Shoin students, however, wrote a petition signed in blood imploring him to return to the university. As a consequence, Honma returned to Shoin University. This event shows the extent to which Shoin students trusted and looked up to Honma.

Honma Ki'ichi and Takagaki Torajirō in the Tōa Dōbun Shoin University era

---

1   Takagaki Torajirō (1890–1985). Born in Hiroshima prefecture, Takagaki graduated from the Tokyo Higher Commercial School (Tōkyō Kōtō Shōgyō Gakkō, later Tokyo College of Commerce, then in 1949 Hitotsubashi University) where he became a professor. He produced impressive research results in the fields of economics and finance.

2nd and 4th Aichi University
president Honma Ki'ichi

3rd Aichi University president
Koiwai Kiyoshi

Honma assumed the post of university president in 1944 under mounting wartime pressures, in a period in which students were being mobilized for wartime service. His role essentially was to oversee the task of closing the school. Indeed, possibly only Honma was equal to this task.

Immediately after the war's end, administrators handed over to the Chinese government the financial records of Tōa Dōbun Shoin University, which administrators had assembled. The institution continued to hope that Shoin students who had been sent to the front and had their education otherwise interrupted by war could return to complete their university coursework. But the only records that administrators were able to take back to Japan in their luggage were student rosters and transcripts for the university-program students.

The night before the GHQ seized the Tōa Dōbunkai

President Honma Ki'ichi had smoothly and efficiently managed the closure of Shoin University in Shanghai. Now, the alumni association (*dōsōkai*) in Japan asked him to re-establish the school in Japan. Honma himself had been wondering how students who had been sent to war zones might complete their educations. He contacted President Saeki Mamoru of the Kureha branch campus asking about a suitable site. By then, Tōa Dōbunkai, the parent organization that oversaw Tōa Dōbun Shoin University, had been disbanded. When Honma returned to Japan in March 1946, he along with Shoin faculty Koiwai Kiyoshi,[2] Kamiya Tatsuo, and Kida Misao found themselves working on their own towards a university revival.

Arao Sei, Nezu Hajime, Konoe Atsumaro and the Path to Aichi University

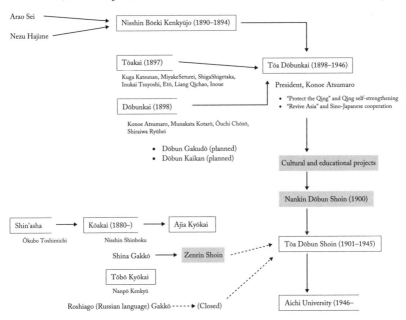

Kamiya Tatsuo was from Takahama City in Aichi prefecture. He had heard about a former Military Preparatory School (Rikugun Yobi Shikan Gakkō) in Toyohashi City that had been spared bombing. He began negotiations with the Nagoya Local Finance Bureau (now the Tōkai Local Finance Bureau) and reached an agreement to use the site. Before relocating, Toyohashi mayor Yokota Shinobu indicated that he would cooperate fully with Honma and welcomed him, saying: "The region produces sweet potatoes, so there is no shortage of food. The

---

2   Koiwai Kiyoshi (1897–1959). Born in Nagano prefecture, Koiwai was a 1922 graduate of the Faculty of Law, University of Tokyo. As a lawyer, he supported Japan's Peasant Movement and the Kansai area Labor Movement. At Honma Ki'ichi's invitation, he joined the faculty of Dōbun Shoin in Shanghai. After the war, Koiwai assisted Honma in establishing Aichi University. He was Aichi University's third president.

people of Mikawa [the eastern part of Aichi prefecture] will be proud to cooperate with you in any way we can."

One dilemma was that the Allied General Headquarters (GHQ)[3] had regarded Tōa Dōbun Shoin as a "spy school" (*supai gakkō*) serving the former Japanese military. Rather than using the name Tōa Dōbun Shoin University, therefore, the founders took the prefectural name Aichi 愛知—which literally means "love of knowledge"—and called the new university "Aichi University." Under these circumstances, Aichi University could not be called a restoration of Tōa Dōbun Shoin University but had to be publicized as a brand-new institution.

Commemorative graduation photo taken outside Aichi University's main campus building in Toyohashi in 1951

The institution faced other intractable problems. Faculty and staff were being brought over from Shanghai. But what about books? Tōa Dōbunkai [a rich repository for books related to China and records related to Tōa Dōbun Shoin] was seized by GHQ at the beginning of the occupation. Kamiya Tatsuo and others at the Kureha branch campus, hearing about GHQ plans for requisition, rushed to Tokyo. The night before final seizure of the building, Tōa Dōbunkai director Makita Takeshi and others loaded about forty thousand books on China including Dōbunkai copies of student Big Trip reports onto

---

3   GHQ (Rengōkokugun Sōshireibu 連合国軍総司令部). Situated in Tokyo, General Headquarters ("GHQ") was managed by the Supreme Commander for the Allied Powers (SCAP). Its task was to implement the Potsdam Agreement. Until 1951, General Douglas MacArthur was Supreme Commander. Under his authority, the democratization of Japan proceeded through its new constitution, dismantling the military, breaking up the zaibatsu, and introducing agricultural land reform.

a truck for safekeeping. Those rescued items, along with another ten thousand books purchased at second-hand bookstores, became the main library collection at the university's opening. Absent this fortuitous event, the rich materials derived from a Tōa Dōbun Shoin education over the years might have been stashed away somewhere by U.S. authorities and Aichi University might have never been born.

The faculty of the new university came from the Kureha campus along with faculty from Shanghai, including Koiwai Kiyoshi, Suzuki Takurō, Tsunochi Naokazu, Miyoshi Shirō, Kuwajima Shin'ichi, Kida Misao, and Kanamaru Kazuo. After this initial transfer, GHQ prohibited further hiring of Shoin faculty. However, thanks to Ministry of Education directives to admit faculty and students repatriated from overseas, exceptional faculty such as Ōuchi Takeji[4] and Akiba Takashi[5] from Keijō Teidai [Imperial University of Seoul] and Taihoku Teidai [Imperial University of Taipei] ended up at Aichi University.

As a result of these efforts, on November 15, 1946, only one year after the war's end, Aichi University received formal government approval under the pre-reform (*kyūsei* 旧制) educational system. Starting in January 1947, the first cohort of students began classes. Between 1947 and 1950, a total of 138 students from the pre-reform undergraduate program (*kyūsei gakubu*) and 66 students from the old preparatory program (*kyūsei yoka*) enrolled at Aichi University. Altogether students from around eighty different schools enrolled. Some had been mobilized during the war and had been unable to study. Some returned from mainland Chinese, Taiwan, and Korean universities or entered directly from various high schools and professional schools around Japan. Others simply craved knowledge. Thus, Aichi University took on the appearance of a university for the whole of East Asia. A medical track was established as part of the preparatory program, which was unique,

---

4 Ōuchi Takeji (? –1946). A former professor at Keijō Teikoku Daigaku (Imperial University of Seoul), Ōuchi taught statistics and economic geography. He was hired by Aichi University, but before he could take up his post as director of the *yoka* preparatory division, he died.

5 Akiba Takashi (1888–1954). A graduate of the Faculty of Social Sciences, University of Tokyo, Akiba became a professor at Keijō Teikoku Daigaku (Imperial University of Seoul), teaching sociology. In Britain and France where he studied, he pursued Cultural Anthropology. At Aichi University, he founded the Sociology Department in the College of Arts and established the Community General Research Center (Sōgō Kyōdo Kenkyūjo).

and soon doctors who had started their studies at Aichi University made their professional debuts.

Honma Ki'ichi felt a special responsibility toward students who had been deployed to the front (*shutsujin*). Meanwhile, he invited the internationalist scholar and statesman, Hayashi Kiroku,[6] former president of Keio Gijuku University (today Keio University) to serve as first president of Aichi University. To ensure that the school was financially viable, Honma sold some of his property.

Editing the *Chū-Nichi dai jiten* [Chinese-Japanese Dictionary]

The mission statement (*setsuritsu shu'i sho*) of Aichi University declared that it would embrace the new era and seek to contribute to world culture and peace, promote "the nurture of international people" (*kokusaijin no yōsei*), and "make contributions to local society." In the aftermath of defeat, Japan was isolated from the international community and its local communities devastated. For its day, Aichi University's founding statement was forward-looking and epoch-making.

The idea of "nurture international people" was at the very soul (*tamashii*) of Tōa Dōbun Shoin in Shanghai; as mentioned above, the Shoin emphasized nurturing international sensibilities (*kokusai kankaku*). Proceeding in this vein, Aichi University quickly established an Institute of International Affairs (Kokusai Mondai Kenkyūjo). The name was new: Meant to carry on the work of the China Research Division (Shina Kenkyūbu) of the Shoin era, the new division had to change that name because GHQ would not permit the use of Shoin-era names. At the same time, the university was located in an outlying region outside

Aichi University's first president, Hayashi Kiroku

---

6   Hayashi Kiroku (1872–1950). Born in Saga prefecture, Hayashi graduated from Keio Gijuku University, which was followed by study in Europe, 1901–1905. A student of Law and Politics, his research emphasis was diplomatic history. From 1923 to 1933, he served as president of Keio Gijuku University. A director of Tōa Dōbunkai, he was first president of Aichi University, 1946–1950.

of Japan's six major cities. To strengthen ties to its locality, the university established a Community General Research Institute (Sōgō Kyōdo Kenkyūjo) and a Chūbu Regional Institute of Industry (Chūbu Chihō Sangyō Kenkyūjo).

Aichi University also carried forward a major Tōa Dōbun Shoin project, the compilation of *Chū-Nichi dai jiten* [Chinese-Japanese Dictionary]. At Tōa Dōbun Shoin, Chinese language study was systematic and comprehensive. A Chinese language textbook series, *Kago suihen* 華語萃編 [Chinese Language Lessons] was the first genuine Chinese language textbook for Japanese, and included a combination of formal and practical phrases and sentences. Starting from book one, the final book of the series—Book Four—was published in 1933.

An editorial meeting for *Chū-Nichi dai jiten*. Suzuki Takurō is second from right. Imaizumi Juntarō is on far left.

Until the twentieth century, *Chūgokugo* (spoken Chinese language) referred to local dialects that were mutually unintelligible outside one's region. People communicated across dialect regions by "brush conversations" (J. *hitsudan*; Ch. *bitan*) using standardized written forms (J. *kanji*; Ch. *hanzi*). One of the spoken dialects gaining most prominence was the "language of officials" of Beijing (*Beijing guanhua*) spoken by upper classes [that is, by Beijing residents or elites educated in Beijing]. Chinese grammar had not been studied scientifically, and phoneticization known as *zhuyin zimu* (phonetic alphabet)—the use of phonetic symbols to aid in pronunciation such as *katakana* to aid in Japanese pronunciation of Chinese characters—was only beginning to be used in the Republican period after 1911.

The *Kago suihen* textbook series was based on *Beijing guanhua* pronunciation and designed for rote memorization. The Chinese language has many sounds absent from spoken Japanese, and so upperclassmen orally taught lowerclassmen. Pronunciation drills sounded like the caw-ing of crows. As a consequence, Tōa Dōbun Shoin came to be called the "Crow School" (*karasu gakkō*). This language education tradition car-ried over to Aichi University in Japan.

The above methodology of language education was unique to Tōa Dōbun Shoin, which invented it. However, still lacking was a good Chinese-Japanese dictionary. In around 1933, a Chinese Language Research Society (Kago Kenkyūkai 華語研究会) consisting of Shoin faculty started to compile a Chinese-Japanese dictionary. Those most enthusiastic included Suzuki Takurō, Kumano Shōhei, Nozaki Shunpei, and Sakamoto Ichirō. By the end of the war one dozen years later, about 140,000 information cards had been filled out along with about 70,000 to 80,000 vocabulary items. These cards were all confiscated by the Chinese Nationalist government, and later transferred to the gov-ernment of the People's Republic of China.

In 1953, Honma Ki'ichi, while second president of Aichi University (1950–55), through the good offices of Uchiyama Kanzō, chairman of the Japan-China Friendship Association, approached Guo Moruo,[7] president of the Chinese Academy of Sciences, seeking return of the note cards. Although unable to get his wish, the following year the materials were sent to the Japan-China Friendship Association on the repatriation ship, *Kōan Maru*. With that, Aichi University was able to resume compilation of the dictionary. The decision to return the materi-als to Japan is said to have been the decision of an old "Japan hand," Prime Minister Zhou Enlai.[8] After normalization of relations between

---

7   Guo Moruo (1892–1978). Guo Moruo went to Japan in 1914 and completed his studies at the Medical Faculty of Kyushu Imperial University in Fukuoka, where he focused on foreign languages and literature. Back in China, he joined the Chinese Communist Party in 1927. After participating in the failed Nanchang communist uprising of August 1927, Guo fled back to Japan where for ten years he immersed himself in research on Chinese ancient history. At the start of China's War of Resistance against Japan, 1937–45, Guo returned to China. After 1949 until his death in 1968, he was president of the prestigious Chinese Academy of Science.

8   Zhou Enlai (1898–1976). After graduating from Nankai Middle School in Tianjin, Zhou studied in Japan for two years from 1917, returning to China in 1919 some-what disillusioned about Japan. [Trans. note: Content of this footnote has been adjusted.] In China, Nankai was elevated to a University in August 1919, and Zhou was in the first class. Expelled for political activism in 1920, he left China and from 1920 to 1924 travelled widely in Europe as a paid correspondent, during which time in 1921 he joined a communist party cell. After returning to China,

Japan and China, Aichi University signed academic and educational agreements with Zhou's *alma mater* Nankai University in Tianjin, followed by Beijing Second Foreign Languages University [now Beijing International Studies University].

Aichi University immediately established a Chinese-Japanese Dictionary Compilation Center led by Suzuki Takurō and supported by the younger Imaizumi Juntarō, with the active participation of Japan-China research specialists. The new government of China [after 1949] introduced simplified Chinese characters as well as the Pinyin romanization system, requiring a difficult restructuring of the dictionary. Securing a budget for publication was yet another difficult challenge. Under the leadership of President Honma, the first edition was published in 1968. The second edition came out later under Professor Imaizumi. Then, in 2010, the third edition was completed and published. Large numbers of copies of the first edition were donated to China, making Aichi University the best known Japanese university in China.

his role in the Chinese Communist Party grew in complex ways. Most significantly, from 1949 until his death in 1976, he was China's premier, widely admired and loved.

Chapter 10. A Leap into the Future

A global vision

The year 2011—the 65th anniversary year of the founding of Aichi University—marked the 110th anniversary of the founding of Tōa Dōbun Shoin and came nearly 120 years after the establishment of Nisshin Bōeki Kenkyūjo. Aichi University's postwar history had already surpassed the 45-year history of Tōa Dōbun Shoin.

In 1946, when Aichi University was established under the old university system (*kyūsei daigaku*), it was the Chūbu region's very first university of law and literature (*hōbunkei daigaku*). Then, in 1949, when Japan moved to its new university system (*shinsei daigaku*), Aichi's academic fields were expanded from just the Law and Economics Faculty (Hōkei Gakubu) of Shoin University to incorporate the old lecture-course system (*kōza sei*) of the Faculty of Literature (Bun Gakubu) of the two prestigious colonial Imperial Universities (Teikoku Daigaku) of Keijō (Seoul, Korea) and of Taihoku (Taipei, Taiwan) [both repatriated to Japan]. Aichi's course offerings were now suddenly expanded to twelve major fields in four academic areas (*gakka*): Social Sciences, Philosophy, History, and Literature. Included among these major fields were Eastern Philosophy (Tōyō Tetsugaku), Eastern History (Tōyōshi), and Chinese Literature (Chūgoku Bungaku). In the Social Sciences, Professor Akiba Takashi and other faculty returnees continued their research focused on East Asia. Aichi's broad focus on East Asia was trailblazing in Japan at the time.

The Faculty of Law and Economics was at the very heart of Tōa Dōbun Shoin University's curriculum and included courses on economics, management, and Chinese law and politics. Aichi University carried forward much of this China research, research which in turn became a nucleus of its Institute of International Affairs (Kokusai Mondai Kenkyujo).

Aichi president Honma Ki'ichi (president, 1950–55; again 1959–63) had a grand dream for Aichi, part of which grew out of Tōa Dōbun Shoin's one-time Division of Agriculture and Industry (Nōkōka). Honma wanted to establish a Faculty of Agriculture and a Faculty of Fisheries geared to local resources, a Faculty of Medicine in partnership with the National Toyohashi Hospital, a Faculty of Engineering, and an affiliated high school. In the ensuing years, the plan proceeded almost to fruition, according to Honma's daughter Tono'oka Akiko.

The newly-completed Aichi campus in Sasashima Live
24 district near JR Nagoya Station

But tragedy struck in January 1963. That month thirteen students of
the university Alpine Club,[1] mostly freshmen and sophomores, lost their
way in a heavy snow storm on Mt. Yakushidake. President Honma said
that if they made it back alive, they would all shave their heads [in
thanksgiving, like Buddhist monks]. But when word came that all had
perished, Honma resigned his presidency—and his dreams never saw
the light of day.

While the search continued for the lost students, Honma declared
that "lives are more important than the university." This comment got
widely reported throughout Japan whereupon condolences and donations poured in from everywhere.

The "Aidai Incident"[2] also occurred during Honma's presidency. In
1952, two policemen unlawfully entered the campus. While one police-

---

1   Alpine Club (Sangaku Bu 山岳部) Tragedy. In January of 1963, a year notorious for
     its heavy snow, thirteen first- and second-year student members of the Alpine Club
     lost their lives after getting lost in a mountain blizzard. Aichi President Honma's
     declaration that "Lives are more important than the university" inspired Toyama
     Prefecture to establish the country's first alpine rescue team.
2   [Trans. note] Aidai Incident (Aidai Jiken 愛大事件). In the 1950s, university cam-
     puses were tense: the influence of communist supporters grew on campus and
     the Japanese Communist Party refused to outright reject violent revolution. The
     police were monitoring and investigating universities as bases for anti-government
     activities, which led to confrontations with students. On May 7, 1952, two police-
     men stole onto Aichi's Toyohashi campus where they were confronted by students.
     While one escaped, one was captured and had his gun and log book removed by
     students.

man escaped, students tied up the other and took away his logbook and gun. After resigning as president, Honma continued to advocate for the students, and the students were acquitted as "innocent" when the case made its way through the courts.

All of these events demonstrate President Honma's sensibilities and foresight.

The Cold War set East against West. Even then, research on China [on the wrong side of the Cold War] continued at the university. During the presidency of Makino Yoshirō (12th president, 1988–92) the idea grew that China research in its many guises should be consolidated under an independent College (*daigakuin*), effectively establishing Japan's very first university-based China Research Division (*kenkyūka*). As part of this initiative, Aichi established a new research track within the Humanities for the interdisciplinary study of China. I, as chairman of the preparatory committee for an independent China Research Division (Chūgoku Kenkyūka), negotiated with the Ministry of Education (Monbushō) over several years for authorization to establish a PhD program. A university Research Division focused on a single country was unprecedented in Japan and faced a huge barrier at the Ministry. After two years of debate around the question of a program centered on "China Studies" (Chūgokugogaku), final permission was granted in 1991. Behind our success lay the existence of Tōa Dōbun Shoin and its storied history, which broke through Japan's thick walls of resistance.

In 1997, Japan's first Faculty of Modern Chinese Studies (Gendai Chūgoku Gakubu) was established at Aichi University. Drawing on the Shoin tradition, the university offered its students Chinese-language instruction *in situ* at Nankai University in Tianjin (China) at its new "Aichi University Hall." The program also instituted an on-site field research program in China.

Later, in connection with the Twenty-first Century Centers of Excellence ["COE"] Program of the expanded Ministry of Education, Culture, Sports, Science and Technology (Monbu Kagaku Shō), Aichi Professor Kagami Mitsuyuki took the lead in developing Aichi's International Center for Chinese Studies (ICCS; Kokusai Chūgokugaku Kenkyū Sentā). Under this arrangement, Aichi cooperated with Nankai University and Renmin University of China (RUC) through its PhD program to produce TV broadcast seminars; to institute a system of dual degrees; and to grant students of the two Chinese universities PhD degrees from Aichi University.

Meanwhile, Aichi University had opened two branch junior colleges with Evening Divisions (Yakan Bu) in Toyohashi and Kurumamichi, Nagoya City in 1951. This afforded young working people the opportunity to pursue further studies, and many Aichi graduates entered local government agencies, legal offices, and private businesses around Aichi prefecture and in the city of Nagoya. Later, daytime divisions (Hiruma Bu) were established. As part of these efforts, a Nagoya campus was established in Miyoshi, a small city formerly under the jurisdiction of Nagoya. This new campus included Faculties of Law, Management, and Modern Chinese Studies. The main Aichi University campus in Toyohashi also housed the two Faculties of Economics and Literature, along with a junior college and a new School of International Communications.

In April 2012, in the Sasashima Live 24 District just south of the Japan Railways (JR) Station at Nagoya, a new Nagoya campus with the five Faculties of Law, Economics, Management, Modern Chinese Studies, and International Communications was established. The new campus set its sights on East Asia, North America, and Europe, implementing the globally-oriented education to which the Tōa Dōbun Shoin aspired.

Dramatic changes after the fall of the Berlin Wall

In 1989, the wall separating East and West Berlin came down and, two years later, the Soviet Union collapsed. These events shook the socialist ideological foundations that formed the intellectual underpinnings of the East-West Cold War after World War II. These changes influenced ideological worlds of politics and academics in Japan and brought about dramatic changes in my own work environment.

Prior to these developments, I had been preoccupied with researching and reprinting the Big Trip records of Tōa Dōbun Shoin. Scarcely anyone—whether inside or outside academia—paid any attention to the subject of Tōa Dōbun Shoin as an institution. The view that Tōa Dōbun Shoin had been a "spy school" during Japan's war with China prevailed among scholars, and very few researchers made any effort to understand the actual situation. "Shoin Studies" faced a wall as impenetrable as the Berlin Wall.

After the fall of these walls, my writings sparked interest in the Japanese media about the extensive, detailed investigations of Shoin students, and ultimately in Tōa Dōbun Shoin itself. China, because of its economic reform and opening, also began to take notice. Influential newspaper and TV stations frequently featured Tōa Dōbun Shoin, and interest grew outside of academia. Shoin alumni themselves began to tell their stories.

Starting in the latter half of the 1980s, Koyūkai, the Shoin alumni association, recognized that graduates were aging and started an endowment fund that raised more than one hundred million yen. With additional funds from Kazankai[3] (the postwar successor of Tōa Dōbunkai) and from Aichi University, in 1991 a Tōa Dōbun Shoin Memorial Fund Committee was set up, which initiated a round of specific activities. In 1993, the Tōa Dōbun Shoin Memorial Center at Aichi University (Aichi Daigaku Tōa Dōbun Shoin Daigaku Kinen Sentā)

An exhibition room at the Tōa Dōbun Shoin Memorial Center at Aichi University

---

3   Kazankai 霞山会. Its predecessor Tōa Dōbunkai was the parent organization that oversaw Tōa Dōbun Shoin; Tōa Dōbunkai was shut down by GHQ in early 1946. Kazankai [Kazan was an honorific name for Konoe Atsumaro], established postwar as a private non-government entity from 1948, gradually resumed the work of Tōa Dōbunkai, focusing on cultural and educational interchange. Today, the organization conducts diverse activities ranging from Chinese-language classes at Tōa Gakuin [East Asia Academy] to interchanges related to study abroad and academic activities.

was founded, which then became the base of the Memorial Fund Committee.

Meanwhile, Shoin graduate and son of Yamada Junzaburō, Yamada Junzō, held Japan's largest collection of Sun Yatsen-related materials, with which he hoped to open a Sun Yatsen Museum. Due to illness, he instead donated all his materials to the Aichi Memorial Center. Center Director Imaizumi Juntarō sorted the materials and in 1998 opened an exhibition in the old main building of the Toyohashi campus.

In 2006, after I became director of the Center, the Ministry of Education, Culture, Sports, Science and Technology funded our Center through its Open Research Center Project. Under this designation, we organized and completed exhibitions on the history of Tōa Dōbun Shoin, on Sun Yatsen and the Yamada brothers, and on the history of Aichi University (including the exhibitions in the President Honma Memorial Room). We sponsored symposia and lectures and organized massive amounts of historical materials, digitizing many of them.

To build awareness of Tōa Dōbun Shoin and Aichi University, we sponsored exhibitions and lectures in cities such as Yokohama, Tokyo, Fukuoka, Hirosaki, Kobe, Kyoto, Yonezawa, Nagoya, and even Chicago. Visitors responded very positively to the displays of items from aristocratic families [such as the Konoe and Nabeshima families] and Shoin students. The first exhibition in Yokohama centered on Shoin publications proved particularly popular, drawing 25,000 visitors. The Memorial Center at the Toyohashi campus continues activities; research-ers from China, Taiwan, Europe, and

A booth at the Yokohama exhibition

North America, students, and study groups visit regularly. Audio guides are available in the three languages of Japanese, English, and Chinese.

Cosmopolitanism

While far from exhaustive, this book depicts the lives and times of Tōa Dōbun Shoin founders, leaders, and students who built ties between Japan and China from the end of the nineteenth century through the first half of the twentieth century. It also speaks of Aichi University, the successor of Tōa Dōbun Shoin.

Both Tōa Dōbun Shoin and its predecessor Nisshin Bōeki Kenkyūjo were constantly buffeted by dramatic changes in world affairs, though their central mission would never waver. Meanwhile, Japanese repatriated from China and elsewhere in Asia after the war shared a sense of Japan's war responsibility (*Nihon no sensō sekinin*) and felt trapped ideologically, so they held their silence. Thus, the role and achievements of Tōa Dōbun Shoin and of its graduates with respect to modern Japan-China relations merit further research.

Three individuals in their twenties with grand dreams, Arao Sei, Konoe Atsumaro, and Nezu Hajime, transformed the idea for a school like Tōa Dōbun Shoin into a reality. How they realized those dreams is explored in some detail in this book. Arao and Konoe died young, so it was up to Nezu to develop their ideas into concrete reality. Because of Nezu, the Shoin spirit (*Shoin no seishin*) never flagged.

The Aichi University Commemorative Hall housing the Tōa Dōbun Shoin Memorial Center

The founding of a school in a foreign country, the teaching of a business curriculum designed to develop trade with that country, and the emphasis on mastery of that country's language and on-the-ground realities—in other words, an education that stressed mastery of the actual business ways and culture (*shō shūkan*) of a foreign country—was unprecedented. The school was a product of the youthful free-thinking of its founders.

I and others of Aichi University's International Center for Chinese Studies (ICCS) were involved in signing exchange agreements with more than ten institutions of higher learning in Europe, including Oxford, Cambridge, Heidelberg, Leiden, London, and the École des hautes études en sciences sociales in Paris. On our visits, these institutions had all heard of Tōa Dōbun Shoin and were most welcoming, whereas they were not familiar with Aichi University. However, when we pointed out *Chū-Nichi dai jiten* (Big Chinese-Japanese Dictionary) sitting on their shelves they immediately understood the relationship between the university and Tōa Dōbun Shoin. Invited speakers from Europe and North America at symposia sponsored by the Tōa Dōbun Shoin Memorial Center of Aichi University have spoken of a perceived threat among western Powers about the founding of Tōa Dōbun Shoin. Meanwhile, leading American universities similarly recognize that Tōa Dōbun Shoin presented a profound challenge to western Powers, and have come to view the Shoin as a global phenomenon.

The considerable talents of former Shoin graduates are also receiving attention. These talents are not unrelated to the cosmopolitan education they received in the international city of Shanghai on the China mainland. [Trans. note: In Japanese minds, continental China is often contrasted to "insular" Japan.] In my many meetings with Shoin graduates they would engage in vigorous debate; then the air would clear and their mutual respect remain. [Trans. note: Japanese rarely engage in noisy debate for fear of permanent disaffection.] This kind of cosmopolitanism, common elsewhere in the world, is characteristic of Shoin graduates.

That Tōa Dōbun Shoin was labeled a "spy school" in postwar Japan is deeply unfortunate. Nonetheless, Shoin graduates kept their mouths shut and refused to protest against this prejudicial view was probably wise. The earliest corrective to this prejudice was by historian of modern Japan, Kurita Hisaya. His assessment of the school (1993) has proved farsighted. [See Reference and Related Works.]

In Japan today, criticism of fickle politics and naïve diplomacy continues to grow, bringing the story of Tōa Dōbun Shoin, the vast international talent the school nurtured, and its ultimate relevance for today into fine focus.

Postscript

This book—*Building Ties between Japan and China: The Lives and Times of Tōa Dōbun Shoin Founders, Students, and Leaders*—was initially published as a series in the evening editions of the three dailies *Chūnichi shimbun*, *Tōkyō shimbun*, and *Hokuriku chūnichi shimbun*. Appearing in sixty installments, the series came out five days a week, Monday through Friday, from October 3 to December 28, 2011.

Much of the original content had to be cut or simplified by the newspapers due to space and layout considerations. To prepare this book, I went back and filled in and even added new material. Additionally, because of the vast array of people and events in the book, I added glosses, photographs, and maps to make the content more intelligible. At the back, I added two appendices: "Reference and Related Works" and "Chronology of Events Related to Tōa Dōbun Shoin."

The story of Tōa Dōbun Shoin (later University) told in this book is really the prelude to Aichi University. Aichi University carries Shoin DNA. However, this story transcends a single institution to embrace the modern histories of Japan and China and the history of interchanges between the two. Beyond just Japan and China, even the West comes within in its scope.

I took on the newspaper serialization project driven by one grand hope: I wanted a wide range of people to read and appreciate this story. As an educational institution, Tōa Dōbun Shoin was unparalleled in the world. Situated in a foreign country, every student was expected to master the language of that country and to profoundly understand the territory in which he lived. Japan's imperial universities in Korea and Taiwan at the time completely ignored the local languages, something also true of Christian missionary schools established abroad by western Powers. Tōa Dōbun Shoin took the position that its relationship with its host country should be founded on a basis of equality. Other aspects of the institution set it apart from its peers. Three young men in their twenties—Arao Sei, Konoe Atsumaro, and Nezu Hajime—came up with ideas that resonated with Japanese and Chinese with youthful and enterprising spirits. Viewed from today's perspective, the group showed an astonishing imaginativeness, practicality, and adaptiveness.

Researchers after World War II—captives of Cold War ideology—insisted on calling Tōa Dōbun Shoin a spy school, a prejudicial label that stuck. I feel a sense of shame at this narrow-mindedness. Thus, this book is intended to re-examine the ideas of Arao, Konoe, and Nezu, and in the process, reconsider Japan-China relations. Beyond that, the Shoin offers some lessons for Japanese young people and political authorities in government who feel a sense of stagnation in post-bubble, deflation-prone Japan. Young people's interest in the outside world and international awareness is in decline. Government agencies watched passively as Chinese tourists dramatically increased without engaging with them in a meaningful way.

In terms of analysis, the two traditional academic frameworks of Japanese History (Nihonshi) and Oriental History (Tōyōshi) are unable to comprehend the existence and development of Tōa Dōbun Shoin. In fact, Japan's relationship with China is merely one example of this phenomenon. Ever since Meiji, Japan has entered into international relations that cannot be understood within such traditional frameworks. Now, by positioning Tōa Dōbun Shoin at the forefront of Japan-China relations, that relationship can be assessed more clearly. A reassessment of the Shoin would show that if Japan is going to see the world through a more international lens, its existing frameworks for seeing the world have to be rebuilt.

Shoin graduates, trained at the interface of the Japan-China relationship, were educated to be "cosmopolitan" (*cosumoporitan*) in outlook. After the war, however, any activities to develop Japan-China relations were curtailed by the Cold War's Bamboo Curtain. Looking today at the direction relations with China are taking, the postwar sidelining of Shoin graduates is most regrettable. Nonetheless, these graduates' energy was transmogrified into energy that drove Japan's postwar rapid economic growth around the world. This fact needs to be more broadly recognized.

Meanwhile, through their Big Trips (*dai chōsa ryokō*), Shoin students became deeply knowledgeable about China and Southeast Asia and left behind vast records about their travels. Their work deserves recognition. In effect, this group of pioneers engaged in Area Studies (*chi'iki kenkyū*), a concept popularized after World War II and a full half-century before the idea took root in the west. Because Japan lost the war, the prewar achievements of Shoin students were ignored for ideological reasons. We know, however, that the results of these Shoin field investigations that relentlessly sought new insights and research findings, are not so easily dismissed. Great interest in those results among Chinese researchers today attests to this fact.

While my specialty is geography, I have spent the past three decades researching Tōa Dōbun Shoin and immersing myself in its murky depths. My conviction that the institution must be reassessed grows directly out of that research. Certainly, Tōa Dōbun Shoin has important connections to Aichi University, my home institution. But beyond that, Tōa Dōbun Shoin has an existence that was Asian, indeed global. I want this book to acquaint large numbers of people with the fascinating aspects of the Tōa Dōbun Shoin.

Since becoming involved with Tōa Dōbun Shoin, I have enjoyed the counsel and cooperation of a great number of alumni and others connected to the institution. Many were affiliated with the Koyūkai Alumni Office. Aichi University staff and graduates also generously assisted. Finally, the daughter of former president Honma Ki'ichi of Tōa Dōbun Shoin University, Tono'oka Akiko, was helpful on an almost daily basis.

In China, many at Shanghai Jiao Tong University deserve mention, starting with Vice-President Li Jianqiang and Professor Ye Dunping of the University History Research Office, and including Professors Mao Xiangyun, Sheng Yi, and Chen Hong, Assistant Professor Ou Qijin, and Researcher Sun Ping. I would like to acknowledge Niki Kenji of the University of Michigan and Professor Douglas Reynolds (1944–2020) of Georgia State University in the United States, along with Professor Marianne Bastid-Bruguière of École des hautes études en sciences sociales, Paris. I learned much through academic interchanges with these individuals.

I would like to acknowledge Mr. Kojima Kazuhiko from the *Chūnichi shimbun* who first came to me with the idea of writing a series about Tōa Dōbun Shoin. He generously shared his time when he had little to spare. Komatsu Taisei of the newspaper's Publications Department also encouraged me through the publications process. Aichi

University and its several alumni associations provided ongoing assistance.

For the second edition, Nozaki Yōhei, also of *Chūnichi shimbun*'s Publications Department, helped with modifying the cover design and with adding the new index. Finally, to Aichi University graduate Chiga Shinzaburō who carefully proofread the entire final manuscript, my profound thanks.

Finally, I end with a note of thanks for the translation of my book by Douglas Reynolds and Paul Sinclair. Author of the major work *East Meets East: Chinese Discover the Modern World in Japan, 1854–1898*, Douglas Reynolds was the foremost researcher and authority on the Sino-Japanese relationship. Paul Sinclair, an excellent researcher on business language education, has been unendingly interested in Tōa Dōbun Shoin. To them I express my deepest gratitude for introducing my book to the world. If this book can be read by many and can help raise interest in the Tōa Dōbun Shoin, an institution that acted as a bridge between China and Japan, it will be my greatest honor.

To all of you, my deepest thanks and profound appreciation.

Fujita Yoshihisa
June 2020

Chronology

Year	Events related to Tōa Dōbun Shoin	Other events
1859	• Arao Sei born in Owari domain	
1860	• Nezu Hajime born in Kōshū domain	
1861	• Makino Nobuaki born in Satsuma domain (Kagoshima)	
1863	• Konoe Atsumaro born in Kyoto	• International Settlement established by Great Britain and United States in Shanghai
1868	• Yamada Yoshimasa born in Tsugaru domain	• Imperial Rule restored (Ōsei fukko) in Japan; capital transferred to Tokyo
1870	• Shiraiwa Ryūhei born in Mimasaka, Okayama prefecture	
1874	• Negishi Tadashi born in Wakayama prefecture	
1875		• China's Guangxu Emperor ascends the throne
1876	• Yamada Junzaburō born in Tsugaru, Aomori prefecture	
1878	• Nezu Hajime enters Rikugun Kyōdō-dan [Army Military Academy], graduates at top of class	
1879	• Nezu Hajime enters Rikugun Shikan Gakkō [Army Officer Training Academy]	
1880	• Kishida Ginkō opens Rakuzendō store in Shanghai	
1884	• Konoe Atsumaro titled Prince	
1885	• Konoe Atsumaro studies abroad in Austria and Germany (until 1890) • Nezu Hajime enters Rikugun Daigakkō (Army War College)	

Year	Events related to Tōa Dōbun Shoin	Other events
1886	• Arao Sei goes to Qing China for first time; opens Hankou Rakuzendō branch store	
1889	• Arao Sei returns to Japan	• Constitution of the Empire of Japan (Meiji Constitution) promulgated
1890	• Nisshin Bōeki Kenkyūjo founded (Nanjing Road, Shanghai)	• *Shanhai nippō* (Shanghai Daily) first Japanese-language newspaper established in Shanghai
1892	• *Shinkoku tsūshō sōran* published	
1894	• First Sino-Japanese War begins; Nisshin Bōeki Kenkyūjo closes	• Japan sends troops to Korea to quell Donghak Peasant Uprising
1895	• Nezu Hajime enters life of seclusion in Kyoto	
1896	• Sheng Xuanhuai opens Nanyang College in Shanghai (later Shanghai Jiaotong University) • Arao Sei dies in Taipei, Taiwan	• Japan-China Treaty of Commerce and Navigation signed in Qing China
1897	• Tōakai established	
1898	• Dōbunkai established, then merged with Tōakai to become Tōa Dōbunkai • *Tōajiron* (East Asia Review) inaugurated	• Kang Youwei and Liang Qichao flee to Japan
1899	• Prince Konoe Atsumaro visits Governor General Liu Kunyi in Nanjing • Tōkyō Dōbun Shoin founded	• Yamada Yoshimasa meets Sun Yatsen in Tokyo
1900	• Konoe Atsumaro recruits students throughout Japan for Nankin Dōbun Shoin (Nanjing Common Culture Academy) • Nezu Hajime called out of seclusion by Prince Konoe • Ajia Kyōkai merged into Tōa Dōbunkai • Nankin Dōbun Shoin founded, moved to Shanghai for fear of Boxer Rebellion disruptions	• Boxers enter Beijing; Powers dispatch troops to Beijing • Sun Yatsen flees to Japan
1901	• Tōa Dōbun Shoin founded in Shanghai; Nezu Hajime becomes new headmaster	

1902	• Sugiura Jūgō appointed stand-in head-master	• Anglo-Japanese Alliance conclud-ed
1903	• Nezu Hajime resumes post of Shoin headmaster	• Huang Xing creates Huaxinghui in Changsha
1904	• Prince Konoe Atsumaro dies • Japan declares war on Russia • Yamada Junzaburō serves as translator for Japanese regiment during Russo-Japanese War	
1905	• Five graduates of Shoin's second enter-ing class survey China's far west on Russia's border	• Sun Yatsen establishes Tongmenghui in Tokyo • Japan signs Treaty of Portsmouth with Russia
1906	• South Manchurian Railway Company established; Gōtō Shimpei is first Director	
1907	• Count Nabeshima Naohiro named new president of Tōa Dōbunkai • Students from Shoin's fifth class inau-gurate Big Trip tradition under Negishi Tadashi • Faculty member Ōmura Kin'ichi com-poses Shoin school song	• Shiraiwa Ryūhei's Nisshin Kisen Kaisha [Japan-China Steamship Company] opens shipping route to Changsha, Hunan • Publication of 12-volume *Shina keizai zensho* begins • Japanese Residents' Association of Shanghai founded
1908	• Meiji Emperor makes imperial dona-tion to Shoin	
1909	• Nezu Hajime, as president of Tōa Dōbunkai, succeeds in striking out phrase "Protect China" (*Shina o hozen su*) from mission statement	
1910	• Shoin celebrates 10th anniversary	
1911	• Admiral Tōgō Heihachirō and General Nogi Maresuke visit Shoin campus	• 1911 Xinhai Revolution erupts at Wuchang • Duanfang assassinated
1912	• Qing Dynasty collapses	• Tongmenhui reorganized as Guomindang (Kuomintang [KMT]—Chinese Nationalist Party)
1913	• Campus buildings burned down ac-cidentally during Second Revolution, students take refuge in Nagasaki; new	• Sun Yatsen flees to Japan • World War I begins

Year	Events related to Tōa Dōbun Shoin	Other events
	campus planned for Haskell Road, Shanghai	
1914	• Agriculture and Industry Program (Nōkōka) set up at Shoin	
1915	• Construction begins for new Shanghai campus in Xujiahui • Ishii Itarō passes national Foreign Service Examination of Japan	• Japan presents Twenty-One Demands to Yuan Shikai
1916	• Publication of 18-volume *Shina shōbetsu zenshi* begins	• Yuan Shikai dies after failed attempt at imperial restoration; Li Yuanhong succeeds as President
1917	• Xujiahui campus completed	• USSR founded in Russia
1918	• Chinese Student Division (Chūka Gakusei Bu) approved • China Research Division (Shina Kenkyūbu) established • Political Science (Seijika) program halts recruitment of students	• World War I ends • Rice riots in Japan
1919	• Big Trip deferred by China's May Fourth Movement anti-foreign mayhem • Chinese Student Division's building construction completed	• May Fourth Movement begins in China • March First Incident occurs in Korea
1920	• Agriculture and Industry Program (Nōkōka) ends recruitment of new students • Chinese Student Division enrolls Preparatory Program (Yoka) 1st class • China Research Division publishes first issue of *Shina kenkyū* • Tōa Dōbun Shoin celebrates 20th anniversary • Nezu Hajime 60th birthday celebration held • Shoin degree program extended to four years; new school year begins in April • Big Trip travel routes reach 200	• Japan-Russia Association School established in Harbin
1921	• Shoin elevated to a Higher Specialized School under Higher Specialized Schools Law (Kōtō Senmon Gakkō Ryō)	• Chinese Communist Party established in Shanghai • Anglo-Japanese Alliance cancelled

	• Chinese Student Division students accepted into regular Shoin program • Tenshin Dōbun Shoin founded in Tianjin • Daily journal (*nisshi*) added to the Big Trip report requirement	
1922	• Tōa Dōbunkai registered as non-profit foundation (*zaidan hōjin*) with Baron Makino Nobuaki as President, Prince Konoe Fumimaro as Vice President, and Shiraiwa Ryūhei as chairman of the board • Kankō Dōbun Shoin founded in Hankou	
1923	• Nezu retires as Shoin headmaster; Ōtsu Rinpei new headmaster	• Yada Shichitarō becomes Japanese Consul General, Shanghai
1924	• Graduation ceremony skipped because of change to four-year study system	• Sun Yatsen gives "Pan-Asianism" (*Dai Ajia shugi*) speech in Kobe • Chinese Guomindang (Nationalist Party) holds first national convention • First United Front between Guomindang and Chinese Communist Party
1925	• Chinese Student Division head (*buchō*) Ōmura Kin'ichi dies; Sakamoto Yoshitaka succeeds	• Sun Yatsen dies
1926	• Prince Konoe Fumimaro becomes new president of Tōa Dōbun Shoin	• China's Northern Expedition begins
1927	• Nezu Hajime dies • Hu Shi gives speech at Shoin	• Global financial crisis helps cause bankruptcy of Suzuki Shōten • Anti-Japanese movement gains strength in China
1928		• Jinan Incident occurs in China
1929	• Inukai Tsuyoshi and Tōyama Mitsuru lecture at Shoin	• Japan recognizes Chinese Nationalist Government • Wall Street stock market crash
1930	• Shoin celebrates 30th anniversary; publication of *Tōa Dōbun Shoin sanjūnen shi* (30th Anniversary of Tōa Dōbun Shoin History) • Shoin students go on strike	• Shina 支那 [term offensive to Chinese] replaced by Japanese government with Republic of China 中華民国 • Northern Expedition advances

Year	Events related to Tōa Dōbun Shoin	Other events
	• Eight Shoin students detained for distributing anti-war pamphlets to Japanese Marines in Shanghai • Nezu Hajime biography *Sanshū Nezu sensei den* published • Chinese Student Division enrolls 10th entering class	• Anti-Chiang Kaishek Northern Government of Yan Xishan, Feng Yuxiang, and Wang Zhaoming founded • Shanhai Nihon Shōgyō Gakkō (Shanghai Japan Commercial School) founded
1931	• Konoe Fumimaro resigns as headmaster • Acting headmaster Ōuchi Chōzō promoted to headmaster • Lu Xun lectures on campus • Chinese Student Division Preparatory Program (Yoka) halts recruitment of new students	• Manchurian (Mukden) Incident occurs • Shanghai Natural Sciences Institute founded with Boxer Indemnity money • China bond market crashes
1932	• Shoin students withdraw to Nagasaki, return to Shanghai later that year	• Manchukuo (Manshūkoku) declared a country
1933	• Chinese Language Research Society (Kago Kenkyūkai) prepares ambitious dictionary project *Ka-Nichi jiten* (Chinese-Japanese Dictionary) • *Kago suihen* Chinese language textbook series completed with vol. 4 • Left-wing Shoin students arrested	• Lytton Commission arrives in Shanghai to investigate Japanese actions in Manchuria
1934	• Konoe Atsumaro memorial service held on 30th anniversary of his death • Chinese Student Division marked for closure	
1935	• Sei-A Jinja enshrinement ceremony held on Shoin campus	• Mao Zedong comes to power
1936	• Prince Konoe Fumimaro appointed new president of Tōa Dōbunkai; Viscount Okabe Nagakage appointed new chairman of the board • Chinese cultural organizations hold consultatiions with Shina Kenkyūbu	• February 26 Incident in Japan
1937	• Shoin students serve as military translators • Xujiahui campus looted and burned down by Chinese forces during the Second Shanghai Incident	• First Konoe Cabinet formed • Seat of Chinese Communist Party established at Yan'an • Marco Polo Bridge Incident occurs • Second Shanghai Incident occurs

1938	• Shoin utilizes Jiaotong University buildings, establishes temporary campus	• Nakayama Masaru appointed Professor at Kenkoku University, Manchukuo (1938–45) • Application to promote Shoin to university status submitted • Supported by Japan, rival "Reformed Government of the Republic of China" established in Nanjing
1939	• Tōa Dōbun Shoin raised to University (Daigaku) status	• Nomonhan Incident occurs in China
1940	• Ōuchi Chōzō appointed university president and Shoin headmaster • Honma Ki'ichi appointed head of University Preparatory Program (Yoka), also Shoin head teacher (kyōtō) • Shoin celebrates 40th anniversary	• Second Konoe cabinet formed
1941	• Undergraduate Division (Gakubu) established; preparatory committee formed to plan affiliated Specialist Division (fuzoku Senmon Bu) • Hayashide Kenjirō appointed new Director of Students for both preparatory and Shoin programs • Graduation of 38th class moved up	• Japan declares war on U.S. and Great Britain; Dai Tōa Sensō (Greater East Asia War / Asia-Pacific War) begins
1942	• Graduation of 39th class moved up • Prince Konoe Fumimaro appointed new president of Tōa Dōbunkai; Tsuda Shizue new chairman of the board; Ichinomiya Fusajirō new managing director	• Ministry of Greater East Asia (Dai Tōa Shō) set up
1943	• New Specialist Division utilizes site of Hujiang University, East Shanghai • Graduation of 40th class moved up • Yada Shichitarō appointed new university president; Honma Ki'ichi resigns posts as director of preparatory program and head teacher • Shoin University students sent off to war	• University students in Japan sent off to war • Admiral Yamamoto Isoroku killed in the Pacific
1944	• Honma Ki'ichi appointed new university president	• Wang Zhaoming (Jingwei) dies in Nagoya

Year	Events related to Tōa Dōbun Shoin	Other events
	• Six Shoin students working at Jiangnan Shipyards killed in American bombing raid	
1945	• Kureha (Toyama) branch campus opened, closed at war's end • Kureha campus reopened, closed in November • Shanghai campus taken back by Chinese military	• Japan surrenders unconditionally
1946	• Students and faculty in Shanghai's Hongkou district repatriated to Japan • Tōa Dōbunkai disbanded of its own accord • Former Shoin president Honma and faculty Koiwai Kiyoshi and Kamiya Tatsuo discuss reestablishing Shoin • Aichi University gains government authorization on November 15 • Hayashi Kiroku appointed first university president • Aichi University student transfer procedures and entrance exams commence	• Manchukuo collapses • Japanese Emperor gives up claim to divinity in Imperial Rescript • General election held; agrarian reforms begin • New Japanese postwar constitution promulgated
1947	• Kazankai donates 35,000 books to Aichi University • Aichi University begins classes for Preparatory division (yoka; 440 students) and undergraduate (gakubu) division • Faculty of Law and Economics (Hōkei Gakubu; with Department of Law and Department of Economics) established • Aichi University extension classes (kōkai kōza) begin	• Fundamental Law of Education promulgated (educational reform under Occupation forces)
1948	• Aichi University Institute of International Affairs (AIIA; Kokusai Mondai Kenkyūjo) founded • Aichi Daigaku shimbun [Aichi University News] begins publication	
1949	• New System for Colleges and Universities (Shinsei Daigaku) law approved and instituted • Aichi Daigaku approved under the	

	New System, with Faculty of Law and Economics (two Departments: Law and Economics); and Faculty of Letters (Bun'gakubu; with Department of Social Sciences); plus courses in law, economics, literature, and attached higher education courses • Nagoya branch school offers law and politics courses and higher education courses • Aichi University celebrates 3rd year anniversary	
1950	• Department of Literature (Bungaku Ka) under Faculty of Letters teaches literature courses for Japanese, Chinese, English, German, and general • Two-year college established • Honma Ki'ichi appointed second university president • Community Research Institute (Sōgō Kyōdo Kenkyūjo) established	• Korean War breaks out • Sino-Soviet Treaty of Friendship, Alliance, and Mutual Assistance signed
1951	• Nagoya branch school moved to Kurumamichi, Nagoya	• San Francisco Peace Conference held • Japan-America Security Treaty signed
1952	• "Aidai Incident" occurs	
1953	• Research Institute of Industry in Chubu District (Chūbu Chihō Sangyō Kenkyūjo) established • Graduate Program instituted with Department of Law and Department of Economics	
1954	• Negishi Tadashi, initiator of Shoin field research in 1901, receives the Japan Academy Prize for his 1953 book *Chūgoku no girudo* (The Guilds of China) • Notecards for *Ka-Nichi jiten* dictionary project returned by China	
1955	• *Ka-Nichi jiten* publications committee formed • Koiwai Kiyoshi appointed 3rd University President	"1955 System" [allows LDP (Liberal Democratic Party) to dominate Japan's party politics until 1993]

Year	Events related to Tōa Dōbun Shoin	Other events
	• History Department (majors in Japanese History [Nihonshi] and Oriental History [Tōyōshi]) and new Literature Department in Faculty of Letters established	
1957	• Graduate Program, Department of Law [Hōgaku Kenkyūka] adds new doctoral course	
1958	• Philosophy Department (majors in Oriental Philosophy [*Tōyō tetsugaku*] and Western Philosophy [*Seiyō tetsugaku*]) established as new courses in Faculty of Letters • Chinese Law and Politics and Chinese Economy established as new courses in Faculty of Law and Economics	• China's Great Leap Forward (to 1962)
1959	• Honma Ki'ichi appointed fourth university President	
1960		• New Security Treaty signed • Ikeda Cabinet introduces Income-Doubling Plan
1963	• Thirteen members of university Alpine Club lose lives in blizzard on Mt. Yakushidake, Toyama prefecture • Honma resigns as President	
1965		• U.S. Vietnam War begins
1966		• Great Proletarian Cultural Revolution begins in China (to 1976)
1967	• History Department of Faculty of Letters offers new geography major • Itō Kikuzō, Shoin graduate and Beijing bureau chief for *Chūnichi shimbun* awarded the Vaughn Award for International Reporting	
1968	• *Chū-Nichi dai jiten* [Chinese-Japanese Comprehensive Dictionary] published	
1973	• Academic delegation to China; Aichi University visits Nankai University in Tianjin	• Okinawa returned to Japan (1972) • Japan-China Joint Communique signed

		• Oil Shock begins • Tanaka Kakuei Cabinet releases "A Plan for Remodeling the Japanese Archipelago" (*Rettō kaikaku seisaku*)
1974	• Beijing University Social Sciences Group visits Aichi University	
1976	• Aichi sends "Third Student China-Friendship Delegation" to China	
1977	• Graduate Program adds Department of Business Administration master's course	
1978	• Graduate Program adds Department of Business Administration doctoral course	
1979		• Japan-China Treaty of Peace and Friendship signed • Second oil shock occurs • China's "reform and opening" policy begins
1980	• Aichi University and two Chinese universities—Nankai University and Beijing Languages Institute (now Beijing Language and Culture University)—sign agreements for academic research and exchanges	
1988	• Nagoya campus opened in Miyoshi, Aichi	
1989		• Berlin Wall falls
1990	• *Chūgoku seikei yōgo jiten* [Dictionary of Chinese Political and Economic Terms] published	• East and West Germany unify
1991	• Graduate program adds Department of Chinese Studies and Department of Humanities (majors in Japanese Culture, Regional Social Systems, and Western Culture) master's courses • Tōa Dōbun Shoin Memorial Foundation established	• Japan's economic bubble bursts
1993	• Aichi University Tōa Dōbun Shoin Memorial Center (Aichi Daigaku Tōa Dōbun Shoin Daigaku Kinen Sentā) founded	

Year	Events related to Tōa Dōbun Shoin	Other events
	• Graduate Program adds Regional Social Systems doctoral course in Department of Humanities	
1994	• Graduate Program adds Department of Chinese Studies and Department of Humanities (majors in Japanese Culture and Western Culture) doctoral courses	
1996	• Aichi University celebrates 50th anniversary	
1997	• Faculty of Modern Chinese Studies (Gendai Chūgoku Gakubu) founded	
1998	• Tōa Dōbun Shoin Memorial Center Exhibition Hall inaugurated • "Nankai-Aidai Kaikan" [Nankai-Aichi University Hall] completed at Nankai University • Faculty of International Communication founded	
2001	• Shoin 100th Founding Anniversary celebrated at Toyohashi and Nagoya campuses • Koyūkai (Shoin Alumni Association) members join Aichi University Alumni Association as "special members" • Graduate School of Law (Hōka Daigaku-in) founded • Honma Ki'ichi sculpture installed at entrance of Aichi University Memorial Hall	
2002	• International Center for Chinese Studies ("ICCS"; Kokusai Chūgoku-gaku Kenkyū Sentā) established after its selection by Ministry of Education, Culture, Sports, Science and Technology (Monbu Kagaku Shō) as a Twenty-first Century Global "COE" (Center of Excellence)	
2006	• Graduate School of Accounting founded • Aichi University Tōa Dōbun Shoin Memorial Center funded by Ministry	

	of Education as "Open Research Center" (to 2010)	
2007	• Koyūkai (Shoin Alumni Association) holds disbanding ceremony, August 24 • Koyūkai disbands, end of September	
2011	• Faculty of Regional Policy (Chi'iki Seisaku Gakubu) founded	
2012	• New Nagoya campus established at Sasashima Live 24 Redevelopment District (near Nagoya Station)	• Japan-China normalization of diplomatic ties celebrates 40th anniversary

Reference and Related Works*

Aichi Daigaku Gojūnenshi Hensan I'inkai 愛知大学五十年史編纂委員会 [Editorial Committee for Aichi University Fifty-year History], comp. *Aichi Daigaku gojūnenshi: tsūshihen* 愛知大学五十年史、通史編 [Fifty Years of Aichi University: A General History]. Toyohashi: Aichi University, 2000. 966 p.

———, comp. *Tairiku ni ikite* 大陸に生きて [Living in China]. Nagoya: Fūbaisha, 1998. 256 p.

Aichi Daigaku Sangakubu Yakushidake Sōnanshi Hensan I'inkai 愛知大学山岳部薬師岳遭難誌編纂委員会 [Editorial Committee for Aichi University Mount Yakushi Disaster Album], comp. *Yakushi* 薬師 [Mount Yakushi]. Toyohashi: Aichi University, 1968. 247 p.

Aichi Daigaku Shōshi Hensan I'inkai 愛知大学小史編纂委員会 [Editorial Committee for Short History of Aichi University], comp. *Aichi Daigaku shōshi: Rokujūnen no ayumi* 愛知大学小史: 六〇年の歩み [Short History of Aichi University: A Sixty-year Journey]. Matsudo: Azusa Shuppan, 2006. 231 p.

Aichi Daigaku Tōa Dōbun Shoin Daigaku Kinen Sentā 愛知大学東亜同文書院大学記念センター [Aichi University Tōa Dōbun Shoin University Memorial Center]. *Ōpun Risāchi Sentā nenpō* オープン・リサーチ・センター年報 [Bulletin of the Open Research Center]. Toyohashi: Aichi Daigaku Tōa Dōbun Shoin Daigaku Kinen Sentā, 2006 to 2010. Vols. 1–5 contain a variety of relevant papers and reports. Materials related to the history of Aichi University can also be found in *Aichi Daigaku shi kenkyū* 愛知大学史研究 [Studies on Aichi University History], Vols. 1–3. Both journals were published by the Memorial Center.

———. *Aichi Daigaku sōseiki no gunzō* 愛知大学創成期の群像 [Images of the Founding Era of Aichi University]. Nagoya: Arumu, 2007. 53 p.

———. *Aichi Daigaku Tōa Dōbun Shoin Sentā: Shūzō shiryō zuroku* 愛知大学東亜同文書院大学記念センター: 収蔵資料図録 [An Illustrated Guide to Materials Housed at Aichi University Tōa Dōbun Shoin University Memorial Cen-

---

* [Trans. note] This list of references is organized alphabetically by title, author, or compiler. Following the lead of author Fujita Yoshihisa, it includes the number of pages of each title. To showcase the role of key institutions, this list often leads with proper names such as Nisshin Bōeki Kenkyūjo, Tōa Dōbun Shoin, Tōa Dōbunkai, Kazankai, and Aichi Daigaku or Aichi University.

ter]. Toyohashi: Aichi Daigaku Tōa Dōbun Shoin Daigaku Kinen Sentā, 2003. 59 p.

_____. *Tōa Dōbun Shoin kara Aichi Daigaku e no ayumi* (DVD) 東亜同文書院から愛知大学への歩み [The Journey from Tōa Dōbun Shoin to Aichi University]. Aichi Daigaku Tōa Dōbun Shoin Daigaku Kinen Sentā, 2008. A DVD. This content can also be accessed via Youtube.

Arao Sei. See Inoue Masaji.

Fujii Shōzō 藤井昇三. *Son Bun no kenkyū: Toku ni minzoku-shugi riron no hatten o chūshin toshite* 孫文の研究: とくに民族主義理論の発展を中心として [Studies of Sun Yatsen: With Special Emphasis on the Development of His Theories of Nationalism]. Tokyo: Keisō Shobō, 1966. 293 p., 9 p.

Fujioka Kikuo 藤岡喜久男, trans. *Giwadan: Chūgoku to Yōroppa* 義和団: 中国とヨーロッパ [The Boxer Movement: China and Europe]. Tokyo: Tōgensha, 1967. 258 p. Translation of G. Nye Steiger. *China and the Occident.* New Haven: Yale University Press, 1927. 349 p.

Fujita Yoshihisa 藤田佳久. Fujita's publications list begins with his monumental five-volume series (1994–2011) based on meticulous study of Tōa Dōbun Shoin student graduation-thesis reports from their mandatory "Big Trips" (*dai ryokō* 大旅行; *dai chōsa ryokō* 大調査旅行). All five volumes appear solely under the authorship of Fujita Yoshihisa.

Vol. 1: *Chūgoku to no de'ai: Tōa Dōbun Shoin Chūgoku chōsa kiroku, dai ik-kan* 中国との出会い: 東亜同文書院中国調査記録、第一巻 [Encounters with China: Accounts of Tōa Dōbun Shoin China Study Trips, Vol. 1]. Tokyo: Taimeidō 大明堂, 1994. 284 p.

Vol. 2: *Chūgoku o aruku: Tōa Dōbun Shoin Chūgoku chōsa kiroku, dai ni kan* 中国を歩く: 東亜同文書院中国調査記録、第二巻 [Walking Around China: Accounts of Tōa Dōbun Shoin China Study Trips, Vol. 2]. Tokyo: Taimeidō, 1995. 847 p.

Vol. 3: *Chūgoku o koete: Tōa Dōbun Shoin Chūgoku chōsa kiroku, dai san kan* 中国を越えて: 東亜同文書院中国調査記録、第三巻 [Going Beyond China: Accounts of the Tōa Dōbun Shoin China Study Trips, Vol. 3]. Tokyo: Taimeidō, 1996. 689 p.

Vol. 4: *Chūgoku o kiroku-suru: Tōa Dōbun Shoin Chūgoku chōsa kiroku, dai yon kan* 中国を記録する: 東亜同文書院中国調査記録、第四巻 [Documenting China: Accounts of Tōa Dōbun Shoin China Study Trips, Vol. 4]. Tokyo: Taimeidō, 2002. 580 p.

Vol. 5: *Manshū o kakeru: Tōa Dōbun Shoin Chūgoku chōsa kiroku, dai go kan* 満州を駆ける: 東亜同文書院中国調査記録、第五巻 [Running Around Manchuria: Accounts of Tōa Dōbun Shoin China Study Trips, Vol. 5]. Tokyo: Fuji Shuppan 不二出版, 2011. 607 p.

_____. *"Maboroshi" de wa nai Tōa Dōbun Shoin to Tōa Dōbun Shoin Daigaku* 「幻」ではない東亜同文書院と東亜同文書院大学 [No, Not a Phantom: Tōa Dōbun Shoin and Tōa Dōbun Shoin University]. Included in *Tōa Dōbun*

Shoin Daigaku to Aichi Daigaku: 1940 nendai; Gakuseitachi no seishun gunzō 東亜同文書院大学と愛知大学: 一九四〇年代・学生たちの青春群像 [Tōa Dōbun Shoin University and Aichi University: The 1940s; Portraits of Young Students], Vol. 1. Kobe: Rokkō Shuppan, 1993.

_____. *Tōa Dōbun Shoin daichōsa ryokō no kenkyū* 東亜同文書院中国大調査旅行の研究 [Studies of Tōa Dōbun Shoin China Study Trips]. Tokyo: Taimeidō, 2000. 349 p.

_____. *Tōa Dōbun Shoinsei ga kiroku shita kindai Chūgoku* 東亜同文書院生が記録した近代中国 [Modern China as Recorded by Tōa Dōbun Shoin Students]. Nagoya: Arumu, 2007. 61 p.

_____. *Tōa Dōbun Shoinsei ga kiroku shita kindai Chūgoku no chi'iki zō* 東亜同文書院生が記録した近代中国の地域像 [Regions of Modern China as Portrayed in Tōa Dōbun Shoin Student Reports]. Kyoto: Nakanishiya Shuppan, 2011. 330 p.

Hatano Yōsaku 波多野養作; comp. Minagawa Hatsuko 皆川初子. *Shiruku rōdo Meijino hitori tabi: Nichi-Ro sensō makki ni Gaimushō no itaku ni yori okuchi shisatsu shita ichi Nihon seinen no kiroku* シルクロード明治の一人旅: 日露戦争末期に外務省の委託により奥地視察した一日本青年の記録 [A Solo Trip on the Silk Road During the Meiji Period: A Young Man's Account of an Observation Trip Commissioned by the Ministry of Foreign Affairs at the End of the Russo-Japanese War]. Shinjukai/Sōzō Shuppan, 1985. 339 p.

Hayashide Ō o Shinobu-kai 林出翁をしのぶ会 [Committee to Commemorate the Venerable Hayashide [Kenjirō], comp. *Tōhō kunshi* 東方君子 [A Venerable Man of the East]. [n.p.]: Hayashide Ō o Shinobu-kai, 1973. 195 p. [Hayashide Kenjirō was a graduate of the 2nd (1902) entering class of Tōa Dōbun Shoin.]

Inoue Masaji 井上雅二. *Kyojin Arao Sei* 巨人荒尾精 [Arao Sei: A Giant]. Tokyo: Sakura Shobō, 1910. 358 p. (Enlarged ed. by Murakami Takeshi 村上武, re-printed by Tōkō Shoin Shuppanbu and Tokyo: Ōzora Sha, 1997.)

Ishii Itarō 石射猪太郎. *Gaimukan no isshō* 外務官の一生 [My Life as a Diplomat]. Tokyo: Chūo Kōron Shinsha, 1986. 521 p. Ishii was an early graduate of Tōa Dōbun Shoin.

Jiaotong Daxue xiao shi, 1896–1949 交通大学校史, 1896–1949 [A History of Jiaotong University, 1896–1949]. Comp. Jiaotong Daxue Xiaoshi bian 交通大学校史編 [Editorial Committee for a History of Jiaotong University]. Shanghai: Shanghai Jiaoyu Chubanshe, 1989. 536 p.

Kato Katsumi 加藤勝美. *Aichi Daigaku o tsukutta otokotachi: Honma Ki'ichi, Koiwai Kiyoshi to sono jidai* 愛知大学を創った男たち: 本間喜一、小岩井淨とその時代 [The Men Who Built Aichi University: Honma Ki'ichi, Koiwai Kiyoshi and their Era]. n.p.: Aichi Daigaku, 2011. 528 p.

Kazankai. See under *Tōa Dōbunkai shi* (three titles).

Kazankai gojūnenshi: Zaidan hōjin Kazankai sōritsu gojusshūnen kinen shuppan 霞山会五〇年史: 財団法人霞山会創立五〇年周年記念出版 [A Fifty-Year History of Kazankai: A Commemorative Publication on the Fiftieth Anniversary of the Kazankai Foundation]. Comp. Kazankai Gojūnenshi Hensan I'inkai 霞山会五〇年史編纂委員会 [Editorial Committee for a Fifty-Year History of Kazankai]. Tokyo: Kazankai, 1998. 255 p.

Kessoku Hiroharu 結束博治. *Jun naru Nihonjin: Son Bun kakumei to Yamada Yoshimasa/Junzaburō* 醇なる日本人: 孫文革命と山田良政・純三郎 [Pure Japanese: The Brothers Yamada Yoshimasa and Junzaburō and the Sun Yatsen Revolution]. Purejidento Sha, 1992. 331 p.

Kishida Ginkō den 岸田吟香伝 [Kishida Ginkō: A Biography]. Comps. Kusachi Tamotsu 草地保 et al. Okayama-ken Asahi-chō Kyōiku I'inkai 岡山県旭町教育委員会 [Okayama Prefecture Asahi-chō Education Committee], 1989. 70 p. For a digest version of this material see Sugiyama Sakae 杉山栄. *Senkūsha Kishida Ginkō* 先駆者岸田吟香 [Kishida Ginkō: Pioneer]. Reprint ed. Tokyo: Ōzora Sha, 1993.

Konoe Atsumaro 近衛篤麿. *Konoe Atsumaro nikki, dai ni kan* 近衛篤麿日記、第二巻 [Konoe Atsumaro Diary, Vol. 2]. Comp. Konoe Atsumaro Nikki Kankōkai 近衛篤麿日記刊行会編 [Publication Committee for the Konoe Atsumaro Diaries]. Kajima Kenkyūjo Shuppankai, 1968. 537 p. Konoe's published diaries, in five volumes, span the period February 1895 to March 1903.

Kosaka Ayano 小坂文乃. *Kakumei o purodyūsu shita Nihonjin* 革命をプロデュースした日本人 [The Japanese who Started a Revolution]. Tokyo: Kōdansha, 2009. 276 p.

Koyūkai 滬友会 [Shanghai Friends Association]. Koyūkai, significant in its meaning, is the name of the alumni association of Tōa Dōbun Shoin graduates. It was active in compiling materials for publication. See below under Tōa Dōbun Shoin Koyūkai Dōsōkai hen; *Shanhai Tōa Dōbun Shoin*; *Tōa Dōbun Shoin Daigaku shi*; and other publications with Tōa Dōbun Shoin in the lead title.

Kurita Hisaya 栗田尚弥. *Shanhai Tōa Dōbun Shoin: Nit-Chū o kaken to shita otokotachi* 上海東亜同文書院: 日中を架けんとした男たち [Shanghai Tōa Dōbun Shoin: Boys Who Bridged Relations between Japan and China]. Tokyo: Shin Jinbutsu Ōraisha, 1993. 299 p.

Miyazaki Tōten 宮崎滔天; annotated by Shimada Kenji 島田虔次 and Kondō Hideki 近藤秀樹. *Sanjūsannen no yume* 三十三年の夢 [My Thirty-three Years' Dream]. Tokyo: Iwanami Shoten, 1993. 500, 7 p.

Nakamura Tadashi 中村義. See under Shiraiwa Ryūhei.

Nakayama Masaru 中山優. *Nakayama Masaru senshū* 中山優選集 [Selected Works of Nakayama Masaru]. N.p.: Nakayama Masaru Senshū Kankō I'inkai 中山優選集刊行委員会 [Publications Committee for Selected Works of Nakayama Masaru], 1972. 430 p.

Nashimoto Yūhei 梨本祐平. *Shingai kakumei* 辛亥革命 [China's 1911 Revolution]. Tokyo: Yūzankaku Shuppan, 261 p.

Negishi Tadashi 根岸佶. *Chūgoku no girudo* 中国のギルド [Chinese Guilds]. Tokyo: Nihon Hyōron Shinsha, 1953. 488 p. (Reprint ed., Tokyo: Ōzora Sha.)

_____. *Shina girudo no kenkyū* 支那ギルドの研究 [Research on Chinese Guilds]. Tokyo: Shibun Shoin, 1931. 442, 22 p.

_____. See also *Shina keizai zensho*.

Nezu Hajime. See Tōa Dōbun Shoin Koyūkai Dōsōkai, comp. *Sanshū Nezu sensei den*.

Nishidokoro Masamichi 西所正道. *"Shanhai Tōa Dōbun Shoin" fūunroku: Nit-Chū kyōzon o oitsuzuketa gosennin no erītotachi* 「上海東亜同文書院」風雲録: 日中共存を追い続けた5000人のエリートたち [Shanghai's Tōa Dōbun Shoin in Turbulent Times: Five Thousand Elites Who Pursued Co-existence between China and Japan]. Tokyo: Kadokawa Shoten, 2001. 323 p.

Nisshin Bōeki Kenkyūjo 日清貿易研究所 [Japan-China Trade Research Institute], comp. *Shinkoku tsūshō sōran: Nisshin bōeki hikkei* 清国通商総覧: 日清貿易必携 [Commercial Handbook of China: Essentials of Japan-China Trade]. 3 vols. Shanghai: Maruzen Shōsha Shoten, 1892. 1060, 665, 60, 15 p.

Nisshin Bōeki Kenkyūjo, Tōa Dōbun Shoin enkakushi 日清貿易研究所、東亜同文書院沿革史 [A History of Nisshin Bōeki Kenkyūjo and Tōa Dōbun Shoin]. Comps. Matsuoka Kyōichi 松岡恭一 and Yamaguchi Noboru 山口昇 (with Shanghai Tōa Dōbun Shoin). Tokyo: Tōa Dōbun Shoin Gakuyūkai, 1908. 167, 64 p.

Ochi Makoto 越知専. *Honma-izumu to Aichi Daigaku: Jitsureihen, sono shinzui o jitsuwa kara manabu* 本間イズムと愛知大学: 実例編、その真髄を実話から学ぶ ["Honma-ism" and Aichi University: Understanding the Essence of the Institution Through Real Stories and Real Examples]. Toyohashi: Aichi Daigaku Tōa Dōbun Shoin Daigaku Kinen Sentā, 2008. 60 p.

_____. *Honma-izumu to Aichi Daigaku: Shiryōhen, sono shinzui o Kokkai shōgen kara manabu* 本間イズムと愛知大学: 資料編、その真髄を国会証言から学ぶ ["Honma-ism" and Aichi University: Understanding the Essence of the Institution through Collected Speeches in the Diet]. Toyohashi: Aichi Daigaku Tōa Dōbun Shoin Daigaku Kinen Sentā, 2008. 39 p.

Ōshiro Tatsuhiro 大城立裕. *Asa, Shanhai ni tachitsukusu: Shōsetsu Tōa Dōbun Shoin* 朝、上海に立ちつくす: 小説東亜同文書院 [Standing in Shanghai in the Morning: A Novel about Tōa Dōbun Shoin]. Tokyo: Kodansha, 1983. 261 p.

Sankei Shinbunsha サンケイ新聞社 [Sankei Shimbun]. *Higeki no Chūgoku tairiku: Shō Kaiseki hiroku* 1 悲劇の中国大陸: 蔣介石秘録 1 [The Tragedy of the Chinese Mainland: Secret Documents Relating to Chiang Kaishek, 1]. Osaka: Sankei Shimbunsha, 1975. 255 p.

Sasamori Gisuke Shokanshū Hensan I'inkai 笹森儀助書簡集編纂委員会 [Editorial Committee for Correspondence of Sasamori Gisuke], comp. Sasamori

Gisuke Shokanshū 笹森儀助書簡集 [Compilation of Sasamori Gisuke Correspondence]. Aomori: Tōō Nippō Sha, 2008. 372 p., 31 p.

Shanhai Tōa Dōbun Shoin tairiku dairyokō kiroku: Jitsuroku Chūgoku tōsa ki 上海東亜同文書院大陸大旅行記録: 実録中国踏査記 [Records of Shanghai Tōa Dōbun Shoin Big Trips: Notes from Field Investigations of China]. Comp. Koyūkai 滬友会. Shin Jinbutsu Ōraisha, 1991. 355 p.

Shina keizai zensho 支那経済全書 [Comprehensive Survey of the Chinese Economy]. Comp. Negishi Tadashi 根岸佶. 12 vols. Tokyo: Tōa Dōbunkai, 1907–1908.

Shina shōbetsu zenshi 支那省別全誌 [Comprehensive Gazetteer of the Individual Provinces of China]. Comp. Tōa Dōbunkai. 18 vols. Tokyo: Tōa Dōbunkai, 1917–1920. (Reprint ed. Tokyo: Hara Shobō, 2012.)

Shinshū Shina shōbetsu zenshi 新修支那省別全誌 [New and Revised Comprehensive Gazetteer of the Individual Provinces of China]. Comp. Tōa Dōbunkai. Halted at 9 vols. Tōa Dōbunkai, 1941–1944. (Reprint ed. Tokyo: Hara Shobō, 2012.)

Shiraiwa Ryūhei 白岩龍平 and Nakamura Tadashi 中村義. *Shiraiwa Ryūhei nikki: Ajia-shugi jitsugyōka no shōgai* 白岩龍平日記: アジア主義実業家の生涯 [The Diary of Shiraiwa Ryūhei: The Life of an "Asianist" Entrepreneur]. Tokyo: Kenbun Shuppan, 1999. 697, 30 p. Shiraiwa was a graduate of Nisshin Bōeki Kenkyūjo.

Steiger, G. N. See Fujioka Kikuo.

Tai-Shi kaikoroku (ge) 対支回顧録 (下) [Memoirs Concerning China, Vol. 2]. Comp. Tōa Dōbunkai. Tokyo: Tōa Dōbunkai, 1936. 1520 p. (Reprint ed. Tokyo: Hara Shobō, 1968.)

Zoku tai-Shi kaikoroku (ge) 続対支回顧録 (下) [Memoirs Concerning China, Continued, Vol. 2]. Comp. Tōa Dōbunkai. Tokyo: Tōa Dōbunkai, 1941. 1316 p. (Reprint ed. Tokyo: Hara Shobō, 1973.)

Takei Yoshikazu 武井義和. *Son Bun o sasaeta Nihonjin: Yamada Yoshimasa to Yamada Junzaburō (Shashin shū)* 孫文を支えた日本人: 山田良政・純三郎 (写真集) [The Japanese Who Supported Sun Yatsen: Yamada Yoshimasa and Yamada Junzaburō (Collected Photographs)]. Nagoya: Arumu, 2011. 68 p. Besides the Arumu photographs, Tōa Dōbun Shoin Memorial Center has other photographs in booklet form.

Tōa Dōbunkai, comp. *Tōajiron* 東亜時論 [East Asia Review]. Tokyo: Tōa Dōbunkai, 1898–1899. (Reprint ed., Tokyo: Yumani Shobō, 2012.)

_____, comp. See also *Shina shōbetsu zenshi*; *Shinshū Shina shōbetsu zenshi*; *Tai-Shi kaikoroku*; and *Zoku tai-Shi kaikoroku*.

Tōa Dobunkai hōkoku 東亜同文会報告 [Tōa Dōbunkai Report]. Comp. Tōa Dōbunkai Chōsa Hensanbu 東亜同文会調査編纂部 [Tōa Dōbunkai Research Editorial Department]. Tokyo: Tōa Dōbunkai, 1900–1910. (Reprint ed., Tokyo: Yumani Shobō. 2011.)

Tōa Dōbunkai jigyō hōkokusho 東亜同文会事業報告書 [Tōa Dōbunkai Activities Report]. Comp. Tōa Dōbunkai. Tokyo: Tōa Dōbunkai. (Published biannually in volumes of 100–200 pages.)

Tōa Dōbunkai shi: Meiji, Taishō hen 東亜同文会史: 明治、大正編 [History of Tōa Dōbunkai: Meiji and Taishō Periods]. Comp. Tōa Bunka Kenkyūjo 東亜文化研究所 [East Asia Culture Research Institute]. Tokyo: Kazankai, 1988.

Tōa Dōbunkai shi: Shōwa hen 東亜同文会史: 昭和編 [History of Tōa Dōbunkai: Showa Period]. Comp. Kazankai 霞山会. Tokyo: Kazankai, 2003. 1272 p.

Tōa Dōbunkai shi ronkō: Zaidan Hōjin Kazankai sōritu gojusshūnen kinen shuppan 東亜同文会史論考: 財団法人霞山会創立五〇年周年記念出版 [Studies in the History of Tōa Dōbunkai: Commemorating the Fiftieth Anniversary of the Kazankai Foundation]. Tokyo: Kazankai, 1998. 361 p.

Tōa Dōbun Shoin. See also Shanhai Tōa Dōbun Shoin.

Tōa Dōbun Shoin, comp. *Sōritsu sanjusshūnen kinen: Tōa Dōbun Shoin shi* 創立三十周年記念: 東亜同文書院誌 [Commemorating the Thirtieth Anniversary of the Founding of Tōa Dōbun Shoin]. Shanghai: Tōa Dōbun Shoin, 1930. 116 p.

Tōa Dōbun Shoin Daigaku shi 東亜同文書院大学史 [History of Tōa Dōbun Shoin University]. Comp. Koyūkai 滬友会, 1955. 338 p.

Tōa Dōbun Shoin Daigaku shi: Sōritsu hachijusshūnen kinen shi 東亜同文書院大学史: 創立八十周年記念誌 [History of Tōa Dōbun Shoin University: Commemorating the Eightieth Anniversary of Its Founding]. Comp. Daigakushi Hensan I'inkai 大学史編纂委員会 [University History Editorial Committee]. Tokyo: Koyūkai, 1982. 775 p.

Tōa Dōbun Shoin gakusei tairiku dairyokō mitsuwa 東亜同文書院学生大陸大旅行密話 [Unknown Tales of Big Trips by Tōa Dōbun Shoin Students]. Comp. Koyū Henshū I'inkai 滬友編集委員会編 [Koyu Editorial Committee]. Tokyo: Koyūkai, 1991. 498 p.

Tōa Dōbun Shoin Koyūkai Dōsōkai hen 東亜同文書院滬友会同窓会編 [Tōa Dōbun Shoin Koyūkai Alumni Association], comp. *Sanshū Nezu sensei den* 山洲根津先生傳 [Biography of Nezu Hajime]. Tokyo: Nezu Sensei Denki Hensanbu, 1930. 490 p. (Reprint ed., Tokyo: Ōzora Sha.)

Tōajiron. See under Tōa Dōbunkai, comp.

Watanabe Ryūsaku 渡辺龍策. *Tairiku rōnin: Meiji romanchishizumu no eikō to zasetsu* 大陸浪人: 明治ロマンチシズムの栄光と挫折 [Continental Adventurers: The Glory and Frustrations of Meiji Romanticism]. Tokyo: Banchō Shobō, 1967. 265 p.

Yamamoto Shigeki 山本茂樹. *Konoe Atsumaro: Sono Meiji kokkakan to Ajia-kan* 近衛篤麿: その明治国家観とアジア観 [Konoe Atsumaro: His Views of the Meiji State and of Asia]. Kyoto: Mineruva Shobō, 2001. 310 p.

Yamamoto Takashi 山本隆. *Tōa Dōbun Shoin sei* 東亜同文書院生 [Tōa Dōbun Shoin Students]. Tokyo: Kawade Shobō Shinsha, 1977. 270 p.

Author

Fujita Yoshihisa. Born in Aichi Prefecture in 1940, Fujita graduated with a bachelor's degree from Aichi University of Education and a masters and PhD from Nagoya University, specializing in geography. After serving as an Assistant Professor in Nara University, he moved to Aichi University in 1979. He served at Aichi until March 2011 as a professor in the university's Faculty of Letters. He also served as the Director of the Tōa Dōbun Shoin Memorial Center in Aichi University. His research has centered on the field work performed by the students at the Tōa Dōbun Shoin.

Translators

Douglas Robertson Reynolds. Born in 1944, Reynolds graduated with a PhD from Columbia University in 1975. Reynolds became a pioneering scholar on Sino-Japanese interchange at the end of the nineteenth and in the early twentieth centuries. Long regarded as an expert on the Tōa Dōbun Shoin, Reynolds spent his career in the history department at Georgia State University. Reynolds passed away in 2020 from cancer, just as the translation of this book was being completed.

Paul Sinclair. Born in 1969, Sinclair lived for extended periods in Osaka, Nagoya, Beijing and Taipei. He has a bachelor's degree from the University of Saskatchewan, a master's degree from the University of Toronto (Ontario Institute for Studies in Education), a PhD from the Osaka University of Foreign Studies (now Osaka University), and an MBA from the University of Alberta. He has been interested in the Tōa Dōbun Shoin since encountering the school in graduate studies in Toronto. Sinclair is Associate Professor in the Faculty of Business at the University of Regina.